MW00334733

The Global Lab

The Global Lab

Inequality, Technology, and the New Experimental Movement

ADAM FEJERSKOV

UNIVERSITY PRESS

Great Clarendon Street, Oxford, OX2 6DP,
United Kingdom

Oxford University Press is a department of the University of Oxford.
It furthers the University's objective of excellence in research, scholarship,
and education by publishing worldwide. Oxford is a registered trade mark of
Oxford University Press in the UK and in certain other countries

First Edition published in 2022

Impression: 1

Published in the United States of America by Oxford University Press
198 Madison Avenue, New York, NY 10016, United States of America

British Library Cataloguing in Publication Data
Data available

Library of Congress Control Number: 2022930161

ISBN 978-0-19-887027-2

DOI: 10.1093/oso/9780198870272.001.0001

Printed and bound in the UK by
Clays Ltd, Elcograf S.p.A.

Preface

During the 1990s, I lived a carefree life in the small Greenlandic town of Qeqertarsuaq, just north of the Arctic Circle and bordering the western edges of the ice sheet. The winter months were long and dark, the sun rarely rising and the depression of darkness always seemingly ready to creep in. But in summer, the world turned on its head and the magic of the midnight sun kept us awake for days before sleep eventually found us. I was seven when my parents brought me and my younger brother from our native Denmark and Copenhagen to the 800-something small town in the beautiful icy wilderness. A large plane carried us to Kangerlussuaq, and a propeller further north to Ilulisat, where we encountered the highlight of the trip: the great round-nosed Sikorsky helicopter. Far from the military macho tales of Black Hawk Down, this Sikorsky brought us across a pristine (if deadly, I would learn) blue and green ocean of icebergs and crystal-clear water. Despite the regular school fights in *Greenlanders-versus-Danes* fashion, my years in western Greenland was a privileged life of dog sledding, eating seal blubber for lunch in the mountains, and catching ammassat, a small fish that arrives by the millions on the banks of the black and icy beaches, once a year. But such privilege was not common in Qeqertarsuaq, a town low on jobs and suffering from hardship. Greenland was my first memory of meeting poverty and a striking testament to how the destructive force of colonialism permeates as far North as one can make it on this planet.

It was the inequality of power inherent in any colonial relationship that drove Denmark, supported by both Save The Children Denmark and the Danish Red Cross[1], to remove a group of twenty-two Greenlandic children from their homeland in 1951 and install them in Denmark. In a social experiment meant to lay the ground for a new bilingual school system, the children, all of them the same age as me when I first arrived in their country, were taken from their parents and sailed to Denmark where they would be indoctrinated to learn the Danish language and culture. Destined to be pioneers of a new Greenland that distanced itself from its Inuit heritage and embraced Denmark as its self-image of modernity. As one of the involved politicians formulated the intentions: 'we wish to create from the Greenlander a good Danish citizen'. It didn't take long for the involved parts to see that the experiment failed to produce positive results, and the children were either offered away for adoption or placed in orphanages, none of them returned to their parents. One of the only remaining children has since told of how meeting her parents again a few years after her removal was a devastating experience. She had forgotten the language of her people, her parents not understanding a word she said to them. Like the other children, she was seen as a traitor of culture, embracing the ways of the colonial ruler, despite having no say in her removal.

The story of the Greenlandic children and their removal is close to my heart, framing and shaping my own understanding of what my privileged presence in their country meant. But also because of its nature as a historical testament to how ideals of modernity, progress, and the pursuit of a greater good, may derail in the sacrifices made to seek such. Experimentation is a powerful methodology and mindset that has driven discoveries and break-throughs across sciences and industries over the past millennia. It is a strong political and moral force that structures and shapes both the present and future for people around the world. Rarely deterministically and often instead in ways we may not understand or imagine from the outset. That uncertainty and unpredictability is also why we must remain focused on explicating and disentangling the hierarchies of knowing, influence, and power that may arise as experimentation is manifested in practice. Which is what I attempt to do here. The inspiration for this book originates from years of research on con-temporary private foundations, in particular the Bill and Melinda Gates Foundation, where I first encountered a strong combination of practices of experimentation and ideas of technological innovation. It is from observing those very same narratives and trajectories across other fields and among actors where I would otherwise not have expected them – and from spending extensive time at their imagined point of origin, Silicon Valley, and at their sites of manifestation – that I pursue an aim here of opening up what experi-mentation looks like today and what are its implications. The book builds on extensive research that has taken me around the world, where observations and interviews have provided insights into practices of experimentation by a diverse cast of actors. A large fieldwork grant from the Carlsberg Foundation, contributing solely to writing this book, specifically made possible visits to the US, East Africa, and South Asia.

Throughout the writing of the book, I have insistently been reminded that none of us can think to stand outside science (and sciences of experimentation not least) and judge it to be good or evil: we are it and it is us.[2] Hence, any criticism must begin with ourselves. An outsider's perspective such as that

I have pursued here may be seen as easy and a way of escaping the pointing of any fingers inwards. The book, much likely due to my own blindness, has obviously been constructed from and with my Western epistemic privilege. I have tried not to preserve or convey any sensation of a hierarchy of centre and periphery in my own interpretation of the both constructed and practised relationship between what I refer to as the Global North and the Global South. While serving the purposes of explanation and simplicity, these two concepts of differing spatial, social, political, and cultural contexts and materialities should visibly not be taken as absolutes. In the same way that I only concern myself with a fraction of what can be said to represent the Global South (along the way undoubtedly reproducing unfortunate stereotypes of this part of the world as one of despair and destitution), the approaches and makings of the book's movement should not come to be taken as an absolute. The categories of Global North and Global South, and their use, quickly run into forms of essentialization that obscures the plurality of these two vast and elusive concepts. I use them here as tools to explain positionalities within power relations.[3] And just as discourses of Western dominance in themselves risk a eurocentrism that neglects the agency of the Global South,[4] the perspectives furthered by me also risk victimizing people who may not want to be victimized. Experimental situations are not settings where individuals either have agency or they do not—being the two extremes of these subject positions—but ones in which we must acknowledge the complexity of the relations of power we are all part of. That is exactly what merits a study of contemporary experimental practices and ideas.

What ensues, with all the ignorance and mistakes that come from trespassing disciplines and geographies as I do here, is all my responsibility and fault. Even so, I am inspired by the excellent works of colleagues who are too many to cite here, but whose ways of thinking and writing can certainly be found throughout the book. I am grateful to international colleagues, whether in academia, journalism, or in the professional fields I explore in the book, who have aided me, sometimes in my writing and other times by opening crucial access to places, people, and organizations. I am also grateful to my Copenhagen-colleagues—in particular Luke Patey—who have been with me throughout the process of publishing this book, as well as Ole Winckler Andersen, Rens van Munster, Johannes Lang, Lars Engberg-Pedersen, Tobias Hagmann, Rasmus Hundsbæk Pedersen, Marie Kolling, Erik Lundsgaarde, Dane Fetterer, Hayel Celik-Graversen, Therese Bostrup, Kirstine Lund Christiansen, Karl Møller, Thomas Glud Skjødt, Maiken Bjerrum, Lars Kristian Mathiesen, Annette Holm, Augusta Janum, Clara Johansen and many others who have encouraged me and supported the project. At Oxford University Press I'm grateful for the support I've received from Katie Bishop, Henry Clarke, Adam Swallow, and not least Erin O'Reilly, for wrestling with the manuscript and displaying their sense of detail.

Towards the end of writing this book, the world suddenly found itself in one of the most striking experiments in decades, as we attempted to respond to the Covid-19 pandemic. A dire reminder of what some people have and what others do not—what difference it makes where you are born, and to whom—the pandemic has been a failure of multilateralism and global cooperation. At the same time, for many, it has been a return to mutualism and the progressive nature that is afforded by what is close to us, whether in our neighbourhoods or in our families. For me, it was a reminder of the source from which everything that truly matters flows, and I'm forever grateful to my family, and in particular to Janni, Bror, and not least Billie who was born into a world of chaos and everyday experimentation, for their unrelenting support and love.

Notes

1. In 2010, Save the Children and the Red Cross both apologized for their participation in the experimental programme, and so too did the Danish Government in 2020. See Rud, S. 2017. *Colonialism in Greenland: Tradition, Governance and Legacy.* Palgrave Macmillan.
2. As Louise Amoore skilfully reminds us in Amoore, L. 2020. *Cloud Ethics: Algorithms and the Attributes of Ourselves and Others.* Duke University Press.
3. Fonseca, M. 2019. Global IR and western dominance: moving forward or Eurocentric entrapment? *Millennium* 48(1): 45–59.
4. See Alejandro, A. 2018. *Western Dominance in International Relations? The Internationalisation of IR in Brazil and India.* London: Routledge.

Contents

1

The Global Lab

'This year's prize is about alleviating poverty' Professor Göran Hansson, Secretary General of the Royal Swedish Academy of Sciences explains to the room of journalists and continues in Swedish: 'the Academy has decided to award the prize for 2019 to Abhijit Banerjee, Esther Duflo and Michael Kremer'. In honour of Alfred Nobel, the three professors are awarded the highest honour for economists 'for their experimental approach to alleviating global poverty' that is radically 'changing how public bodies and private organisations work'. The Academy explains further that 'this year's Laureates have shown how the problem of global poverty can be tackled by breaking it down into a number of smaller—but more precise—questions at individual or group levels. They then answer each of these using a specially designed field experiment. Over just twenty years, this approach has completely reshaped research in the field known as development economics'. British news media *The Guardian* chipped in with their interpretation of the Academy's award as well: 'The Academy said the winners had shown there was a need to adopt new approaches in the fight against poverty that were based on field trials rather than prejudice or the failed methods of the past'.[1] The three Nobel-recipients are the intellectual and institutional spearheads of a group of economists known in equal part collegially and satirically as the *randomistas*. The group is so named for their unrelenting affinity for conducting random-ized controlled trials (RCTs), a pronounced form of scientific experiment, among poor people in the Global South. In her ceremonial interview, Esther Duflo, the group's scientific superstar, laid bare their grand ambitions: 'Our goal is to make sure that the fight against poverty is based on scientific evi-dence', and 'the three of us stand for hundreds of researchers who are part of a network,...and thousands of staff and of course all of the partners and the NGOs and governments that we have worked with. So, it really reflects the fact that it has become a movement, a movement that is much larger than us.'

This book is about a movement that prescribes to logics of experimentation as it practises the Global South as a laboratory, with profound social and political ramifications. A movement that is propelled by the present accomplishments of the randomistas, but whose web extends far beyond, as a whole host of organizations and companies are experimenting with new drugs, emerging technologies, biometric humanitarian solutions, and radical policies and methodologies for social change in the Global South. Some of these pursue promises of great revenue in the global bioeconomy while others are in the business of doing good, but they are bound together by a strong mindset of experimentation. Throughout the book, we will meet at least four main protagonists, together making up the core of the movement: philanthropists, economists, pharmas, and humanitarians. Private foundations such as the Bill and Melinda Gates Foundation experiment with new technologies and radical change as they test innovative toilets or condoms or attempt to alter social norms in poor communities, basing their actions on what they see as objective models of change emerging from experiments, reducing the messy real world to formulae. Pharmaceutical companies have moved their experiments with new drugs to 'emerging markets' that provide abundant human subjects ready to partake in clinical trials to overcome diseases for which they often cannot afford treatment, pushing both experimental methodologies and stabilizing experimental practices as everyday care. The randomista economists likewise conduct randomized controlled trials and similar methodologies brought in from the natural sciences to experiment with solutions for social problems, driven by similar scientific desires of reducing complex realities to a set of logical causal chains. Finally, humanitarian actors, including private charities and United Nations (UN) organizations, pursue what they see as radical and innovative approaches to saving lives in disasters and emergencies through new technologies, from testing cargo drones and big data, to the registration and ordering of refugees through biometric data, iris scans, and blockchains-this is an introduction of emerging technologies that essentially functions as experimentation.

It was during periods of living on the US West Coast that I was initially familiarized with this emerging movement of experimentation. From entrepreneurial engineers in the heart of Silicon Valley and overtly optimist programme officers working in Seattle for the Gates Foundation, I heard repeated dreams of using experimentation to radically change the lives of the world's poor. These were complemented by harsh criticism of existing ways of combatting poverty that were seemingly based on *old-fashioned* and *ideological* concerns that were the opposite of the clean scientific nature of the new experimental project. I remember I found the fervour and commitment with which these people argued both fascinating and worrying. Still, it was not until I began to meet experimental proponents and subjects, from East Africa to South Asia that I began to realize both the extent of a movement on the rise and the deep relationship between experimentation, uncertainty, and inequality. All experiments are caught between, on the one hand, the uncertainty of knowing the potential consequences or the ignorance that lies in not being able to imagine these, and, on the other hand, choices about how to proceed and conduct experiments. Sometimes unwisely acted upon through a veil of ambiguity, sometimes through a troubling logic of subordination. The book examines the imagined universal and sometimes unquestioned value of scientific and technological progress to show the inequality inherent in experimental practice. It explores the political and social ramifications of scientific efforts, no matter how value neutral, objective, or apolitical these see themselves as being, and in particular the construction of difference and the inequality of experimentation that is found in the erection of imaginary walls between *us* and *them*, between living and dead laboratories. And between development and inertia. We will follow a movement that is on the rise across fields that may seem distant from each other but that are in fact bound together. Across its diverse endeavours runs a common thread: a belief in the necessity of conducting scientific and technological experimentation for the sake of progress. The movement's actors are inspired not least by core logics emanating out of Silicon Valley about the need for fast-paced radical change, societal disruption, and technological innovation as progress.

Today then, practices of experimentation have emerged as a major force in the pursuit of progress and modernization. This book explores a newfound interest in the practice of experimentation in the Global South at the intersections of polity, biology, knowledge, and the circumstances of material, social, and digital life. It aims to explore the oft-hidden geometry of power relations between those who aim to help and those who receive, sometimes wilfully and at other times forcefully.[2] We will meet a peculiar mix of protagonists, from Bill Gates and Silicon Valley idealists who see it as their call to push exponential technologies to the boundaries of the possible, to economists whose uncompromising views on science lead them to hold experiments as the only source of truthful evidence, to organizations who specialize in enrolling, organizing, or monitoring vulnerable populations. They may represent different worlds and industries, but they converge around experimentation in the Global South conducted in the name of notions of development, science, and policy.[3] We will move across geographies and scales, from Southeast Asia and Africa to Silicon Valley, in order to explore the interplay between global forces, ideas, and local circumstance and consequence, addressing questions of what experimentation looks like today in the Global South, who practises it, and to what ends? What types of progress are imagined through it, and who benefits from these futures?

*

One of the earliest and most widely discussed disputes on the nature and impact of experimentation took place between the seventeenth-century philosophers Thomas Hobbes and Robert Boyle. Boyle belonged to a group of British scientists that would eventually form the Royal Society, the UK's national academy of sciences today. A devout advocate and central historical face of experimentation, Boyle and his fellows saw the matter of fact as the foundation of knowledge; as absolute, permanent, and as holding what they called 'moral certainty'. Facts were like holding up a mirror against nature to simply see that which is given and beyond dispute. And only obtainable through experimentation. His own famous experimental programme was that of the air pump, allowing him to explore the nature of air, the vacuum, and the relationship between pressure and volume of gas in closed systems. Thomas Hobbes' innate scepticism drove him to become a critic of Boyle's work and approach, challenging the legitimacy of the experiments and the view that they created unquestionable matters of fact. But his views were largely discredited as the experimentalists and their newly founded Royal Society gained widespread prominence in the European scientific community. Reduced to its core, the dispute between Hobbes and Boyle almost four hundred years ago encapsulates contemporary discussions on the form and ambitions of experimentation. Their intellectual debate was not only one of science but one of social order and assent in Restoration England, Boyle's experimental practice taking the form of an ideological programme as much as a scientific one, deeply situated in the social and political context of the time.[4] Should authority emerge from a more democratic public sphere or through the isolated centralized character that was the monarch, they implicitly struggled over. The present experimental movement we explore here in the same way sets forth not just a scientific but a political and moral vision for development and progress in the Global South and beyond.

What is an experiment—is it a method, a logic, or a course of action? *Ex* comes from the latin 'out of' and 'periculum' has the meaning 'a (dangerous) trial'. *Expiri* also means to try something, in the same category of experience. Fifteenth-century British philosopher Francis Bacon was among the earlier thinkers to ponder over the nature of the experiment, but he didn't make a clear distinction between observation as experience and experimentation as a method,[5] which has since become a dominant way to consider experiments.

In the sciences that see themselves as *hard*, experimentation is about looking at the evidence, proposing a hypothesis that explains the evidence, creating a trial that tests the ability of the hypothesis to confirm, predict, or explain the evidence, and use the results of the trial to refine the hypothesis. This is a scientific *method*, as positivists such as Karl Popper would put it, designed to falsify theories. In the medical realm, where it is perhaps most widely practised, an experiment is seen as 'an act whereby the investigator deliberately changes the internal or external environment in order to observe the effects of such a change', as the World Medical Association describes it. For the French physiologist Claude Bernard, who is credited with initiating modern experimental medicine with his 1865 *Introduction to Experimental Medicine*, the basis for science and knowledge was the experiment and in particular the method of comparison accentuating the difference between what one expects to see and what one then finds through trialling.

Andrew Conway Ivy, known in his time as the 'conscience of U.S. science' and appointed representative of the American Medical Association at the 1946 Nuremberg Trials that saw Nazi doctors prosecuted for inhumane experiments during the war, articulated a similar approach to experimentation and knowledge production: 'All science or knowledge has two aspects, the descriptive and the experimental. Knowledge is obtained by describing and systematizing things and processes which are observed to occur in Nature and by designing and executing experiments to reveal the nature of things and processes observed'.[6] In practice, the medical approach came to be to trial both subjects taking a specific experimental therapeutic and subjects not taking it, to objectively study the effects of the intervention. The clinical trial was born from such ideas and would come to be known for its use of methods such as the selection of control groups, the randomization of subjects, and the blinding of scientists to make them unaware of which patients received a placebo. But crucially also its post processing evolved, using mathematical and statistical methods to control for change. The word clinical, fundamentally meaning a process conducted as though in a clinic, has developed to informally denote something performed with excellence and precision.[7] In a hierarchy of the quality of practices, proponents of the clinical trial and the closely related RCT thus see it forming a golden standard, the scientific method par excellence taking precedence over everything else; the pinnacle of not just biomedical but all forms of research design.[8]

It is perhaps of little surprise then that experimentation has travelled from clinical medicine to almost all other sciences over the past hundred years and more, just as we will see its migration across organizations and professional worlds. Not least facilitated by its focus on, at heart, causation and finding the relationship between cause and effect. Beyond observation, experiments see the researcher inducing a change and then observing the outcome and consequences of that change. The burden of proof is on the researcher to show that she can separate and manage variables in such a manner that the effects of these are not spoiled by confounding factors. British philosopher and utilitarianist John Stuart Mill, who formulated his own ideas on experimentation around the same time as Claude Bernard, held that to understand either cause or effects, we must isolate one or the other and change the circumstances to see the consequences. Mill maintained that we could either observe or experiment our way to such knowledge, and that while both hold value, the problem with observations is that observing b to follow a does not necessarily mean that a actually causes b. Correlation does not imply causation, as the first teaching of 101 statistics classes goes. This problem is also referred to as *internal validity*, meaning uncertainty surrounds the isolated case. In theory, experiments make up for this by allowing scientists in their labs to have some degree of control over the circumstances. In certain experiments, this is theoretically sufficient to make claims of causality valid, such as when a clinical study is meant to tell us something about the effects of a cancer treatment in blood cells. But in cases where experiments are meant to say something about or affect people in the real world, so-called *external validity* becomes a problem for the experimenters, simply because the laboratory context does not mirror the real world.

Real-world experimentation was key in facilitating the migration of experimental practices to the social sciences. Political scientist Harold Gosnell famously pioneered field experiments in the 1920s by trialling the determining factors of voter turnout in Chicago. In the same city and around the same time, sociologists who were part of what would become known as the *Chicago School* conducted experiments on programmes of social work, later helping to spur the so-called golden age of experimentation in US social policy during the 1960s. Albion Small, the first Professor of Sociology at the University of Chicago famously claimed that 'All life is experimentation. Every spontaneous or voluntary association is an experiment....Each civilization in the world today, each mode of living side by side within or between the several civilizations is an experiment.'[9] These words were repeated in the late twentieth-century work of sociologists such as Ulrick Beck and Bruno Latour, who both held that the world itself is a laboratory. To Beck, science had long since forfeited its exclusive right to judge what signifies an experiment, as research left the laboratory and spilled out into society.[10] As it moves out of the laboratory, modern science transfers both risks and potential gains directly into society. Experimentation, in this view, not only forms a method but may be understood as a distinguishing feature of modern society, breaking with forms of knowledge discovery existing prior to the seventeenth century.[11] The transfer of randomized experiments from medicine to the social sciences is not without its issues though, Latour held. In clinical trialling, the so-called confounding factors are easier to identify and remove than they are in the social sciences. While a certain protein or a protein level for a subject can be manipulated and measured to have been so in a clinical trial, it is difficult to ensure that a variable has been completely ruled out in the social world. The same can be said for a treatment given in an experiment. While a medical doctor can control the treatment by changing the dosage or the specific drug, social scientists have a harder time ensuring a streamlined treatment because of human agency and understanding.[12]

In reality then, experiments are not clean, clinical, and ordered scientific processes, whose results form a mirror against nature to expose given truths. As we were taught decades ago, science and the scientific process—which to the outsider appears logical, ordered, and coherent—in fact constitute a constant struggle to produce order from disorder.[13] There is no control inherent in scientific methods, only tools that help to assemble or build a performance of control. In the laboratory, these efforts to produce order are one thing, but in the field, in the real world, they are something else entirely. There are scientific words for why field experiments possess an even higher degree of chaos to be ordered than lab experiments: problems of compliance, deviation from assignment, self-selection, or interference between units.[14] Taken together, what these record is simply the story of how the real world does not easily offer itself up for the kind of manipulation that a lab perhaps does. People are not machines, and even in medicine, there is little stability. Returning to Andrew Ivy, even after the therapy of a disease is discovered 'its application to the patient remains in part experimental. Because of the physiological variations in the response of different patients to the same therapy, the therapy of disease is, and will always be, an experimental aspect of medicine'.[15]

Despite the way historical accounts of experimentation often situate the scientist as a lone explorer of truth and knowledge—an individualized authority and miracle *man*—we appreciate today the messy and complex interlinkages, networks, and knowledges that together often form the hybridity of experimentation. Such appreciation concerns the construction and execution of an experiment as much as it does its implications. Experiments are not just open-ended explorations of scientific issues, but instead they are vested with strategic interests and purpose.[16] This perception feeds a core question asked here—whom do the experiments benefit? RCTs and other experiments are deeply political and whenever the experimental movement talks of a 'golden standard', these are attempts to render hierarchic the structures of knowledge, challenging relativism or pluralism. But experiments and all that they produce, as for all other methodologies, can be as biased as any other form of knowledge. They, too, work as symbolic assets or instruments of communication that deliver knowledge, carry value, and produce authority across their many different forms and shapes.

The different forms of experimentation that this book covers also move across a spectrum. Some are deliberately done for the purpose of inferring knowledge; others are simply done on the fly with little systematic or scientific thought given to them. Some are expansive in that their immediate success generates larger and larger experimentation, and some are narrow or isolated. Some of the experiments in the book are social, aiming to study how local systems, norms, or practices can be most effectively disrupted, often based on a belief that a community or social group is maintaining a harmful or undesirable practice. Some are economic or political, pursuing systematic evidence on how to increase employment or the likelihood that local farmers will adopt new varieties of genetically modified seeds. Central to many of the experiments we will encounter is technology, borne out of the idea that exponential or radical technologies can bring social and economic progress swiftly and effectively. Technologies—whether biomedical, humanitarian, or digital—that are not dead but very much alive, are sometimes given life by those who use them in experiments or aim to introduce them, and sometimes assume a life themselves as shapers of future political goals. All of the book's experimental practices then share the common denominator that they are conducted for something more than just scientific purposes. They are done for commercial ends, to influence social and economic policy, or perhaps to render more bureaucratically effective the management of vulnerable populations.

Because of these tangible social and political effects of experimentation, we must approach it from a perspective broader than that pertaining only to a scientific method. We can call it a political programme, a higher-order logic, or just a mindset. The purpose is to say that methods are alive and that beyond its practicality of scientific technique, experimentation is a structuring way to perceive the world's being and our understanding of it. Not does it only shape and produce science, but also social, economic, and political life. When World Bank economists run a trial to find the most effective measure for forcing tenants to pay for water in Nairobi slums, they not only conduct an experiment in which thousands of vulnerable people have their vital access to water cut off but may also end up legitimizing such measures going forward.[17] Experimentation then forms a vocabulary of action and discourse; a set of shared values about knowledge, change, and about social and political life. And specific material practices such as RCTs give way for broader assumptions about what knowledge has legitimacy, and how social and political work ought to be shaped. By approaching experimentation as something much broader than a scientific method, we can include experimental implementation that may not be conscious of or explicit about its experimental nature. Not all social experiments are acknowledged as such,[18] just as those involved may not understand their participation as experimental. But that does not mean they cannot be fundamentally experimental, perhaps even extending those risks into society.

We must therefore move our analytical gaze from narrow conceptions of the experiment as a scientific method to experimentation as a political practice, fundamentally shaped by uncertainty and ignorance, as a trial or a venture into the unknown.[19] Uncertainty means multiple future possibilities for outcomes; that not everything can be known. As we move towards a knowledge society, we don't deterministically reduce unknowns but instead see surprises and unexpected events increase.[20] More new knowledge also means more ignorance. In the lab, uncertainty means repeated attempts at construing the experiment to ensure satisfactory results or negate unforeseen consequences between chemical agents. When involving vulnerable populations in practices of experimentation, uncertainty is added a further dimension of the risk of human harm. Many of the experimental practices explored here may come with good intentions—to understand how to incite economic growth, increase school attendance, or treat diseases. But the interventions themselves may be experimental to a degree that shows a devaluation of other peoples. Through the book, we will see the risk here in retaining the Global South as a laboratory of inequality where subjects are easily accessible and legitimated by scientific aims, often because they are caught in poverty or otherwise disadvantaged. Trials may become the only available medical treatment for disadvantaged groups, and experiments in one country suddenly structure access to education and health in another very different place. The tension between abstract notions of progressing science or knowledge, and respect for the individual subject who may not see any immediate or longer-term benefit from experiments, looms large. It matters very much, then, where, how, by, and on whom experimentation is conducted.

*

> In a solitary chamber, or rather cell, at the top of the house, and separated from all the other apartments by a gallery and staircase, I kept my workshop of filthy creation; my eyeballs were starting from their sockets in attending to the details of my employment. The dissecting room and the slaughter-house furnished many of my materials; and often did my human nature turn with loathing from my occupation, whilst, still urged on by an eagerness which perpetually increased, I brought my work near to a conclusion.[21]

Mary Shelley gives surprisingly little attention to the laboratory of the perhaps most famous fictional scientist, Victor Frankenstein, in her 1918 novel. Still, we are left with the gist of laboratory life. The lab is removed from the rest of society by way of both a gallery and a staircase, separating what goes on inside and who can enter from everyone who is not a scientist. The work of the scientist is solitary and even as he is startled by the discoveries and experiments, he conducts (the laboratory is certainly a *ghastly kitchen*, as Claude Bernard described it), Frankenstein has an inborne fervour to reach scientific absolutism; to bring his work to conclusion.

Historians of science tell us that laboratories are traditionally seen as the *where* of science, the realm in which the scientist roams, uncovering the truths of nature and man piece by piece. The laboratory is where observations and experiments are made into scientific facts and lifted above questions of falsification,[22] providing a 'consequence free' space in which the implications of the manipulation and the research cannot escape the premises and entail real-world consequences.[23] As *truth-spots*,[24] laboratories are often taken to purport a controlled space, allowing for procedures that can be manipulated by scientists, and whose placeless form allows them to replicate the same methods everywhere.[25] The same inputs produce the same outputs because of the, in theory, stable qualities of the lab.[26] It thus contrasts both uncontrolled spaces and the inexistence of a specified procedure of producing knowledge. The laboratory is nowhere, and it is everywhere, as a homogenous, universalized space, removed from geographical place. This perceived objective locality is seen to give way for generalization and replication, the two cornerstones of what the laboratory is thought to produce. While sometimes private and secret, for experimental scientists such as Boyle whom we have just met, it was also theatrical, open to spectators, important to the general acceptance of results produced there, and through the witnessing of experiments.[27] That does not mean it was an inclusive space, quite the opposite, often reserved for doctors, most of whom were white men. And although surely in use for millennia in the form of workshops (Aristotle likely had his own), laboratories as we think of them today rose together with experimental medicine and the quest for comparisons, not least through the controlled manipulation of animals, giving scientists a comparability they didn't have with autopsies. Formal scientific laboratories emerged in the mid-nineteenth century, quickly becoming a hegemonic space for the production of scientific knowledge and, by World War II, the laboratory had become a regular site for the systematic testing and development of therapeutics and bioweapons alike.

If the laboratory is artificial, ordered, and inconsequential in idealized scientific theory, the *field* is seen as natural, disordered, and consequential.[28] Such is not the reality, of course.[29] The knowledge produced in even the most hermetically closed labs will surely escape the premises, if not in the form of an infected rat, then perhaps more likely in the hands or through the reports of scientists, something that has equally real consequences. Across scientific fields, from economics to biomedicine to political science, experiments increasingly take place outside the laboratory, a development captured by the growing volume of published research applying the term 'field experiment' to its efforts. In 1990, some six hundred pieces of research included this specific term, growing to more than twenty thousand over the next few decades. The ambition in field experiments is to have science face the real world outside the artificial lab, employing manipulation and random assignment in investigating behaviours in naturally occurring contexts. If observational scientists study a card game as spectators, experimental scientists in the field take on the role of dealers, manipulating events.[30] At the very least, this puts to the test ideas about reproducibility; the contexts and conditions of formal laboratory settings may perhaps be reproduced, but what happens when experiments are conducted out in the social world, with its inherent complexities and factors that we do not see or are able to explain? Researchers are biased, but methods never lie, is the argument to counter such questions. They are transparent, replicable, and decontextualized.

Even so, in environments not wholly controlled by the researcher, the lines between anticipated and unforeseen consequences are fluid. Not least because in the *real* world, science forms a social practice rather than a dead mechanical scheme. Knowledge does not float around in the contexts where it is pursued, waiting to be found. It is constructed by those who venture out, and shaped by historical and social factors bound to any place and time. Through the diverse interventions considered in the book, scientific or not, but surely experimental, we see how treating the real world as a laboratory fit for experimentation often works to exacerbate existing power dynamics. Experiments may change the life-courses of people, both for the better and the worse, and equally for those directly or indirectly involved. Historically, the real-world environments or *labs* of experimentation have inherently been unequal and coercive ones, conducive to identifying, recruiting, and exploiting human subjects. The prison, itself an experiment of social reform and punishment, was a popular laboratory of accessible experimental subjects, from supporting state efforts of war to fulfilling the commercial aims of pharmaceutical companies. The colonial realms of African lands were treated this way too. With the rise of germ theory, in itself stigmatizing the poor by cultivating an understanding that certain diseases resided overwhelmingly with the *ugly classes*, colonies became the setting for large-scale disease eradication campaigns by authorities such as the French Pasteur institution. West Africa, French Indochina, or Tunisia formed colonial *theatres of proof* as experimental medicines were tested for their efficacy, the results compared and confirmed before being brought back to Europe,[31] where there was no guarantee they would be published or used scientifically. Local communities were seen as 'reservoirs of disease' with ample subjects from which to extrapolate scientific findings. But as for anyone looking behind the closed doors of the ordered laboratory, colonial rulers and doctors quickly realized that the control they had envisioned was not so easy to acquire. Resistance, defiance, and the natural complexity of life stood in the way for their dreams of experimentation, and not only in medicine, but with instruments of government at large: fingerprints, identification documents, and other methods introduced to govern and organize spaces and people.

In employing the Global South as a laboratory of experimentation today, no matter whether the aim is commercial or to directly inform policy and practice, fundamental notions of race, bodies, and ethics take centre stage.[32] We cannot, for one, consider experimentation by predominantly Western organizations and companies around the world without paying attention to race as a social category of difference and of hierarchy. The idea of race did not travel from some objective discipline of science but was rather a concept picked up by scientists from folk or popular ideas about human differences.[33] The human differences that biological conceptions of race attempt to make spill over into economic, social, and cultural differences of race that we as humans all too easily fall into, and these are supported by medical practices, institutions, and some parts of 'science' that equate race with social groups, who share norms and values. The concept of race has been through different processes of scientification by way of disciplines such as anthropology or craniometry,[34] tied to the nexus between categorization, census, and empire.[35] Race was the meeting with others that Europeans made during colonialization, employed as a way to describe the difference between majorities and minorities in society, shaping privilege, hierarchies, as well as power and conflicts between groups. But until the seventeenth century, race was mainly used to describe families or nations, perhaps entire regions, or continents, or to denote all of mankind, as in 'the race of man'. By the eighteenth century, race was increasingly employed to describe biologically different kinds of humans as ethnologists applied taxonomy to study people, derived from research on animal breeding and a growing understanding of animal subspecies. The Swedish 'naturalist' Carl Von Linné famously categorized Africans as *Homo afer*, arguing that black men had a separate evolutionary track from white that saw them 'ruled by caprice'. *Homo sapiens americanus*, native americans, were 'ruled by superstition'; *Homo sapiens asiaticus*, Asians, were 'ruled by ritual'; and *Homo sapiens europaeus*, Europeans, were 'ruled by intelligence'. These efforts formed part of a general order of science and attempts to organize and hierarchize the world from a polygenist perspective. And the racist and racialized views were strengthened by the rise of the late nineteenth-century eugenicists, increasingly institutionalizing ideas of race and difference into bureaucracies from 'science'.

The way race is used in epidemiological or clinical research today as a classification of population, sometimes maintained by funders or by history, has little to do with the idea of ancestry just as it is held by many that the limited biological variances between such constructed categories can likely not justify their use.[36] Such categories are not only descriptive but importantly attributive. By actively employing them, certain groups are ascribed specific qualities, making racialization real and informing the wider construction of diseases in clinical research. Consider an example in which the prevalence of a disease is investigated in a particular region of a country. If one of the main race categories consists mainly of immigrants living in a precarious situation or in poverty, then those 'environmental' factors are sure to influence the prevalence of the disease. But if these factors are not taken into account by the researchers, the entire racial category can easily be attributed a greater prevalence of the disease, not because of environmental factors but because of racialized ones. Biogenetic material then will always be infused with social meaning, and scientists are not objective carriers of truth but co-constructors of socioeconomic and historical understandings of race.[37] Subpopulation descriptors such as 'Asian woman' or 'black man' can help draw attention to important social differences in the name of fostering equality, but they are also categorizations that may be used towards political aims of ordering or exclusion.[38] The exclusion dilemma—that overinclusion can mean exploitation while full exclusion can come to imply indifference or failure of representation—is pertinent for discussions of experimentation and something we will return to. Race may be a human invention and a social construct, but it persists to permeate all sides of contemporary social, cultural, and economic life, from biology books to birth certificates and blood tests,[39] and there is little truth to any perceived difference between the biological being 'real' and the social being constructed. At the heart of race, then, are ideas about difference. And not just about what types of differences, but what the differences give way for, what they legitimize, so to speak.

Similar perceptions of difference apply to discussions of bodies. Pharmaceutical market strategies often revolve around constructing the body as abstracted so as to establish a collective need across the human race for a specific medicine. This abstraction then supports the purposes of experimenting—since medication is seen as benefiting the body in abstracted form (i.e. all of us) its exploration is both laudable and necessary. In reality of course, some bodies are worth more than others to the industry, and the outcome post-trial never becomes access in the same abstracted way the body is seen when justifying global trials. Post-trial, the body once again becomes co-constructed with socioeconomics: if you cannot afford the medicine, you are likely not granted access to it. In contrast to these pharmaceutical views, others have argued that there is no abstracted body. Only this body or that body; mine or yours. Bodies may be 'real' and share organs and tissue and flesh, but that does not make them alike,[40] and they certainly don't experience the same implications of poverty, medicine, or social experimentation.

Throughout history, the body of the colonized was both a body of difference and a body of experimentation. Embodied extraction and the collection and accumulation of research material for scientific experiments was widespread, as white doctors gladly risked their lives to extract intimate fluids and samples from local populations. In colonial Africa during the nineteenth and early twentieth centuries, samples of blood, tissue, or limbs became part of a sprawling bioeconomy in which local populations had their bodies exploited by medical doctors who could use the research material for their own careers, for the empire, or commercially by selling it to third parties. Subjects obviously received no cut of the business, as if it was a business they even wanted to become involved in in the first place. The work seldom led to therapeutic discoveries, and if it did, hardly ever ones accessible to the local population who had facilitated those results. In Tanganiyka, present-day Tanzania, experimentation—often involving the drawing of blood as well as post-mortems—came to be associated with the nocturnal, witchcraft, and black magic. When rumours of cannibalism spread in the aftermath of a German doctor arriving in the Kingdom of Kiziba, part of German East Africa at the time, to draw samples from plague-infected victims, the doctor summoned the person suspected responsible for spreading the rumour and had him hanged.[41] The research material collected was essentially data and in theory not very different from the dozens of items of personal information that corporations today can crowdsource from social media to commercialize. The material and the social body are mutually constitutive,[42] but today, this relationship also includes the digital body. What happens in the digital realm has physical or biological consequences and vice versa. When refugees are asked to give up their biometric characteristics upon arrival in refugee camps, a denial to let their biological body be digitized could have consequences for the receipt of life-saving aid.

This situates issues of ethics at the centre. Over the past hundred years, early German ethical rules (disregarded during the two World Wars, obviously) helped develop the Nuremberg code,[43] which inspired the Declaration of Helsinki and other ethical protocols such as the guidelines of the Council for International Organizations of Medical Sciences (CIOMS), the Convention on Human Rights and Biomedicine, and the famous Belmont report. Today, we understand the core concerns of these frameworks as pertaining to non-maleficence, beneficence, respect for autonomy, and justice in experimentation. These are notions that obviously go through many layers of translation as they are inscripted into (or disregarded in) experimental protocols. Informed consent is one such material practice of ethics that stands as almost unbreakable, fundamentally concerned with making sure that subjects understand exactly what they are getting into when agreeing to partake in experiments. 'Respect for persons' is sometimes translated in reductionist terms and taken to mean that consent mainly requires 'information that a rational person would need'.[44] But what is a rational person? One who is cut loose from the constraining conditions of circumstance and not influenced by concerns such as poverty or lack of access to health treatment? What does it mean to volunteer in countries with little or no basic health care and can that consent ever be 'free' or made with 'respect for persons'?

There are many pertinent questions when experiments are taken to contexts where there is no need for coercion, as the structural conditions of inequality themselves facilitate voluntariness. Social or economic conditions greatly influence the risk tolerance of individuals, and while some experiments may be limited to consequences for the individual, larger experiments may also put a collective at risk through consequences that were not foreseen. Principles of justice that remain in some ethical codes are interesting for the way they address access, arguing that subjects should have access to the medicines or treatments once experimented with. Likewise, justice denotes how the benefits of the research should not befall disproportionately to a class or race that does not participate in the research. Nonetheless, we will see here that some groups are systematically incorporated in experimentation because of their relative availability, enabled through pronounced inequalities. Methodological integrity becomes scientific integrity becomes human integrity. So, who partakes in experiments and who benefits from the potential treatment? How much risk is tolerable, and who gets to decide this? There might not be any immediate health risks associated with taking a given experimental drug that is being trialled. But what if the perceived treatment is placebo, or if the trial is cancelled after two months, after which the subject cannot afford access to another form of treatment, making trialling the only *de facto* accessible treatment. There are many questions of ethics at play that experimenters must juggle as they not only wield power over subjects directly in the research but also through the conclusions they draw on the basis of experiments. The conclusions from the trial may very well go on to influence resource allocation at a political level, affecting the local population in ways the experiments do not or could not know. Beginning to understand the nature of experimental practice and conceptions of the Global South as a laboratory, the ensuing question becomes exactly what it is experimentation can produce and what types of knowledge it gives prominence to. In short, why the movement depicted here sees experimentation as such a strict necessity.

*

Do worms affect attendance in schools? In what is now a famous experiment in the *randomista* movement, Berkeley Professor Edward Miguel and Nobel Prize laurate Michael Kremer trialled the effects of treatments for intestinal worms in schools in Kenya in the mid-1990s. Their findings were astounding— a deworming treatment at the cost of only 49 cents per year proved able to bring down absenteeism in the Kenyan schools trialled by 25 per cent. This was seemingly so because worm infections among the children often occurred on their way to school, walking bare footed in places where infected children had defecated. The findings were so authoritative, the authors wrote as they published them, 'that they fully justify subsidizing treatment.'[45] At the time, the Abdul Latif Jameel Poverty Action Lab at MIT or J-PAL as it is known for short today, quickly plotted the findings against other programmes to show that the cost per extra year of education for deworming was a mere $3.50 compared to more than $6,000 in the otherwise successful Mexican Progresa programme that aimed to increase children's education and health through cash transfers. Inaugurated in 2003, J-PAL has since developed immensely and now spearheads the randomista movement. The institution has grown from four affiliated professors and a few projects during its inception year to more than 160 professors and engagement in over 1,000 experiments across the world today. Expanding on the aforementioned experiment ten years later in 2014, French-Indian economist duo and J-PAL leads Abhijit Banerjee and Esther Duflo noted that, based on the available cost-evidence, deworming is twenty times more effective for school attendance than hiring an extra teacher.[46] One must simply look at the numbers, the evidence, to understand that some programmes are much cheaper than others. But their most important conclusion was that policymaking should be about the efficacy of programmes—and that to learn about such we need to cast away a priori knowledge and base ourselves solely on experiments, and ideally multiple experiments at the same time on the same population.

Some of the ideas implicitly or explicitly given weight above mirror the way many organizations of the experimental movement think and work. Questions about 'the evidence' are as frequent as any I have heard while interviewing employees of the Bill and Melinda Gates Foundation through the years—what does the evidence show? Is the evidence 'solid' and systematic? At a meeting with a foundation senior programme officer (PO) in its Seattle headquarters, the talk about her field of work immediately moved to the lack of 'evidence' being produced. When I pushed the subject by asking what in fact constitutes good evidence, the senior PO was very clear: 'we have too much anecdotal knowledge and qualitative work that doesn't tell us enough about the big picture; what works and what doesn't? What is most effective compared to other interventions? We need to gather systematic evidence'. 'Can't a dozen observational cases be seen as systematic', I probed, 'if there are certain similar findings across them?', 'No, we need to know the exact effects and we need to replicate those effects elsewhere to make sure that the conclusions we reach are valid' she responded and ended with the short answer to my final question of how we do that: 'RCTs!'.[47]

The battle for what is scientific evidence and what is not, appears as real today as it was four hundred years ago when Robert Boyle's Royal Society experimentalists came together to confront competing methodological regimes.

Experimentation is seen by its proponents to give way for quantification, generalized, and systematic evidence, comparison, and replication. There are important attempts at establishing authority of scientific knowledge in play in the two illustrations above, from a perspective that not all evidence is equally valid. Both stories hold a pronounced asymmetry of comprehension—some understand and are able to produce knowledge, others are not. Those who do not follow the reason of experimentation simply fail to produce valid and objective knowledge and evidence. Objectivity is stressed as the epitome of science, but is there such a thing as a universality of scientific knowledge? Universal claims certainly have an immediate allure. The laws of nature are the same everywhere, we often assume. Conditions may change, yet causality remains. Newton's laws of motion, as he laid them out in *Mathematical Principles of Natural Philosophy*, the very title of which hints at the perceived objective measure of knowledge, being just one commonly used example of these. Their designation as *laws* means they are seen by a scientific community as universal and natural. What gives them these traits is agreement that they have not been invented or constructed by scientists, they have simply been discovered, as though a mirror has been held up to nature. Objectivity then, lends authority and forms the height of scientific knowledge in many disciplines. But it also carries a deeply moral value by connecting itself to the idea of fairness. Subjective knowledge is seen as biased and thus fundamentally unfair because it will always lean to one side or the other. Fairness in objective scientific knowledge on the other hand seemingly presents a truth detached from political, social, or other localized disturbances—it is a way of making decisions without having to decide. At least it is thought so by its proponents. The famous positivist Karl Pearson put it bluntly: 'those who do not seek truth from an unbiassed standpoint are, in the theology of freethought, ministers in the devil's synagogue'.[48]

If bias is the devil, then quantification may very well be John the Apostle, Jesus' most important friend, for the ways in which numbers help experiments construct their scientific authority. In attempts at rendering society objective through quantification, mathematics is exceedingly important for the way it is thought synonymous with rigour and universality. To the American historian of science Theodore M. Porter, numbers, graphs, and formulae are strategies of communication, used to convey objectivity and validity, just as they are deeply connected to community—to social identities and world views expressed through them. Quantification is a great methodological tool of reductionism and ordering, of making a complex and nonlinear social world seem orderly so that we may direct policy and see it achieve expected results in practice.

When Gates Foundation employees longingly tell me of some of the grand issues they engage in—'if only there was a model for that'—it expresses a deeply rooted yearning for making the nonlinear, linear. As we shall see later, the prestige and power of numbers today cannot be separated from the rise and development of Silicon Valley.[49]

When coupled, objectivity and quantification also form a strategy for dealing with distance and distrust. Being able to compare results is a key foundation for producing evidence from experiments, something observations are thought unable to provide because of bias. Reliance on numbers and quantitative manipulation instead reduces the need for personal trust, with methods seen as easily able to travel beyond the boundaries of locality. Without a need for trust, it doesn't matter who produces the data, furthering impersonality and paving the way for operations on the scale of J-PAL in which the decontextualization of knowledge and solutions to social problems reaches an immense height. Neither does it matter where in the world the data is produced, so long as it addresses the *same* problem. All that is produced can then feed into a collective pool of decontextualized knowledge that may inform decisions anywhere. As Esther Duflo proclaimed when interviewed immediately after winning the Nobel Prize in economics in 2019: 'We keep running into the same problem from place to place to place, in India, in Africa, even in France, we have the same problem. And the solutions, in a sense, then can be the same'.[50] We will return to the question of whether social problems and solutions can ever be the same across scales of time and place.

*

Some actors in the experimental movement are in the business of doing good, others are good at doing business but they each deserve a few more words before we move on to exploring them in the remainder of the book. What follows here, then, is both an account of the experimental movement's key actors, and a primer of how the book's narrative is structured over the next few hundred pages. We start with the next chapter's humanitarians, a group of actors whose inclusion in these discussions likely forms the most provocative claim exactly because their ambitions from the outset are both altruistic and laudable. We are witnessing a massive complexity of protracted conflicts, disasters and crises, and the number of displaced people is at its highest since World War II. For the humanitarian industry—across civil society, multilateral organizations, and private charities—the intent and purpose has always been a stable foundation: to save human lives, provide emergency relief to the most vulnerable, and alleviate suffering among those who have been exposed to conflicts and disasters. But in recent years, new digital technologies have radically altered how the humanitarians identify, prevent, and resolve conflicts and disasters—whether they are human or caused by nature. Mobile phones, geo-data technologies and social networks have made it possible to collect data about when crises occur and how to stop them. Digital payment systems and iris scanners are increasingly used to control the delivery of emergency aid, food, and water in refugee camps. Biometric data from millions of people is collected and employed to identify and follow refugees and migrants as they move across borders. And just as defence forces laud them for their use in situations of war, humanitarians have great expectations for the use of drones to provide relief in service of the poor. All these inventions are made with hopes of success, yet failure is simultaneously seen as a productive force of progress, and the faster the failure the better.

A striking feature of contemporary humanitarianism then is its experimental turn. Humanitarian actors have turned to new and in some instances unproven and untested approaches and technologies, partly because of a growing pressure on them to do more with less resources, and partly because of a growing fashion for the sector to 'innovate itself' through datafication and digitization. As a consequence, almost all humanitarian organizations now have innovation and technology departments working only to experiment with new technologies and innovative approaches to humanitarian work. Many of these technologies are essentially what Harvard Professor Sheila Jasanoff has coined *technologies of hubris*, designed to facilitate ordering and the management of populations, and sourcing their power by way of constructed objectivity pursued through the use of, for example, quantitative or complex statistical analysis.[51] The idea of hubris conveys the significant amount of uncertainty encapsulated in them. It is this inherent inability to wield control over the technologies that makes their use experimental. Like RCTs and clinical trials, the introduction of new technologies is often presented as a logical and ordered process in which the technical and determinist nature of the technologies makes for almost objective processes of implementation. Technologies such as biometric registration systems have a pre-determined and linear form for those who use them. You input biographic information by asking a set of fixed questions that have been decided by people far away from where you are, likely in a headquarters somewhere in the North. The refugee responds, and you then proceed to taking fingerprints and iris scans. It is a mundane effort, whose repetitive and monotonous nature in practice helps to clout unknowns or risks for those who employ them. Even if it essentially captures and documents the central life and biological conditions of a vulnerable human being, the process is bureaucratic and rationally practical, executed as though it were as harmless as completing an annual tax bill. Yet the potential risks lie not as much here in the individual reception of refugees and collection data as in the collective production of a massive amount of sensitive data. It is the distance or decoupling between the mundane bureaucratic capture and the mass-collection of personal and vulnerable information that may lead us to not take seriously the inherent risks in such procedures. Exponential technologies are not uncertain because they are difficult to use or understand in practice, but because of the implications their actions may turn out to have on a grander scale. In **Chapter 2**, we will dive into the corporeal reality of humanitarian experimentation today to understand the relationship between cause and effect, exploring what can be called the politics of demarcation; that by maintaining a focus on the technology itself rather than what it produces, we risk a blindness to fundamental uncertainties and wider implications of such experimental practices.

Vital to the experimental movement are the *randomistas* we met at the beginning of this chapter, so named for their affinity for randomized controlled trials and the supposed golden ability of experiments to generate universal evidence. RCTs began migrating to development economics in the 1980s but had a difficult time manifesting themselves as a true alternative to existing forms of knowledge production back then. As we reached the new millennium, large scale government interventions were increasingly questioned for their apparent inability to produce development, whether the market-oriented policy reforms of the structural adjustment programmes or the surge in UN social sector projects following the collapse of the Soviet Union. This was combined with both a growing focus on the effectiveness and measurability of results in aid, as well as an empirical turn in the field of economics that saw the discipline refocus part of its attention towards exploring causal identification. That is, the documentation of causes and effect as well as the isolation of specific factors or variables in such. Together, these developments pushed forward RCTs as a new way to bring experiments into the real world and helped establish and solidify the work of organizations such as J-PAL, whose two leaders Duflo and Banerjee today form the intellectual face of the movement at large.

The movement has grown immensely since early randomistas suggested developing countries to be ideal testing grounds for the movement. Today, it furthers a dual aim of establishing methodological and theoretical dominance of RCTs and experimentation in generating knowledge on development interventions and their effectiveness, and of mass-institutionalizing the tangible execution of experiments to shape policymaking around the world. In contrast to the political advice of what it considers policy or 'soft' experts, the movement sees itself as based on a mechanical objectivity from the hard sciences thought to remove bias and subjectivity, releasing decisions from any notion of a political nature by presenting them in an envelope of independence and scienticism. The aim is to transform complex and perhaps multi-solution problems of development into technical matters of hard evidence that can, in theory, reduce the uncertainty of social policy and projects. To obtain methodological dominance, the movement has employed diverse strategies of discrediting opponent disciplines, fields of science, and existing approaches to knowledge and evaluation production. Far from a contingent rise to prominence, the randomistas have skilfully and strategically utilized windows of opportunity left open by disciplinary battles in both economics and the development field, and quickly risen to assume positions at the top of the evidence-producing hierarchy for development. As we will see in **Chapter 3**, they have been immensely adept at building institutions and legitimacy around their specific experimental approach, continuously expanding their network and presence, both in elite university settings and on the ground in developing countries, culminating with the 2019 Nobel Prize. From this base, they have moved to fundamentally reshape government and non-state policy and interventions alike. They are, accordingly, a crucial proponent and transmitter of the new experimental regime in the Global South, holding dearly the RCT and its ensuing ways of both perceiving and exercising influence in the world.

Randomistas, as well as the experimental movement at large, benefit greatly from a re-emerging powerhouse of financial and political influence in the Global South—the private foundations. Foundations have been major players in international matters for more than a hundred years, as significant transmitters of science, technology, and value systems from Western to developing countries. They have both financed and directly executed forms of experimentation throughout the Global South, from education curricula in Africa to agri-tech in Asia to policy reforms in Latin America. Yet we are witnessing a new situation today that surpasses even the significant historical baggage. A set of novel foundations and philanthropists have soared to new heights of political influence as they have increasingly turned their foundation activities outwards to the rest of the world. Sometimes referred to as philanthrocapitalists or technophilanthropists because of how they embody the three notions of philanthropy, technology, and capitalism, a new group of hyper actors have emerged with enormous expectations about their ability to change the world, driving what they see as a global social revolution through technological innovation and experimentation. From Mark Zuckerberg to Bill Gates to Jeff Bezos, these individuals have made their fortunes in the digital economy that emerged at the end of the twentieth and the beginning of the twenty-first centuries and now dream of eradicating diseases, educating the poor, and bringing the digital revolution to all corners of the world. Their philanthropic endeavours and private foundations are, like their companies, shaped by logics of societal progress through technological innovation and experimentation.

Steering this train of thought and action today is the Bill and Melinda Gates Foundation. An immense political and economic force investing billions of dollars in medical and social research and experimentation, the foundation is currently shaping the lives of poor people and poor nations around the world. By experimenting with the development of new toilets, vaccines, or birth control to be distributed throughout the Global South, it furthers a view of this part of the world as a form of laboratory in which technical and social experiments and interventions are necessary for social progress. **Chapter 4** opens up the contemporary efforts of private foundations to use the Global South as a laboratory ready for experiments, whether in the form of radically changing social norms or testing new technologies. Actions that build on a knowledge regime not least inspired by the natural scientific and in particular the medical realm, as furthered by another key actor in the movement—global pharmas.

It was John le Carré's 2001 novel *The Constant Gardener*, and its Oscar-winning adaptation to the big screen, that brought clinical trials into the public imagination by portraying a British diplomat uncovering a story of medical experimentation in Africa as the root cause for his wife's murder. Today as then, pharmaceutical companies are major funders, developers, and diffusors of clinical trials and RCTs in the biomedical sphere and beyond. Over the past decades, drug development, production, and distribution has moved from a national and regionally centred activity to a global one. This was initially facilitated by a set of 1975 provisions that saw the US Food and Drug Administration (FDA) open up for data from foreign clinical trials. In the pharmaceutical business, FDA approval is the holy grail of drug development; billions and billions of dollars are invested towards outcome every year, but it is something only forty-eight drugs obtained in 2019. While global clinical trials may not be a new-found phenomenon, the business has expanded immensely over the past few years, looking to approach the 65-billion-dollar mark by 2025, just as it has moved into new fields of trialling. And above all, it is the business that pursues experimental efforts in the Global South with the greatest of force, significantly transformed over the past decades to work across the globe.

Twenty years ago, more than 80 per cent of all FDA Regulated Investigators—a specialist term for those responsible for any clinical investigation of a drug, biological product, or medical device—were based in the United States. Today, that number is approaching less than half, a watershed moment for the globalization of clinical trials as non-US based investigators will soon form the majority. Pharmaceutical companies are increasingly outsourcing and offshoring clinical trial activities to contract research organizations (CROs) throughout the Global South, who are adept at quickly recruiting patients and producing results that are transferrable or translatable to the pharmas on whose behalf they work. Like the civil society organizations of development cooperation, they can access local populations, enlist, recruit, facilitate, and execute implementation in countries that are far from 'home' for many pharmas. For the pharmaceuticals, these developments result from a combined push and pull. 'At home' in the US or Europe, they face difficulties in subject recruitment (more than 95 per cent of US patients don't want to partake in clinical trials), higher standards of care and bars of regulation, and higher costs altogether for the crucial Phase III component of clinical trials that requires up to thousands of human subjects. The pull factors mirror these very well. The Global South provides fast and naïve (the clinical term for subjects who have not received prior medication for their illness) recruitment, a large number of subjects, and a different regulatory environments.[52] And then there are the CROs, whose breadth of services have come to include everything from drug discovery to bioanalytical services and data management, meaning that even mid-size and small pharmaceuticals can increasingly move their trials to regions and countries in the Global South traditionally out of their reach. This is where we will go in **Chapter 5** then, with Thailand as an empirical backdrop, to understand the experimental mindset that inspires the book's other actors to this day, helping to stabilize experimental practice as everyday treatment.

Common to these actors that we will meet through the book's chapters is that they are all deeply related to an epicentre of experimentation today—Silicon Valley. Sometimes directly through partnerships, funding, personnel, or the employment of nascent technology and sometimes by ways of ideas and methodology. Silicon Valley, or perhaps more precisely the core organizations that make up and shape technology startup culture today, have become major diffusors of ideas and practices of experimentation and trialling through mantras such as *fail fast*. In the wake of the United Nations' Sustainable Development Goals and Agenda 2030, startups and their technologies have crashed onto the scene of global development, increasingly deploying their experimental technologies in refugee camps and poor communities and looked to as the new innovators of development. Yet the introduction of all new and radical technologies comes with a veil that clouts our ability to understand their eventual consequences. Some may have few, but others may come to shape societies, social relations, or individual lives in ways we cannot imagine as we develop or begin to introduce them. Some technologies are so new that they have not been tested much in the real world, and others may have been tried out in different places but have never been put to use either in the specific context of humanitarian emergencies or at the scale they are now being put to use. They hold great unknowns and indeterminacies, the outcomes of which we will not know until we eventually face them and will have to appease them. Unintended consequences whose likelihood grows with the speed of scaling and adoption—the quicker we introduce and scale a new technology that has not been trialled elsewhere or combine existing ones to new forms—the greater the scale of potential negative consequences if such emerge. As we will see in **Chapter 6**, the magnitude of any effects also grows as the boundaries between the digital, social, and material body becomes blurred, with little separation of the technological from the social and material.

Over the following chapters, we will venture into sites and organizations of modern technoscience that practices a newfound experimental drive in the Global South. Most of the cases here will evoke questions about inequality, power, or hierarchies of evidence and knowledge. But also, of the evil of necessity. The contexts and circumstances in which the experiments take place are often ones of emergency and of destitution, perhaps begging obvious questions of progress through experimentation or no progress at all. And many of the experimental practices do concern themselves with improving the lives of poor people. But on their way to doing so, they sometimes forget exactly why it is they are experimenting and for whom, risking to maintain rather than confront inequalities. The rest of the book then unfolds the inequality inherent in this experimental regime, both in how it works and what it produces. We start with the radical machine dreams of today's humanitarians.

Notes

1. Inman, P. 2019. Economics Nobel prize won by academics for tackling poverty, *The Guardian*, 14 October
2. See Klein, N. 2008. The Shock Doctrine. 1st edition, Picador; for a brilliant historical account of experimentation in Africa see Tilley, H. 2011. Africa as a living laboratory:

Empire, development and the problem of scientific knowledge, 1870–1950. University of Chicago Press.

3. See also Said, E.W. 1978. *Orientalism*. New York: Vintage Books; Said, E.W. 1994. *Culture and Imperialism*. New York: Knopf; Foucault, M. 1970. *The Order of Things: An Archaeology of the Human Sciences*. London: Tavistock Publications.

4. Shapin, S. and Schaffer, S. 1985. *Leviathan and the Air-pump: Hobbes, Boyle and the Experimental Life*. Princeton, NJ: Princeton University Press.

5. Hansson, S.O. 2016. Experiments: why and how?, *Science and Engineering Ethics* 22(3): 613–32.

6. Ivy, A. 1948. The history and ethics of the use of human subjects in medical experiments, *Science* 108: 2 July.

7. See Merriam Webster.

8. Lock, M. and Nguyen, V.K. 2010. *The Social Life of Organs. An Anthropology of Biomedicine*. Chichester: Wiley-Blackwell.

9. Small, A.W. 1921. The future of sociology, *Publications of the American Sociological Society* 15: 174–93, at 187.

10. Beck, U. 1994. *Ecological Enlightenment: Essays on the Politics of the Risk Society*. Amherst, NY: Prometheus Books, p. 125.

11. Gross, M. 2009. Collaborative experiments: Jane Addams, Hull House and experimental social work, *Social Science Information* 48: 81–95; see Beck, U. 1997. The world as laboratory. In S. E. Bronner (ed.), *Twentieth-century Political Theory*. London: Routledge, pp. 356–66; Latour, B. 2004. *Politics of Nature: How to Bring the Sciences into Democracy*, Cambridge, MA: Harvard University Press.

12. Barrett, C.B. and Carter, M.R. 2014. Retreat from radical skepticism: Rebalancing theory, observational data and randomization in development economics. In Dawn Teele (ed.), *Field Experiments and Their Critics: Essays on the Uses and Abuses of Experiments in the Social Sciences*. New Haven, CT: Yale University Press, pp. 58–77.

13. Latour, B. and Woolgar, S. 1986. *Laboratory Life: The Construction of Scientific Facts*. Princeton, NJ: Princeton University Press; Latour, B. 1987. *Science in Action: How to Follow Scientists and Engineers through Society*. Cambridge, MA: Harvard University Press.

14. Baldassarri, D. and Abascal, M. 2017. Field experiments across the social sciences, *Annual Review of Sociology* 43(1): 41–73; McDermott, R. 2011. Internal and external validity. In J.N. Druckman, D.P. Green, J.H. Kuklinski, and A. Lupia (eds), *Cambridge Handbook of Experimental Political Science*. Cambridge, UK: Cambridge University Press, pp. 27–40; Gerber, A.S. and Green, D.P. 2012. *Field Experiments*. New York: Norton.

15. Ivy, 1948.

16. Bulkeley, H., Castán Broto, V., Maassen, A., et al., 2011. Governing low carbon transitions. In H. Bulkeley (ed.), *Cities and Low Carbon Transitions*. London and New York: Routledge Taylor and Francis Group, pp. 29–41.

17. Coville, A., Galiani, S., Gertler, P., and Yoshida, S. 2020. Enforcing Payment for Water and Sanitation Services in Nairobi's Slums, NBER Working Paper No. 27569, Issued in July 2020.

18. van de Poel, I. 2011. Nuclear energy as a social experiment, *Ethics, Policy & Environment* 14(3): 285–90.

19. Rheinberger, H.J. 1997. *Toward a History of Epistemic Things: Synthesizing Proteins in the Test Tube*. Stanford, CA: Stanford University Press; Gross, M. 2010. The public

proceduralization of contingency: Bruno Latour and the formation of collective experiments, *Social Epistemology* 24(1): 63–74.

20. Gross, M. 2010. *Ignorance and Surprise: Science, Society, and Ecological Design.* Cambridge, MA: MIT Press; Gross, M. and McGoey, L. (eds). 2015. *Routledge International Handbook of Ignorance Studies.* London: Routledge.

21. Shelley, M. *Frankenstein.* London: Penguin Classics, pp. 36–7.

22. Latour and Woolgar, 1986.

23. Krohn, W. and Weyer, J. 1994. Society as a laboratory: the social risks of experimental research, *Science and Public Policy* 21(3): 173–83.

24. Gieryn, T.F. 2006. City as truth-spot: laboratories and field-sites in urban studies, *Social Studies of Science* 36(1): 5–38.

25. Kohler, R.E. 2008. Lab history: reflections, *Isis* 99: 761–8.

26. Guggenheim, M. 2012. Laboratizing and delaboratizing the world: changing sociological concepts for places of knowledge production, *History of the Human Sciences* 25(1): 99–118.

27. Shapin and Schaffer, 1985.

28. Lorimer, J. and Driessen, C. 2014. Wild experiments at the Oostvaardersplassen, *Transactions of the Institute of British Geographers* 39(2): 169–81; see Lemov, R. 2006. *World as Laboratory—Experiments with Mice, Mazes and Men.* New York: Hill and Wang.

29. Knorr Cetina, K. 1999. *Epistemic Cultures: How the Sciences Make Knowledge.* Cambridge, MA: Harvard University Press.

30. Teele, D. (ed.), 2014. *Field Experiments and Their Critics: Essays on the Uses and Abuses of Experiments in the Social Sciences.* New Haven, CT: Yale University Press.

31. Latour, B. 1988. *The Pasteurization of France.* Cambridge, MA: Harvard University Press.

32. Although obviously in incomparable forms to the cruel history just told.

33. See Hudson, N. 1996. From 'Nation' to 'Race': the origin of racial classification in eighteenth-century thought, *Eighteenth-Century Studies* 29(3): 247–64; Saini, A. 2019. *Superior—The Return of Race Science.* Boson, MA: Beacon Press.

34. See Morton, S.G. 1839. *Crania Americana: Or, a Comparative View of the Skulls of Various Aboriginal Nations of North and South America: To Which Is Prefixed an Essay on the Varieties of the Human Species.* Philadelphia: J. Dobson; Nott, J.C. and Gliddon, G.R. 1854. *Types of Mankind: Or Ethnological Researches, Based upon the Ancient Monuments, Paintings, Sculptures, and Crania of Races, and upon their Natural, Geographical, Philological, and Biblical History.* Philadelphia, PA: Lippincott, Grambo.

35. Hacking, I. 2005. Why race still matters, *Daedalus* 134(1) (Winter): 102–16.

36. See Morning, A. 2011. *The Nature of Race: How Scientists Think and Teach about Human Difference.* Berkeley: University of California Press; Epstein, S. 2007. *Inclusion: The Politics of Difference in Medical Research.* Chicago, IL: University of Chicago Press.

37. Montoya, M.J. 2011. *Making the Mexican Diabetic: Race, Science, and the Genetics of Inequality.* Berkeley: University of California Press.

38. Epstein, 2007.

39. Morning, 2011.

40. Michael, M. and Rosengarten, M. 2012. Medicine: experimentation, politics, emergent bodies, *Body and Society* 18(3–4): 1–17.

41. Malloy, P. 2014. Research material and necromancy: imagining the political-economy of biomedicine in Colonial Tanganyika, *The International Journal of African Historical Studies* 47(3), 425–43.

42. Butler, J. 1993. *Bodies That Matter: On the Discursive Limits of 'Sex'*. New York: Routledge.

43. Vollmann, J. and Winau, R. 1996. Informed consent in human experimentation before the Nuremberg code, *British Medical Journal* 313: 1445–7.

44. Martin, M. and Schinzinger, R. 1988. *Engineering Ethics*, 2nd ed. New York: McGraw-Hill; see also Dussel, E.D. and Vallega, A.A. 2012. *Ethics of Liberation in the Age of Globalization and Exclusion*. Durham: Duke University Press.

45. Kremer, M. and Miguel, E. Worms: identifying impacts on education and health in the presence of treatment externalities, *Econometrica* 72(1): 159–217.

46. Banerjee, A. and Duflo, E. 2009. The experimental approach to development economics, NBER working paper, No. 14467.

47. Interview with Senior Programme Officer, Bill and Melinda Gates Foundation, March 2019.

48. As Quoted in Porter, T. 1995. *Trust in Numbers*. Princeton, NJ: Princeton University Press.

49. Mirowski, P. 2002. *Machine Dreams: Economics Becomes a Cyborg Science*. Cambridge: Cambridge University Press; Porter, 1995.

50. See Nobel interview with Esther Duflo, available at: https://www.nobelprize.org/prizes/economic-sciences/2019/duflo/interview/.

51. Jasanoff, S. 2003. Technologies of humility: citizen participation in governing science, *Minerva* 41: 223–44.

52. See also Goldacre, B. 2013. *Bad Pharma: How Drug Companies Mislead Doctors and Harm Patients*. New York: Faber & Faber; Shah, S. 2006. *The Body Hunters: Testing New Drugs on the World's Poorest Patients*. New York: New Press.

2

Humanitarian Machine Dreams

On the morning of 30 August 2017, Burmese security forces approached the village of Tula Toli in the Maungdaw Township. The soldiers helicoptered in the day before were supported by armed Rakhine villagers who had received uniforms and weapons from the forces. Hundreds of unarmed Rohingya Muslims were trapped on the banks of the river surrounding Tula Toli as security forces and villagers approached and opened fire on the defenceless group. Some tried to swim across to the other shores and were killed in the water. The families could not move and tried to defend their children. The men were killed first, with guns, machetes, and clubs. The children were killed in front of their mothers or thrown into the bamboo huts that had been set ablaze. The women were raped, hacked, and many of them killed over the next few hours, the village of some 300 structures burned to the ground. Hassina, a 20-year-old woman, desperately tried to hide her 1-year-old girl under her shawl, but a soldier noticed, wrestled the girl from her mother and threw her into a burning hut.[1]

From late 2016 to the end of 2017, almost a million people belonging to the ethnic minority Rohingya, living in Rakhine State in Myanmar's north-western region, fled the country. Tens of thousands were killed at the brutal hands of the Tatmadaw, Myanmar's armed forces, who murdered, raped, and burned their way through Rohingya villages. The official cover from the government was the pursuit of a Rohingya insurgent group known as Arakan Rohingya Salvation Army or ARSA, and that only a few targeted killings of terrorists had taken place. In reality, it seems to have been an ethnic cleansing and genocide, following a pattern that had seen the ethnic minority persecuted by the Myanmari government and nationalist Buddhists since at least the late 1970s. As State Counsellor, Aung San Suu Kyi, the Nobel Peace Prize winner and formerly political prisoner, watched in silence as the slaughter unfolded.

At a press conference in New York City in early 2018, Yanghee Lee, Investigator for the UN Fact-Finding Mission on Myanmar, exclaimed that social media had 'substantially contributed to the level of acrimony and dissension and conflict', and that in Myanmar, 'social media is Facebook, and Facebook is social media'.[2] Facebook is a strong part of both public and private life in the country, and the government often uses it to relay information to the public, but the platform had 'turned into a beast, and not what it originally intended', she proclaimed.[3] The UN mission argued that Facebook had functioned as an effective platform for hate speech, misinformation, and false accusations that incited violence against the Rohingya.[4] One of the chain letters making its way online among the Myanmari population with misinformation warned citizens that a Rohingya 'Jihad' was underway, that people should defend themselves, and that the armed forces had already been asked to take up arms against the Muslims. The effect could be felt on the streets and in public transport, with many keeping their children out of school on the day designated in the letter. Other instances saw military personnel posting fake pictures and stories about Rohingya people raping or killing Buddhist women. Upwards of 700 military personnel were tasked with creating fake accounts, including celebrity and news accounts, and spreading anti-Rohingya fake news timed for peak viewership. Many of these Burmese soldiers had gone to Russia for their disinformation training. Not until August 2018 were most of these accounts taken down by Facebook. By then, the covert military propaganda operation had been in operation for years, working from bases in the foothills near the capital of Naypyidaw, and the Rohingya massacres had been carried out.[5] In December of 2021, a group of Rohingya survivors filed a US class-action complaint in California against Facebook, suing the company for reparations worth up to $150 billion, arguing that the company's failure to police content and the platform's design contributed to real-world violence towards the Rohingya community. The immediate response from Facebook, or rather from its mother company Meta, was that it is protected from liability over content posted by users by a US internet law called Section 230, which holds that online platforms are not liable for content posted by third parties.[6]

During the Arab Spring, social media were hailed as pathways to freedom and democracy. Today, that dream and the revolutions along with it, seems to be dead. Recent years have shown that we do not fully comprehend the power and rapid ability of new technologies to shift from good to bad—their true political, human, and social consequences are clouded and may easily change over time. The very same instruments that we thought would bring freedom have now brought death and suffering upon others, as governments and political groups have learned to use social media to their own terrible advantage. New technologies, whose potential and multiple uses we only see and understand as they evolve naturally over time, may have grave consequences for vulnerable populations. There is one place in particular, however, where technological experimentation is continually accentuated as a path to peace and prosperity—the humanitarian industry. The world is witnessing more conflicts, disasters, and crises than perhaps ever before, such as the one in Myanmar, at a time when the number of displaced people is at its highest since World War II. For the humanitarian industry, the intention and fundamental purpose have always been the same—to save human lives, provide emergency relief to the most vulnerable, and alleviate suffering among those who have been exposed to conflict and disaster. But in recent years, new digital technologies have radically altered how humanitarian actors identify, prevent, and resolve conflict and disaster—whether they are human or caused by nature. Digital early warning systems are being developed to predict and analyse humanitarian crises using big data drawn from mobile phones, satellite imagery, or social media, utilizing advances in computing and AI. Digital payment systems and iris scanners are widely used to organize and control the delivery of emergency aid, food, and water in refugee camps. Biometric data are collected and employed to identify and follow refugees and migrants as they move across borders. And just as they are used to cause death and destruction in situations of war, there are also great expectations for the use of 'good' drones to provide relief, medicine, or food in service of the poor.

A new experimental humanitarianism has emerged with supposed omni-improvement of our ability to identify and solve crises in a more effective and accountable way.[7] The World Disaster Report, a major source of humanitarian influence published by The International Federation of the Red Cross, has framed the situation this way: 'New ICT tools for humanitarian action are proposed with the potential to detect needs earlier and predict crises better, enable greater scale, speed and efficiency of response and assistance delivery, enhance the specificity of resource transfers to match the needs of communities at risk, and increase accountability'.[8] Humanitarian actors have turned to these new—and in some cases unproven and untested—approaches and technologies, partly because of a growing pressure on them to do more with fewer resources, and partly because of calls for the sector to 'innovate itself' through datafication and digitization. As a consequence, almost all emergency organizations now employ innovation and technology departments working only to experiment with new technologies and *innovative* approaches to humanitarian and development work. One common feature of most of the new technologies and methodologies tested by the humanitarian sector is that they are experimental.[9] Innovations are made with hopes of success, yet failure is simultaneously seen as a productive force, and the faster the failure the better, allowing the inventers to produce new and better experiments. Some of the technologies may have been tested under stable conditions, sometimes in lab-like situations and sometimes in stable situations in the North. But once they make their way into humanitarian operations, the situations they meet and are expected to function in are so radically different from where they were tested that we can only consider them as new forms of experimenting.

Many of us talk of the potential for cryptocurrencies to change economies and societies but mainly speculate in private, buying Bitcoin, Ethereum, or Dogecoin in the hope of making a lesser or greater digital fortune. And it will take years if not decades for tech-companies to gain public regulatory acceptance to experiment with transferring central parts of our economies to digital ledgers. In humanitarian situations, where needs are desperate and regulations scarce because of the fragile nature of the contexts, the room for experimentation appears wider. Here then, is where we find the true experiments of the new digitized age. The new focus on technology to save lives changes the way we try to help the world's poorest and most vulnerable, making it more or less effective. Technology euphoria and new digital instruments alter core issues about when, who, how, and for what purposes we should help other people. The technological turn, in essence, opens the way for a wide variety of new experimental types and forms of humanitarian interventions, in some situations making access to technology in itself a form of relief. It opens a door to and builds dependence on new actors: startups or other organizations with limited experience in emergencies, whose inclusion and work must also fundamentally be seen as experimental. It changes the relationships between actors, the accountability between beneficiaries and donors, the very form of the relief provided, and our drive to aid others. And the potential risks are certainly not only digital. There are fluid boundaries between the technological and 'real' world of humanitarian efforts, and we increasingly see overlapping and integrated sites of activities, communication, and interaction.[10] And as we will see for the movement as a whole, these changes to contemporary humanitarianism are greatly inspired by ideas and practices emerging out of Silicon Valley—ideas about rapid radical change, willingness to experiment with other people's lives, and the individualization and potential overriding of central social institutions in the name of technological innovation.

*

Nine days. It took the Afghan Islamist movement Taliban roughly nine days in August 2021 to conquer the country's 34 provincial capitals. It started without much fight in the city of Zaranj in the south-western part of the country, bordering Iran and Pakistan, on Friday 6 August. In Helmand province, the US and Afghan armies tried to push the Taliban back with air strikes, but to no avail. A few days later, the group had conquered most of the northern provinces and the strategically important city of Kunduz. In late June, the US intelligence service delivered a conclusion that President Biden and the political elite refused to believe: the Afghan army and government could collapse in just six months. There was no way it could happen so quickly, the American politicians maintained. Unfortunately, reality surpassed imagination when the Taliban arrived in Kabul on 15 August. The Taliban's takeover of the capital culminated in surreal images from the presidential palace's fitness room where Taliban fighters amused themselves with workout equipment they had clearly never seen before, and from a local amusement park where they rode radio cars donning AK-47s.

Kabul Airport became the scene of a tragic end to the international community's twenty-year commitment to Afghanistan. Pictures of desperate Afghans fleeing to the airport quickly reached all countries of the world. So did clips showing Afghans trying to cling to the landing gear of military planes and falling to their deaths high in the air. Images that desperately recalled how it had all started on the corner of Greenwich and Fulton in lower Manhattan, on that fateful day in September 2001. As the Islamists made headway through Afghanistan, they quickly seized expensive military hardware and social media overflowed with images of Taliban fighters posing in full American military gear—the symbolism being beyond belief. Through twenty years of (the most recent) international presence in the country, the Afghan security forces had received hundreds of thousands of weapons and forms of communications equipment, up to 80,000 military vehicles and more than 150 military aircraft. Everything from fully automatic weapons to dozens of Black Hawk helicopters, with their almost mythical status in American culture, to night-vision goggles and heavy artillery, was now in the hands of the Taliban.

Yet it's not weapons worth hundreds of billions of dollars that potentially raise the greatest concern. That dubious honour falls upon another piece of both military and civilian technology called HIIDE or Handheld Interagency Identity Detection Equipment. HIIDEs are handheld biometric cameras that the US military used in the country for years to record and check local Afghans, as a smart and technologized way to confirm who was collaborating with the international coalition. Everything from drivers to interpreters to cleaning staff had their biometric identities checked daily through scans of their irises, with a camera that was able to compare such pictures against a database of cooperating Afghans. This database therefore held extremely sensitive data, which is worth much more to the Taliban than advanced weapons. We know that the group, as one of its first tasks, carried out brutal door-to-door checks of local Afghans in Kabul, precisely to identify people who had collaborated with the international coalition. With that knowledge in mind, embassies used the last days before the Taliban's takeover of Kabul to burn everything under the umbrella of 'confidential documents' that could be misused by the Taliban to persecute locals. USB keys, hard drives, and phones were physically smashed so that they couldn't be accessed, or their memory restored. Before the Taliban reached Kabul, smoke had been rising from the US embassy for several days, as US staff tried to destroy all sorts of confidential materials, yet they still failed to get the biometric cameras out of the way. Access to HIIDE's databases would be a terrible goldmine for the Taliban, putting tens of thousands of people's lives in extreme danger. By the time the Taliban had retaken Afghanistan, the Americans had used the biometric databases and the iris-scanning cameras for years and to such an extent that they had even coined a code-name for their goal of biometrically registering as large a section of the Afghan population as possible: identity dominance.

Many travellers have had their fingerprints taken or looked into a camera that recorded their biological features at an airport, when going through immigration control. Most of us probably didn't think much about it when it happened or even considered its implications, eager as we probably were to go on vacation or pass through quickly to our luggage. It is the essence of biometry, literally 'measurement of life', to collect physiological characteristics of humans in order to register and categorize them. At an airport, it is about monitoring who is moving across the borders of a country. Who comes in and who goes out, who is allowed to enter and who is not. In Afghanistan, biometry served similar aims of control. In refugee camps, it serves a variety of other purposes, and often includes techniques other than fingerprints, such as iris scans. What is common to iris scans and fingerprints, of course, is that in theory these are unique to one human being. No one in the world has the same iris characteristics or fingerprints as you. An iris scanner films video of a person's iris, the muscle that regulates the contraction of the pupil and the eye. A series of algorithms uses mathematical pattern recognition to evaluate and save a person's iris profile, enabling its use for either establishing the identity of a person or for verifying whether a person is who he or she claims to be. The process of iris scanning commonly runs through a series of stages whereby a digital representation of biological features is captured through the scanner's sensor and via algorithms turned into a template that contains less information than the initial picture. These templates are then stored, either on a database accessed through an online connection or locally on a hard drive, and used to match the person with existing templates in the system. The UN's Refugee Agency (UNHCR) has a Rapid Application or RApp with a current standard of capturing ten fingerprints, two iris scans, a photo, and biographic information on family compositions in about six minutes. The iris scan registers up to twenty times more data points than a fingerprint, which in theory increases their safety. However, it is fully possible to manipulate machines that detect and collect such data, just as they may be affected by conditions such as wind and weather. When these systems are used in a system where food and water delivery are controlled through biometrics, technical difficulties may have fatal consequences. And although the expected error rate of iris scans may only be around 3 per cent, in a refugee population of a million, that is 30,000 people.

UNHCR was the first organization to test the new biometric technologies in the early years of the new millennium. In October 2002, a year after US forces invaded Afghanistan, UNHCR attempted biometric registration of Afghan refugees in Peshawar, Pakistan. To get support for repatriation, refugees had to undergo iris registration with UNHCR, who managed the camp. What started in a single voluntary repatriation centre was soon rolled out across many more of these, and it became mandatory for all Afghan refugees to register their biometric identities.[11] Over the next few years, the use of biometric registration was scaled to UNHCR camps in other countries such as Tanzania, Kenya, Ghana, and Djibouti. The initial use of biometrics culminated with an official UNHCR policy in 2013 that describes the technology as a strategic choice for the organization. In the policy, the UN organization estimated that it would register up to ten million refugees over the following ten years, a feat it is well on its way to achieving. The experiments with biometrics no longer concerned whether it was reasonable to use such a system, that decision was already made, but rather how to best develop an effective system to register as many refugees as possible as swiftly as possible. As the Syrian refugee crisis unfolded in 2014 and 2015, we also saw a shift in the biometrics approach that led organizations to focus on regional systems not limited to a single country. That is, the databases and systems used to record and monitor refugees through biometric methods, were used to register movements across countries, not just people who were stuck in camps in a single country.

Today, UNHCR has expanded its biometric system to more than seventy country operations worldwide, from Brazil to Sudan, with eight in ten UNHCR refugees over the age of five now biometrically registered. The organization has based its biometric work on a suite of applications under the umbrella name of PRIMES, an acronym for 'Population Registration and Identity Management EcoSystem'. PRIMES looks to become the single entry-point for all digital interaction between UNHCR and its partners, enabling biometric and biographic registration, case management including protection aspects such as refugee status, assistance in the form of aid, as well as the sharing, managing, and reporting of data. The application portfolio consists of four core modules: ProGres v4 which integrates with state civil registry systems; BIMS (the core Biometric Identity Management System); Dataport, which is a business intelligence tool giving all UNHCR staff access to aggregated statistical data on registered caseloads; and RApp, enabling offline registration and allowing UNHCR to register people in their temporary dwellings and elsewhere outside the camps.

This and other organizations' use of biometric data and similar experimental technologies has a double-sided character. On the one hand, the vast majority of refugees arrive at camps without any form of identification papers, so biometric registration can ensure that the correct help reaches the right recipients in an effective way that limits potential corruption and abuse. Biometric registration can provide a better overview of the nature and size of a humanitarian situation, thus also delivering a more accurate picture of the need for help, which may then be communicated to donors and shape the response and size of assistance delivered. On the other hand, there are a number of issues with the increasing use of biometric technology in the world's humanitarian hot spots. Biometric registration is not just a dead technology that may be used to streamline several workflows. Its use in itself helps to transform what policy objectives a given intervention seeks to achieve.[12] Many humanitarian operations take place in contexts of conflict where the boundaries between humanitarian organizations, state actors, military, and police are gradually blurred. The same applies, for example, to the sharing of data, intelligence, and information, something often takes place among those very same actors, who end up using it for quite different purposes. The boundaries between situations where biometric registration is used to provide relief and security for a refugee, and situations in which it might support a military intervention or a local government's desire to organize and control certain populations, are also fluid. Thus, biometric registration not only helps with the provision of objective and politically neutral forms of emergency relief but may risk being used for political measures such as the monitoring and managing of who travels, across which borders, and when. Databases may, under troubling circumstances, be used to identify targeted individuals or groups and thereby cross the boundary between the humanitarian imperative to help anyone who needs it, and a state's desire to discriminate between people or seek out specific individuals. Instead of protecting people against states, biometric registration technologies may thus come to expand the scope of state influence and control over individuals and groups.

It is important to remember here that nascent technologies are inherently uncertain and often insecure. Insecurities that may turn into harm for intended beneficiaries, and to loss of legitimacy for organizations. The more data that are extracted and collected about beneficiaries, project plans, coordination, funds, operations, etc. the more likely it is that any breach of security will have significant consequences. And some loss of control over information and data is almost a given in any large organization, and even more so in operations executed across many organizations and scales. In all arenas where information has become a key resource, we have seen attempts to manipulate, undermine, steal, or otherwise compromise this valuable resource. If standards and regulatory systems to handle data and information are not fully in place in humanitarian organizations, these efforts and the great turn towards collection, accumulation, and utilization of data must be seen as fundamentally experimental in themselves. In 2016, the four years prior of operation of the UNHCR's Biometric Identity Management System or BIMS was evaluated, the only proper review we have seen publicly. The group of UN investigators from the Office of Internal Oversight Services found a series of concerns that underline the potential risks of using biometric registration.[13] In four out of five of the country operations reviewed, the level of information provided to registered persons concerning their obligations, rights, and protection of their data was below the standard required by UNHCR policies. Essentially, no evidence was found that persons were informed of their rights and obligations. The audit report also showed that data were regularly transferred to governments with no underlying assessments of the level of data protection and with no data transfer agreements. Across all the assessed operations, staff were found to be lacking in sufficient technical capacity or knowledge of relevant UNHCR policies and biometric registrations.

These issues, not least lacking technical and political knowledge to handle the iris scans and ensure data protection, are a good indication of why the use of biometric registration can be seen as fundamentally experimental, but it also calls into question what the collected data are used for. It is difficult, perhaps even for the UNHCR itself, to know exactly who has access to the data collected.

In Kenya, for example, UNHCR has an agreement with the government to share information, not least after 2016 when it found that almost 25,000 Kenyans had registered as refugees in the Dadaab camp. A similar situation is the case in Lebanon, where the organization also shares certain data with the government. If the Syrian government seizes a database of people who have fled from the Assad regime, it is obvious that this could be used to instigate political persecution, just as a similar list is an effective way for the Bangladeshi government to repatriate or push Rohingya refugees out of the country, where the authorities have openly stated they are not welcome. This is a major question to pose about the effort of collecting and registering refugee identities through biometrics. What would happen if the data ended up in the worst possible hands? Throughout history, the registration, classification, and mass surveillance of groups, whether religious, ethnic, or otherwise, have facilitated the worst of humanitarian crimes. ID cards identifying people by their ethnic group effectively served as death sentences during the Rwandan genocide. In Bangladesh, mobile phone operators have been prohibited from selling SIM cards to Rohingya refugees who are required to stay inside camps and not interact with locals. Should data be lost or spread to non-authorized entities, it could enable and support continued discrimination of the ethnic group.

Despite the obvious intention of doing good for other people, these discussions emphasize the difficult relationship between experimentation, technology, and vulnerable populations. The ability to draw refugees into biometric registration is in itself a vast power to wield, not least because once data have been produced it is difficult to contain or delete them. There is also power to gain access to that data and act on it—a power that cannot always be expected to be used for good causes. But there are in addition political and socio-cultural issues associated with biometrics beyond these technologically determinist or instrumental problems that mainly question the operability of the technology. Biometrics in essence changes the scope for and way people are governed, managed, and categorized by organizations and states. As such the fusion of the material body and of technology has resulted in a strong way of governing human beings: biometrics can help to organize where people are staying, where they move to, but also fundamentally questions of life and death, as it serves as an access point to food and water for certain populations. Herein lies an ultimate point of sovereign power. Developments in biometric technology are not only a matter of 'we would like to register and now we can'. It is also very much a case of 'it is now possible to effectively register refugees' identities, and therefore we should'. That is, the technology not only renders possible existing objectives, but fundamentally enables new ones, just as its

experimental form may lead to a set of unintended or unexpected consequences, as a form of function creep, opening up new avenues for action,
intervention, and steps towards ordering (vulnerable) populations.[14]

*

In the village of Thipa in Central Malawi, the local children gathered around a
man carrying a white item with what looked like four small helicopter wings.
Not that helicopters often land in Thipa. The man lifted the object over his
head and told everyone that this was a drone from UNICEF that would help
them improve their lives. There is no word for drone in the local language
Chichewa, so the man used the term 'kandege kakang'ono', which means
small plane.[15] The red sandy earth whirled up around the drone's four winged
engines when the man put it on the ground and turned it on. The crowd
gasped, and everyone took a step back. The drone quickly took off to the sky
and flew over the gathering now enthusiastically clapping and pointing, while
the children tried to follow its movements from the ground. The white
'Phantom' quadcopter employed in Thipa is manufactured by Chinese technology giant DJI, Dà-Jiāng Innovations, based out of Shenzhen, Quangdong
who account for some 70 per cent of the global commercial and civilian
drone market.

Thipa is located in the Kasungu district whose main industry has traditionally been the cultivation of tobacco and now, increasingly, tourism at the
nearly 2,500 square kilometre national park, not far from the village. But one
day in June 2017, Kasungu made its mark on the world map when UNICEF
announced it had designed Africa's first drone corridor there. A 5,000 square
kilometre large 'aerodrome' called Kasungu Aerodrome, where private companies, universities, and others could test drones in the name of development.
In reality, we're talking about permission to fly 'good drones' over a fairly normal populated area and a smaller landing spot, but the news made major
headlines when it was announced. The term 'good drone' is obviously one to
be popularized because we are used to seeing drone technology applied in a
context quite different from the business of saving human lives—war and
conflict.

Today, the military drone industry is a multi-billion-dollar business across
the globe. Although the US, Europe, and Israel have historically been some of
the main developers and producers of military drones, countries across the
world, from South America to Asia, have greatly increased the resources invested
in constructing indigenous drones. When the US invaded Iraq in 2003, it was
with a very limited number of drones or unmanned aerial vehicles (UAVs) as

they are formally known. By 2011 the US Armed Forces operated more than 7,000 UAVs, and today it employs more than 10,000 drone operators alone. In recent years, drones have developed a growing presence in civilian and humanitarian situations, where they have become a central experimental sociotechnical tool of the experimental movement.[16] Experiments have seen drones tested in Latin America to analyse injuries from hurricanes and earthquakes. In Africa, experiments have been undertaken to transport HIV tests and map floods. In Asia, drones have delivered medication, assessed disaster consequences, and delivered real-time information after typhoon Haiyan in the Philippines. After the earthquake in Nepal in 2015, where massive cloud cover made it impossible to use satellite imagery, drones provided pictures that documented the extent of the disaster. When humanitarian actors arrived in Nepal with their UAVs, there were no laws regulating the flying of these, just as there were no laws to protect the privacy of those being filmed and documented. In Guyana and Panama, drones have been used by local tribes near the Amazon River to monitor illegal deforestation and mining, on the millions of acres of savannah and rainforest, something that would not typically be achievable by local authorities with traditional monitoring resources. The Wapishana tribe in Guyana, with the help of the American organization Digital Democracy, has built their own drones that can be repaired with locally available products such as plastic and wood.[17] It is almost unavoidable that the drones crash at some point, and in such instances, it seems smart to not depend on expensive parts needing to be flown in from the US.

Although there are experiments with humanitarian drones across the world, and we even have a 'drones for good' competition in the United Arab Emirates, UAVs are far from a normalized and operationalized part of the humanitarian repertoire. Their use is, not least, still surrounded by a wide range of legal, ethical, and technical questions. Common areas of concern when it comes to using UAVs in humanitarian situations include privacy, as a result of efforts to collect data and conduct surveillance with drones (*who are using the drones and for what purposes?*), and limited transparency and consent of those being filmed or flown over, including the creation of expectations among populations that drone-use will automatically result in humanitarian support. One of the greatest fears comes from drones' military association and the accompanying stigma; simply speaking: civilian drones have an uncanny resemblance to military attack drones.[18] Humanitarian drones may help legitimize military attack drones, but they can also be suspected as such themselves and thus problematic because of their resemblance to military drones.

How can locals know the difference between an attacking predator drone and a humanitarian drone in a chaotic conflict situation? Such uncertain situations can result in confusion, fear, and associated injury. This dilemma is unfolding already in places such as DR Congo or in the Sahel, where UN missions use drones for military purposes, just as the Americans also do in the rest of North Africa, largely keeping local humanitarian organizations from using them for fear of the reaction among the civilian populations. Humanitarian action is built on the principles of humanity, neutrality, impartiality, and independence, and any doubts among people of concern as to whether humanitarian instruments are in fact military ones, would compromise those principles. The relationship is complicated further by the fact that almost all drone technology derives from military technology research and development. Without military UAVs and their derivative effects, we would probably not have humanitarian drones today. So, the question remains whether a piece of technology such as the drone, which is so intrinsically connected to its potential ability to kill and destruct, can be turned into a piece of civic engineering serving humanitarian purposes.

For those who accept the inevitability of drones in humanitarian action, wisely or not, the matter becomes not whether drones ought to be utilized, but rather in what way they should be employed. Here, two opposite worlds of practice emerge—one that introduces the drone as a foreign object in a local circumstance, and one that attempts to construct a form of indigenous drone-use. The first role is the one most widely practised today with UAV-specialists working for humanitarian agencies to bring drones to a humanitarian emergency and carry out certain tasks, likely leaving the area once the funding has stopped or their task has been completed. In the same way as a foreign intervention, this practice brings in exogenous knowledge and expertise, largely disregards local capacity, and leaves once a task has been achieved. Such strong reliance on drones that can only be operated by highly trained specialists also results in prolonging the necessity of foreign intervention. For many humanitarian organizations, this approach to technology is neither uncommon nor surprising. Sitting on technical knowledge and details is of course a business opportunity as it is in any other industry. By becoming a leader in the field of UAVs, a humanitarian agency may position itself as central in any emergency, securing important funding that sustains and secures the organization. At the same time, relying on startups or other tech companies, as many humanitarian organizations do, only increases the privatization of humanitarian UAVs, along with the secrecy of the software of the application programming interface (API) and technical details of the UAVs systems, keeping them away from the public eye. This is contrasted with what we might call a more participatory practice of furthering UAVs. This approach— exemplified by the illustration from Guyana where Digital Democracy helped a local community expand their way of monitoring their part of the rainforest— focuses on community development to translate the technologies and adapt them to local needs and understandings, essentially to create forms of indi- genous drones. It utilizes local knowledge and skill rather than top-down templates, attempting to put power into the hands of those who are to use the technology, and for whom we expect it to bring about transformation. Those are two of the key matters at play for this second approach: the technology must be able to bring about a productive form of change—be transformational— and it must be participatory, not the sole result of an exogeneous intervention.

Now, does a good drone become a *bad* drone, if it puts vulnerable populations' privacy under risk? As with biometric registration, there is an impending risk that information and data collected through humanitarian drones may serve other unintended political objectives. Drones are widely used by the European Border and Coast Guard Agency (formerly known as FRONTEX) in missions such as its European Border Surveillance System (EUROSUR), a key provider of intelligence in EU efforts to 'secure' Europe's border. Here, European drone-producers such as the Italian company Leonardo S.p.A., but also the Israeli Aerospace Industries, fly routes for European Member States to identify movement along the EU border in what is an obvious militarization of these. Intimate information on humanitarian situations in for example North Africa, which is potentially obtainable from humanitarian drones, would be of great value to these efforts of European border control. In such suppositions, efforts taken to support vulnerable populations through UAVs could risk being used to constrain the mobility, and thus livelihood possibilities, of these very same people. This illustrates the core issues of 'good' or humanitarian drones. These technologies expand the realm of humanitarian action, just as they expand public space to include people's homes and grow the array of actors that are considered legitimate in emergencies. In so doing, they risk blurring the boundaries between the private and the public, and between emergency help, population control, and security.

*

On a cold December day in Copenhagen in 2017, I watched as the former Danish Minister of Development Cooperation Ulla Tørnæs took the stage in the Nordic UN City and proclaimed that Denmark, as the first country in the world, was ready to experiment with blockchain as a weapon in the fight for human rights. The media were all over the story, and even the *New York Times* wrote about the innovative Danes who were ready to break with traditional thinking and let new technology fight poverty. The occasion was Denmark's financing of a report entitled *Hack the Future of Development Aid*, exploring how development assistance and humanitarian work would be revolutionized through radical technology.[19] Central for the report was how 'development aid is slow money, whereas crypto is fast money', offering 'entirely new ways to finance innovations, startups, and projects'. According to the report, blockchain in particular offers an opportunity to refocus the emphasis of development aid towards an ability to 'spot high impact startups and support them through investments to scale change', turning 'risk into opportunity by applying exponential technologies to innovate'. One way to tap into the potential for blockchain to encourage change in developing countries is to organize global hackathons to tap into tech talent, where 'prizes can enable the best ideas'. Central to the call made was the idea of experimentation around the world. Denmark 'can bring more developing states into hands-on experimentation', just as development actors altogether 'need to throw themselves into the discussion and into hands-on experimentation, and fast', the report exclaimed. This move represents the key ideas and ideologies of the Silicon Valley movement, furthering what it sees as a systems-wide tech-utopia: 'Instead of allocating funding for different themes, Danida can turn into a platform, onto which actors—startups, local organisations, NGOs etc.—upload their aid offerings. The end user can then log on and request the aid most suited to their needs. It is a future-fit model enabling the most in demand aid to scale.'

The development community's expectations for the use of blockchain in emergencies, not just the Danish ones, are enormous. A blockchain is a list of records or *blocks*, each subsequent one holding information on the blocks before it as well as a timestamp of the modification made, and transaction data. Typically managed by a peer-to-peer network as forms of distributed ledgers, blockchains are heralded for their resistance to modification, meaning they are difficult to manipulate and thus could form ideal systems for transactions of things such as money or property. There is nothing new to the idea of ledgers themselves, having been used as a traditional transactional recording method for thousands of years, all the way back to Mesopotamia. The difference today lies in the digital realm that sees us able to distribute a ledger across a network of computers, each holding a version of the ledger, thus minimizing the risks of manipulation. Its proponents emphasize how blockchains cut out intermediaries, often understood as corrupt bureaucrats or financial institutions that overcharge for transactions, and who eat up large chunks of assistance we would rather send to the world's poorest.[20] Disintermediating, as it is called, is thus thought to make a system more effective and reduce the likelihood for corruption. Funds can in theory be transferred directly from the donor to the recipient without the need for interference from other parties, thereby decreasing both the risk of abuse and transaction costs. Additionally, you can replace paper documents that may be manipulated and modified to match unscrupulous interests with digital ledgers where digital evidence of ownership of land, rights, property, etc. can in theory not be compromised.

A number of organizations are currently engaged in heavy forms of experimenting with blockchain across poor countries. This includes the World Bank, who launched its Blockchain Lab in 2017 with the purpose of partnering with non-profits and tech companies to 'produce proofs-of-concept that may be rolled out in the field'—newspeak for experimentation. It aims to test distributed ledgers within areas such as land administration, supply chain management, health, education, cross-border payments, and carbon market trading. Interestingly, as many blockchain proponents claim that the technology will substitute trust for mechanized transfers of resources, the World Bank holds that distributed ledger technologies have the potential to rebuild trust in institutions that may have lost it. The Bank hopes the lab's efforts will 'trickle' into its development work and argues that blockchain not only holds the potential to reshape individual payment systems but may be used to fundamentally rewire the entire financial infrastructure of developing economies. The only major risk and problem identified by the Bank upon the initiation of this work was the extreme energy consumption that goes into mining and maintaining a comprehensive blockchain. And there is certainly truth to this. Just maintaining the current Bitcoin crypto currency requires more than the entire energy consumption of Ireland, and with every increase in value, the carbon footprint grows dramatically. In August 2018, the Bank launched the world's first bond (bond-i—a nod to Sydney's famous Bondi beach), created, allocated, transferred, and managed all through its life cycle using distributed ledger technology. The blockchain bond was executed in partnership with the Commonwealth Bank of Australia (CBA), developed by the CBA Blockchain Centre of Excellence, and is essentially a debt instrument. Built on Ethereum, the architecture and resilience of the CBA's system were overseen by Microsoft who will run the infrastructure on its Azure cloud computing platform. The bond attracted $110 million in investments from a diverse group, still a relatively low-scale operation given that the bank issues between US$50–60 billion annually in bonds for development.

The World Bank's work is a tangible pilot project in the still evolving humanitarian and development blockchain field. Far more advanced, and above everyone else, however, is the work of UN organizations, many of whom are experimenting with blockchain forms and solutions. One of the organizations experimenting with real projects is the United Nations World Food Program or WFP. Since 2017, WFP has tested a major pilot project in Jordan and Pakistan called Building Blocks where refugees receive financial support inscribed on a blockchain. Instead of providing vouchers or direct food aid, refugee households receive approximately 30 dollars a month on an account associated with their biometric identity and can visit a local supermarket to 'buy' groceries through an iris scan that then records the purchase on a block-chain, making it easy to review transactions and track money wherever it moves. WFP's blockchain system in Jordan utilizes a variant of the Etherium client Parity (a client essentially being the software that secures access to the Etherium network) and is integrated with the biometric identification system provided by IrisGuard.

WFP is supported by tech companies Parity Technologies and Datarella in the project. Parity Technologies are a well-established blockchain infrastruc-ture company founded by a group of key figures from the initial construction of Ethereum and blockchain technology, with offices in Berlin, London, and Cambridge, and developers in nine countries. They are responsible for the Parity client that essentially handles over $50 billion in assets and is a core foundation of the Etherium network. Datarella, a company working out of Germany, provided support in setting up the blockchain-based payment and accounting system for WFP. Before shifting to a blockchain focus in 2015, Datarella was heavily involved in furthering a radical idea and approach called Quantified Self; essentially the concept of measuring various aspects of our bodily functions, our actions, habits, and environment into quantified data that may be sold on to third parties for commercial aims, used by our-selves to track our human 'progress', or be presented to medical doctors to find ideal treatments.

The initiative for the experimental Building Blocks project was taken by Houman Haddad, a finance officer working for WFP.[21] In mid-2016, Haddad came in contact with WFP Accelerator (which is based in Munich, partly explaining the strong German links to Building Blocks), essentially an innov-ations incubator for the organization that supports entrepreneurs with funding and advice for piloting their ideas. He was then paired with Alexandra Alden, a Silicon-Valley based innovation consultant, and together they refined the concept that would become Building Blocks at a boot camp run through Santa Clara-based Singularity University. In January 2017, a one-month pilot was initiated in the Sindh province of Pakistan, relying on text-based mobile voucher codes instead of the iris scanners used later on. We do not know much about the results, but the programme seems to have been surprisingly successful and was quickly scaled up to other countries and a much broader base of refugees. By 2018, it had been expanded to Jordan and especially the Azraq camp housing Syrian refugees some 90 kilometres from the Jordan-Syria border. Today it provides WFP assistance to upwards of half a million refugees, with the aim of covering all Syrian refugees in Jordan, through the blockchain system, and expanding from there.

The purpose, from WFP's perspective, is to ensure transparency and the effective delivery of financial support, and to allow refugees themselves to choose how they use their funds locally. Instead of receiving a predetermined form of emergency food aid, or vouchers that may be compromised, they receive aid on their biometric identity account. According to WFP, transaction fees are reduced by 98 per cent, saving hundreds of thousands of dollars each month. The Building Blocks project is interesting for the ways in which it may be able to liberate resources for use elsewhere but it faces a significant challenge in terms of its potential for data maximization, function creep, and privacy breach. We may, for example, ask whether it is really reasonable to collect highly sensitive biometric and biographic identity information and store it collectively on ledgers that may be private, but that may be compromised? What started as a WFP-only project is now expanding as UN Women has been included and gained co-control over the nodes, again increasing the amount of data collected and stored about individuals, just as it expands the circle of actors with access to the data, potentially increasing the risks that it might fall into the wrong hands. The expansion and associated function creep in which more and more layers of identity data are added into the system, are not a contingent consequence but rather a stated ambition. The Building Blocks design is mostly open source, allowing for customizable applications and its extension into fields such as health and education, where data on refugees can be collected and stored, just as it is transferable across borders. As the Silicon Valley consultant on the project has exclaimed it, 'that's when it starts getting pretty interesting and powerful'.[22] It is also when it starts getting riskier for those whose complete lives are registered and digitized in, as well as ordered and quasi-controlled by, biometric identity files.

WFP's pilot projects are among the most sensible examples, although they also have their own inherent problems. For most organizations, expectations of what blockchain can contribute are often overstated, undermining, or not properly understanding the complexity of the developmental problems they are trying to solve. The idea of having one's human rights 'on a blockchain' that could be accessed on a mobile phone is certainly a real possibility, but its effect in practice is hard to imagine. It is difficult to think of a situation in which Ethiopian prison guards would refrain from beating a political prisoner if the person took out of his phone and demanded his rights. The same applies to the use of blockchain to prove land or property rights. In reality, we rarely see the strong individualization of such rights, as imagined by the blockchain proponents. Research shows that for many people living in extreme poverty, ownership of land or property is typically embedded in social relationships and identities, and thus not necessarily individualized, far more often based on community or family associations. In addition, there is still ample room to manipulate inputs into a blockchain and we are therefore heavily dependent on a transparent and democratic political process for operationalizing blockchains, unless people are to be deprived of the right to their land or property. The individualization we see with the current technology focus means attention is usually directed towards how the individual can utilize the technology to change his or her own life, while the state or public institutions are seen as the big enemy to be 'disrupted' or 'disintermediated' or cut out. This is profoundly problematic, not least because it is the state and its institutions that may fundamentally help to institutionalize and enforce the rights or determine the absence of these. This applies to all of us. If my rights are violated, I don't act autonomously, but I expect certain societal institutions to defend or protect them, one way or another. By circumventing the state in our attempt to find technological solutions in developing countries, we clearly undermine these. A conscious strategy of bypassing the state is not very healthy for democracy or the prospect of building strong and accountable institutions. The state absolutely represents a (frequently ineffective) bureaucracy that is not quick to push for new technologies, but it ideally contains and ensures, after all, fundamental democratic institutions. These may not exist in many developing countries, but nor will they ever do so, if they are pushed out by extreme individualization.

Blockchain, as it appears in its current experimental form, mainly looks to solve problems caused by bad bookkeeping systems and unsafe money transfers. It is difficult to see it foster a revolution of poverty reduction or inequality.

Development is not just about simple resource transfers, but rather about creating lasting social and economic development. There is a significant difference between doing the same things in a new and different way or asking if we are actually doing the right things altogether. If we have a desire to create radical change, there is a need to pose radical questions about the way we think and conduct our development and humanitarian efforts today. The aim should be to not just deliver the same solutions but to do so more efficiently with new technology, albeit that we do not even fundamentally know how to control this technology.

*

'This is not charity', the normcore man in the black polo shirt and washed jeans exclaims from the stage, 'if we don't come up with solutions now and work with companies, private sector, technologists, in clever ways now, we are kind of in a bad place'.[23] The man is Christopher or Chris Fabian, co-founder of UNICEF Innovation all the way back in 2006, when innovation departments were not really in existence in humanitarian organizations. To Fabian, who has since transitioned to lead UNICEF Ventures, the work of UNICEF Innovation is essentially about connecting the needs of humans to profit. That is connecting 50 million refugees on the move because of violence with businesses to 'create stronger businesses and help humanity'. Changing the way UNICEF does its business of helping the world's most vulnerable children means pursuing and experimenting with new technology: 'we think that some of the best solutions for kids come from startups and from the space of technology', as Fabian has explained it. UNICEF needs to 'think like businesses and…work with startups', is how Fabian frames the bleak solution to contemporary human suffering. Some may think that reframing recipients to be consumers is an act of empowerment, but the reality, as we have seen, is often one mirroring our contemporary shopping at online giants, with freedom and choice effectively appearing as *fata morganas*.

Many of the new technologies we've heard about so far have truly taken the humanitarian industry by storm. Virtually all major UN organizations, NGOs, or development organizations today have so-called innovation departments, teams or labs. These departments see it as their task to change 'business as usual'—accelerating, expanding, and scaling up the effect that their organization is already trying to have on the ground. To an organization like the International Federation of the Red Cross and Red Crescent Societies (IFRC), 'accelerating' essentially means experimentation focused on 'multiple parallel designs', 'rapid prototyping and testing', and using 'behavioural science'.

For WFP, innovation is evoked through the mantra of 'Design. Fail. Iterate. Scale', supporting WFP innovators and external startups and companies through financial support, access to a network of experts, and a global field reach,[24] all actions introduced with the aim of bringing about change to the humanitarian ecosystem.

Despite a continuous drive to improve humanitarian action, we had to reach the end of 2000s before humanitarian innovation began to be singled out as a specific area of engagement.[25] For decades, humanitarian actors had been researching new solutions and approaches within the different confines of specific programmes or themes, such as water, sanitation, etc. but these efforts had not been collapsed into distinct programmes for innovation and experimentation. Around 2009 and 2010, the UK's Department for International Development (DFID) began providing exploratory funding for humanitarian innovations, partially inspired by a series of meetings and a report (*Innovations in International Humanitarian Action*) by the Active Learning Network for Accountability and Performance (ALNAP). The Humanitarian Innovation Fund (HIF) was established in 2010 as a non-governmental donor of innovations, and a few years later in 2013, OCHA (the UN Office for the Coordination of Humanitarian Affairs) released a major report charting the field of humanitarian innovation. That same year also saw the World Disaster Report focus on humanitarian technology, and in 2016, innovation was a core theme of the World Humanitarian Summit. The agenda was here to stay, although few organizations were making any significant progress on actual innovations. Today, innovation teams and departments experiment with new—or try to translate and adapt—existing technologies and innovations, so that they can be used meaningfully on the ground or support the development of new cutting-edge technologies. One way in which this is done is by introducing new business models that include much closer cooperation with private actors. Implicitly, they partake in a race to be the foremost organization when it comes to new humanitarian technologies. Being at the forefront of humanitarian innovation and experimentation means increased financial support, whether in the form of direct investments in the organizations' own innovation teams or towards specific projects and collaborations, from donors who would like to be seen as the greatest supporter of the latest and most innovative approaches to saving human lives. These individual vis-à-vis collective problems have formed a central subject of discussion for years, with many actors arguing for a focus on ecosystems of humanitarian innovation that can benefit the sector as a whole, rather than a focus on how individual organizations may 'get ahead' using technological innovations.

The heavy material attention given to developing new products and technologies often entails a disregard for forms of innovation that are more interested in changing organizational, management, or operational processes in humanitarian responses, though this is inherently where unequal structures of influence and power reside and are sustained.[26] It also concentrates attention on the specific organizational context—how may an organization improve its delivery of x to population y in situation z—rather than focusing on the affected populations and communities, letting recipients partake in producing innovations. This is not least reflected in the way the innovation process is interpreted by most humanitarian innovation departments. Commonly across the sector, the innovation process is crudely conceptualized as comprising phases where a problem or challenge is recognized, a solution is then developed or innovated, after which it is put to use. In the current innovation ecosystem, this has meant startups identifying problems or avenues of innovation that may be profitable for them, while at the same time improving organizational responses by humanitarian actors. This creates a preference for top-down technological solutions proposed by mostly Western companies, which are then brought to local contexts and experimented with. In the same way, it refocuses accountability on upwards relationships towards donors, rather than down towards beneficiaries. Innovation is not a given concept that necessarily requires a top-down approach, and notions of social, participatory, or indigenous innovation have gained ground over the past decade, refocusing on utilizing local ecosystems to innovate from the ground up.[27] This is partly because traditional ways of understanding innovation are focused on maximizing profit, whereas innovation in the humanitarian sector is fundamentally about creating social change. Today, however, the clear and obvious inspiration flows from Silicon Valley, whether in the predilection for technology, rapid change, systems disruption, market narratives, or private sector partners in the form of startups. And of course experimentation, seen as a top-down approach, often favours experimentation that tests out exogeneous products in local circumstances, rather than seeing these develop naturally.

As is evident from the opening quotes of this section, the market and humanitarian efforts are seen as closely bound together within the field of innovation. Private sector actors are considered the main source of innovation, which cannot come from 'traditional' and 'slow' actors such as those already established in the humanitarian sector. Despite the differences between commercial markets and the humanitarian industry, these are often fused, such as when Chris Fabian talks of the necessity to innovate products that can both make a profit for private sector actors and 'do good'. And we are not just talking private sector actors of any kind, but most regularly startups, whose inherent goal often remains the disruption of industries, in themselves embodiments of innovation and technological change. Startups do not just refer to any kind of emerging business, but almost always ones affiliated with the growth-euphoria of Silicon Valley, bringing us back to the exceptional focus on innovating and experimenting new technological products. As UNICEF explains concerning their work on drones: 'we want to make sure we are in conversation with these Silicon Valley institutions and are therefore making inroads to ensure future longevity for our corporate partners'. The aim of 'being in conversation' with Silicon Valley also has a very tangible commercial end to it, when organizations like WFP train refugees in specific sets of technical digital skills. In the project bluntly called 'Tech for Food', the aim is to help 'young people affected by conflict in the Middle East reach their full potential through a career in the digital economy', connecting them to demands from the US and Europe. As WFP explains, 'with remote work becoming the norm across many industries, online freelancing offers isolated communities in places like Iraq and Lebanon new opportunities to earn an income and build a brighter future'.[28] It is a very specific set of basic IT skills then, mainly around simple and repetitive services such as data entry or picture annotation. Some of the participants may very well go on to hone their skills in the digital economy, likely through their own individual drive rather than through an institutional push, but most, if using their 'education', will be faced with the routine, physical, and low-paid jobs that characterized the workplace of the last century, and which are now being globalized by Silicon Valley. The WFP training is supported by US companies such as Samasource, who specialize in helping computer vision algorithms recognize shapes, patterns, and objects within images through picture annotation. It might sound fancy, but picture annotation is essentially tagging images for what they show, a major task in the growing artificial intelligence business. Algorithms may need to have millions of pictures tagged to understand a certain task such as knowing soda cans from ice creams, and low-skilled labour is then used to manually tag pictures for what they contain, again and again. Is it a cow, a cup, or a cactus? These tasks cannot yet be done properly by computers themselves and thus require manual labour, here provided in refugee camps, through UN organizations.

*

Humanitarian emergencies across the Global South today appear as key frontiers of technological experimentation with innovation becoming the go-to driver of progress. Humanitarian actors look to the businesses of Silicon

Valley startups as they finance or themselves engage in experiments with new technologies of biometrics, blockchain, or drones. When we reach a point in the Global North when experiments will begin to see commercial stores and bank accounts connected to our personal identities and when both salaries and shopping are written on to digital ledgers, tangible experience with implementing such systems will not be drawn from other Western countries. They will be drawn from the Global South, where such systems are being tested right now, spearheaded by humanitarian actors. This emerging focus on technology not only changes the way we try to help the world's most vulnerable populations. Technology-elation alters core issues about when, who, and for what purposes we should help other people, shaped by Silicon Valley ideas about rapid radical change, a willingness to experiment with other people's lives, fostering individualization, and often overriding of central social institutions.[29]

Humanitarian situations' states of exception, desperation, and emergency legitimizes a 'let's see what works' attitude that foregrounds testing and nascent technologies. And not all forms of experimental practice or attempts at innovating humanitarian work are successful—experimentation that is often centred on testing the effects of products and material technologies. The urgency to respond is what legitimizes intervention, but also what allows for testing unproven technologies. We can refer to these efforts as experimental because we simply do not fully understand their consequences when employed in humanitarian emergencies. Counter to data minimization principles, humanitarian actors extract and collect immense amounts of data, and we do not entirely know what it is being used for. What we do know, is that these data are sometimes stored irresponsibly[30] and risk being compromised by actors who have a strong political or economic interest in obtaining it. And it is a very specific form of experimentation, not least driven by Silicon Valley dogmas of productive failures. For a US startup experimenting with a new digital platform, failure essentially means the inability to function, unexpected errors, or surprising problems for users. Yet in humanitarian emergencies, failure means the inability to deliver vital food aid, lethal conflicts and violence, and the potential compromise of human lives. Unintended leaks of data or privacy information mean new passwords, bad publicity, and—in the worst of cases—bank theft or identity abuse. In humanitarian emergencies, deeply intimate and highly political data in the wrong hands means persecution and conceivable harm.

The growing repertoire of experimental technologies and interventions brings with it new objectives, new actors, and not least new risks. The transformational effect of technology is not a given, and data prospecting and use is not inevitably empowering for vulnerable populations. Instead, the potential risks that unintended consequences, failures, or mistakes may have create new vulnerabilities. Humanitarian responses have always faced the curse of having to deliberately distribute harm by deciding who receives what kind of assistance at what points in time. And resources are always scarce in emergencies. But by introducing new technological innovations, these may come to shape and decide how harm is distributed. If drones can mainly be used under certain conditions, emergencies that do not satisfy these conditions will have to cope without help from the particular technology. And importantly, risks come not only from failure.[31] The successful biometric registration of millions of refugees only works to strengthen this particular regime of refugee and population management. As such, its success facilitates a propagation across countries and continents, while at the same time several elements beyond the technically feasible registration process itself may pose a risk to humanitarian principles and the imperative to do no harm.

There is a great need for the humanitarian industry to innovate, searching out improved solutions that may save lives and make a difference for the world's most vulnerable populations. But there is also a constant need to ask questions about the effects of frontier technologies being experimented with and the inequalities this produces or exacerbates. The humanitarian industry and emergencies are not systems that can easily be hacked and manipulated as a computer program. These are complex systems and arenas where new practices, ideas, and experiments have real consequences for real people. And there is no straight line between technological innovation and experimentation and the well-being of vulnerable populations. There is a strong duality in this technologization of the humanitarian sector. While the pace of innovations and new digitized ideas sometimes seems rapid, and appears to be carrying with it a form that may radically change humanitarian practices, most humanitarian responses to crises still take *traditional* forms and require conventional deliveries of support. Water, food aid, sanitation, shelter, and protection need to be delivered and often depend on traditional infrastructures that cannot be hacked. Efforts have to be coordinated, and there has to be interaction with partners and host governments, to ensure that the aid can be delivered effectively and efficiently.

Experimentation may introduce new technologies and invent solutions that, in theory, should deliver aid more quickly and more precisely fitted to the needs or predict the scale and duration of crises. But these efforts and the technological artefacts they develop do not automatically translate into improved humanitarian action. The next key figures in the experimental movement that we will visit, the development economists known as the Randomistas, know this conundrum all too well: that effects (and potentially detrimental ones at that) are produced beyond those expected and that, once set free, a technology or an experiment can suddenly take on a life of its own and expand outside the control of those who thought they were in charge. If the experimental movement was a startup, the next actor in question would undoubtedly be its Chief Scientific Officer for the ways in which the randomistas see themselves as the pinnacle of scientific practice and experimental competence.

Notes

1. Human Rights Watch. 2017. Massacre by the river: Burmese army crimes against humanity in Tula Toli, December 2017.
2. In its report to the UN Human Rights Council, the independent international fact-finding mission on Myanmar detailed that: 'The role of social media is significant. Facebook has been a useful instrument for those seeking to spread hate, in a context where, for most users, Facebook is the Internet. Although improved in recent months, the response of Facebook has been slow and ineffective. The extent to which Facebook posts and messages have led to real-world discrimination and violence must be independently and thoroughly examined. The mission regrets that Facebook is unable to provide country-specific data about the spread of hate speech on its platform, which is imperative to assess the adequacy of its response.' See Human Rights Council, Thirty-ninth session, 10–28 September 2018, Agenda item 4.
3. BBC. 2018. UN: Facebook has turned into a beast in Myanmar. 13 March.
4. See Mozur, P. 2018. A genocide incited on Facebook, with posts from Myanmar's military, *New York Times* 15 October 2018.
5. Larson, C. 2017. Facebook can't cope with the world it's created, *Foreign Policy* 7 November. Facebook's main response to the allegations made by the UN at the time came in the form of a blogpost by Alex Warofka, a Facebook product policy manager where it was stated that 'The [UN, ed.] report concludes that, prior to this year, we weren't doing enough to help prevent our platform from being used to foment division and incite offline violence. We agree that we can and should do more.'
6. See Culliford, E. 2021. Rohingya refugees sue Facebook for $150 billion over Myanmar violence, Reuters, 8 December.
7. See Sandvik, K.B. 2016. The humanitarian cyberspace: shrinking space or an expanding frontier?, *Third World Quarterly* 37(1): 17–32.
8. IFRC. 2013. *World Disasters Report: Focus on technology and the future of humanitarian action*. International Federation of Red Cross and Red Crescent Societies.
9. See Sandvik, K.B., Jacobsen, K.L., and McDonald, S.M. 2017. Do no harm: a taxonomy of the challenges of humanitarian experimentation, *International Review of the Red Cross* 99(1): 319–44; Sandvik, K.B., Jumbert, M.G., Karlsrud, J., and Kaufmann,

M. 2014. Humanitarian technology: a critical research agenda, *International Review of the Red Cross* 96(893): 219–42.

10. Sandvik, 2016.

11. Jacobsen, K.L. 2017. On humanitarian refugee biometrics and new forms of intervention, *Journal of Interventions and Statebuilding* 11(4): 539–51.

12. See Jacobsen, K.L. 2015. Experimentation in humanitarian locations: UNHCR and biometric registration of Afghan Refugees, *Security Dialogue* 46(2): 144–64.

13. OIOS. 2016. Audit of the Biometric Identity Management System at the Office of the United Nations High Commissioner for Refugees. Report 2016/181.

14. See Ajana, B. 2013. Asylum, identity management and biometric control, *Journal of Refugee Studies* 26(4).

15. UNICEF. Humanitarian drone corridor launched in Malawi, see https://www.unicef.org/stories/humanitarian-drone-corridor-launched-malawi.

16. See OCHA. 2014. Unmanned aerial vehicles in humanitarian response, OCHA Policy and Studies Series, June 2014, 010; Jumbert, M.G. and Sandvik, K.B. 2017. Introduction: what does it take to be good? In K.B. Sandvik and M.G. Jumber (eds), *The Good Drone*. Abingdon & New York: Routledge.

17. Digital Democracy. 2014. We built a drone. 19 December, see https://wp.digital-democracy.org/we-built-a-drone/.

18. See Whetham, D. 2015. Drones to protect, *The International Journal of Human Rights* 19(2): 199–210.

19. Danish Ministry of Foreign Affairs. 2017. *Hack the Future of Development Aid*. Danish Ministry of Foreign Affairs, Sustainia and Coinify.

20. For a general introduction to blockchain in aid, see Pisa, M. 2017. Blockchain and economic development: Hype vs. reality, CGD Policy Paper 107, July 2017. Center for Global Development.

21. Paynter, B. 2017. How blockchain could transform the way international aid is distributed, *Fast Company*, 18 September.

22. Paynter, 2017.

23. Fabian interview with *Ego Magazine*, 22 May 2018. Accessible at: https://www.youtube.com/watch?v=s256FwvgOzU.

24. See https://innovation.wfp.org/innovation-accelerator.

25. Obrecht, A. and Waner, A.T. 2016. *More than Just Luck: Innovation in Humanitarian Action*. HIF/ALNAP Study. London: ALNAP/ODI.

26. Betts, A. and Bloom, L. 2014. Humanitarian Innovation: State of the Art, OCHA Policy and Studies Series, November 2014, 009.

27. Bloom, L. and Betts, A. 2013. The Two Worlds of Humanitarian Innovation, Refugee Studies Centre Working Paper Series No. 94.

28. WFP. 2018. Tech for Food wins big at the 'Innovate for Refugees' awards ceremony in Amman. 31 January 2018.

29. See Inman, P. 2018. Should Africa let Silicon Valley in?, *The Guardian* 19 May.

30. See OIOS, 2016.

31. Sandvik et al., 2017.

3

Randomistas

On the north-eastern banks of Lake Victoria, fishing boats line up waiting to take crews out to sea in the dark hours long before first light hits the shores. But these days business is not booming. Over the past decades, stocks of Nile Perch, the invasive freshwater fish introduced in the 1950s to grow the local fishing industries in the basin and subsequently a major reason for the declining ecological diversity of Africa's greatest lake, have halved because of over-fishing and pollution. Yet, the biggest challenge for the local Kenyan fishermen arrives from some 8,000 kilometres away in Southern China. Chinese aquaculture exports are a success story, and in Kenyan fish markets the farm-raised and widely exported tilapia shares enough resemblance to what fishermen may get from the lake that local buyers either don't spot the difference or choose it for its often two-thirds lower price than the local fish.[1] In late 2018, the Kenyan government imposed an import ban on foreign tilapia, but sanctions only lasted a few months before the Chinese ambassador accused Kenya of instigating a 'trade war' with China. Rumours grew of China threatening to freeze funding for the East Africa railway connecting the port of Mombasa with Kigali through Uganda, for which it provided some 90 per cent of initial funding.

Predictably, many of the local fishermen are struggling to make a living in the shadow of the Chinese trading regime, but that's not a strange situation for many Kenyans living in the Western districts of the country, where several industries are now far from previous heights. Siaya district in particular is one of the poorest in all of Kenya with the majority of its population of one million living below the poverty line, although it comprises a large portion of Kenya's shores on Lake Victoria. In the district's southern parts lies the Rarieda constituency, an otherwise overlooked part of Siaya were it not for its sharp and sharply dressed Member of Parliament Otiende Amollo, elected as a member of the Orange Democratric Movement (ODM) from 2017 onwards. Amollo is known for being a contributing factor when the Kenyan Supreme Court shocked the world and nullified the results of the country's presidential election in 2017, a first ever on the continent and a stunning result considering the 2007 events and violence post-election. For the sake of our story, however, Rarieda is of greatest relevance because, over the past years, an American NGO has been conducting a series of history's largest cash transfer and income experiments there. The experiments have grown through different stages of implementation and have collectively provided tens of thousands of poor Kenyans with thousands of dollars, allowing the organization to both manipulate the local context and observe the economic and social consequences unfold over time.

'So simple, it's genius' American periodical *The Atlantic* praised a new charity by the name of GiveDirectly in 2012.[2] Four years earlier, a group of graduate economics students at Harvard and MIT—Paul Niehaus, Michael Faye, Rohit Wanchoo, and Jeremy Shapiro—had established a private giving circle with the aim of bypassing middlemen, whom they saw as skimming aid projects by supposedly taking a cut at every level before the funding reached beneficiaries. By 2012 their efforts had been professionalized in a US charity built around providing direct unconditional cash transfers to poor Kenyans. The project hit a home run with Silicon Valley moguls, many of whom practically preach disintermediation as a business strategy in their companies, and Google quickly awarded the organization US$2.4 million allowing it to move into Uganda, whilst Facebook cofounder Chris Hughes joined its board. In what feels like the echo of the story of many of the economists we will meet in this chapter, the GiveDirectly founders believe their organization and idea initially met a sceptical development milieu locked in conservative and self-preserving ways, with NGO staff critically inquiring 'If this works, what are we all here for? Why do we have jobs?'. GiveDirectly co-founder Niehaus dismissed what he believed was a monotone approach from existing organizations: 'There's an industry that exists that tries to make decisions for poor people and determine what's best for them.... But the value of that hasn't been proven.'[3] And so, the American charity evidently took a different direction in Kenya.

GiveDirectly's first major experiment with cash transfers in Rarieda, designed as a randomized controlled trial, was initiated in 2011. Villages were selected based on the number of thatched roofs (taken as an indicator of extreme poverty vis-à-vis houses with metal roofs) and of these, some 500 households were randomly selected to receive cash transfers through the M-Pesa mobile service. Some of the households in the *treatment* group would receive the money as a lump sum and some over a period of nine months. The total amount of both was US$404. A quarter of the households in the treatment group were further selected to receive upwards of US$1,500. That is around 75 per cent of annual income for most of the families, delivered as a single transfer. At the same time roughly 500 households in treatment villages functioned as the control group, meaning they participated in the baseline survey but received no money transfers unlike their fortunate neighbours. The researchers didn't visit the control households to explain why their neighbours received a massive transfer of funds and they did not, but the research team explains that 'those who asked were told that they "had not won the lottery"'.[4] And lottery does not have to be a metaphor, as many randomized experiments in the Global South conduct public randomization ceremonies in which a project is first presented to the public and then names are drawn from a container and shown to everyone in attendance. Evidently this is done to support the logics of fairness and transparency, but is also likely to create expectations of benefits while potentially having strong pacifying effects by turning people into willing subjects that have limited rights to contestation later on, naturalizing the presence of the researchers.[5] But that is getting ahead of ourselves and for now lottery is lottery, life is life. Researchers surveyed the households four months before and four months after the programme, with the baseline survey done without informing participants that it was part of an experiment on unconditional cash transfers. The researchers judged that they couldn't ask for consent or disclose the details because this would pollute the scientific purity of the research design.[6]

What is the effect on a set of extremely poor rural communities, if you give half of the families upwards of US$1,500, while others receive zero? GiveDirectly's RCT from the experiment showed an anticipated increase in assets (think livestock, furniture, or metal roofs), consumption and food security among recipients, yet the programme had no effect on health care, education or women's empowerment, and there was no impact on the overall economic environment. In fact, and unsurprisingly perhaps because of its very nature as an experiment benefiting some and not others, the intervention amplified existing inequalities.[7] The doubts unmistakeably rank up. These transfers could sway attention away from public goods to purely individual financial support, potentially leaving little improvement for most of the villagers who have neither electricity nor clean water. There are likewise strong assumptions that they may disrupt established patterns of wealth distribution within a community and create tensions between those who receive and those who do not. And why do you need an experimental approach with control groups to an intervention form we already know fairly well—are we so unsure that giving very poor people a large amount of money is likely better for them than not receiving any, and would it not be more realistic to compare different levels of support without a control group? Still, the potential upside is striking too—what if this experiment could lay the foundation for a future effective delivery of universal basic income (UBI) across not just the developing world but in the well-off parts of the world as well?

For the evidence from the experiment to have any chance of theoretically contributing to our general understanding of universal basic income, it would require a much greater scale. It just so happens that that is where GiveDirectly decided to go next. The latest instalment represents the world's largest cash transfer experiment and will run for twelve years from its commencement in 2017. Two hundred villages or more than 20,000 Kenyans will receive direct cash: some every month for twelve years, some for two years, and some as a lump sum equal to two years of payments. This time too, major backers include Silicon Valley institutions and individuals, pushing UBI as an instrument to disintermediate development agencies and implementors, or bypass government services in efforts directly targeted at citizens. The experiment will complement other unconditional cash trials currently underway, including by investment firm and legendary startup 'school' Y-Combinator. Needless to say, the experiment will run as a randomized controlled trial. In charge of the RCT will be MIT star economist and randomista co-commander-in-chief Abhijit Banerjee. How is it that the experimentalist affinities of RCTs have managed to become so dominant in the field, despite econometricians persuasively arguing that the evidence these methods provide is not guaranteed to be any more foolproof than other forms of evidence? Next, we open up the randomista movement that is as bound together by political concerns as it is by scientific or methical concerns about the necessity of experimentation in the Global South. We explore the main personages and actors driving forward this supposed experimental revolution of our understanding of the effectiveness of development and social policy and examine the rhetorical and political strategies employed by the top people from the experimental movement, to recruit allies and convince audiences of the superiority of their experimentation.[8]

*

Evidence discussions have raged in global development for more than half a century, but the randomistas, slowly emerging in the 1990s and picking up speed over the past decade, have lifted these to a whole new level. Wanting to clear the air between opposing perspectives in development economics on aid and large-scale government interventions, the randomistas emerged suggesting that instead of for or against, we should be discussing when, how, and under what conditions aid works. They also advised that the path to such evidence was through a single methodology and only that methodology: randomized controlled trials. The rise of the randomistas, however, has been anything but confined. Scientifically, RCTs have come to 'entirely dominate development economics' as the Nobel Academy concluded in 2019, pushed forward by elite US institutions such as the Abdul Latif Jameel Poverty Action Lab (or J-PAL for short at MIT), Innovations for Poverty Action (IPA) at Yale, and the Center for Effective Global Action (CEGA) at Berkeley. Together, these form a network of hundreds of researchers and thousands of staff and students all around the world and are responsible for more than a thousand different randomized experiments conducted in the Global South over the past decade. They make up an immensely strong group with an aptitude for turning science into policy and action, shaping government, non-profit, and commercial efforts from Kerala to Kenya. The story of the randomistas' rise is a story of how a research programme became a policy programme, carrying social, cultural, and political implications far beyond its self-image as an objective chaser of truth. To some, this was a revelation of effectivizing development aid in a business that has a bad habit of repeating past mistakes and practising organizational conservatism, and to others it was a cautionary tale rather than a success story.[9] We start from the inborne criticism of the prevailing development milieu that fuelled a behavioural economic revolution in the field.

'How costly is the resistance to knowledge?' Abhijit Banerjee asked in an early 2006 commentary on 'making aid work' as a prelude to his 2007 book of the same name, targeting conventional development donors for their apparent 'institutional laziness', as he described it.[10] The rise of the randomistas was instigated and made possible by at least two simultaneous if different sets of changes inside and outside the discipline of economics. We will return to what occurred inside the economics discipline later in this chapter. Outside the discipline, the political and scientific field of global development saw growing questions about the ability of development aid to induce measurable societal change in the wake of relative disappointment for many of the large-scale government and development bank programmes implemented through the 1980s and 1990s. The 1990s saw the gradual waning of the 'Washington Consensus', leaving room in particular for private foundations and NGOs, who were seen to be more politically independent than governments and public aid agencies,[11] at least in theory. For many of these, RCTs are a fit for isolated project interventions that operate with limited scope and a specific set of objectives, where they can test changes to different variables in a somewhat bounded form. Think of questions such as what happens to enrolment for girls if we make education free or charge a small amount, rather than whether or in what forms education has an effect on poverty levels. The NGOs proved to be much more flexible and willing to try experimental interventions or innovative changes to existing work, it would turn out,[12] not least spurred by their competitive field. This fragmented field of development increasingly facilitated the coming of different logics from other scientific or policy fields than those traditionally affiliated with development, witnessing a massive diversification of actors and ideas. This can be coupled with other developments in the aid field such as the growing international focus on measurable results and aid effectiveness during the start of the 2000s that culminated with the OECD DAC (Development Assistance Committee) Paris Declaration on Aid Effectiveness from 2005.[13] Growing concerns over value for money and cost-effectiveness on the donor side led more than a hundred countries to formally pursue performance assessments, results-oriented reporting, and monitoring frameworks. This was followed up by the 2008 Accra Agenda for Action, which reaffirmed that development partners 'will work to develop cost-effective results management instruments to assess the impact of development policies and adjust them as necessary'.[14] As such, randomistas had both disorganization and a growing technocratic consensus in development available to them as they were making moves to position themselves.

Banerjee's early criticism of the established development milieu did not take aim against just any development institution but perhaps the most powerful one, the World Bank, claiming it was knowledge resistant and built on lazy thinking because its evaluation practice at the time did not utilize the randomistas' methodological weapon, the RCT.[15] But the sweeping critique from the new development economists extended far beyond just the Bank. The diagnosis was straightforward: contemporary development thinking and interventions were overly dominated by notions of contextuality and politics, undermining the potential of policy to follow 'scientifically proven' programmes and prescriptions. Most of the programmes implemented were seen as built on simplified ideologies and an ignorance of the realities of 'the field',[16] born out of politics rather than a reflection of actual objectively identifiable needs. It was a strong narrative of how 'old development bureaucracies are protecting their organizational self-interest and hence are not using the rigorous techniques available to evaluate the outcomes from their projects and hence wasting taxpayer money and not doing good for the poor'.[17] The prevailing regimes of expertise in development were seen as opinion-based, seniority- and anecdote-based,[18] wrought with unproven political advice of policy or 'soft' experts: 'what goes for best practice is often not particularly well founded', Banerjee voiced.[19]

The randomistas, in contrast, were able to provide a very different road to a different truth. Based on self-perceived mechanical objectivity, they articulated a regime of evidence thought to remove bias and subjectivity, maintaining that they could release decisions from their political nature by presenting them in an envelope of independence and scienticism. The evidential truths delivered by the development economists were scientific and smart, and 'largely independent of "expert" knowledge that is often regarded as manipulable, politically biased, or otherwise suspect'.[20] Things were indeed looking to change, it seemed: 'attitudes are changing. A number of large foundations, including the Bill and Melinda Gates Foundation,...have shown a strong commitment to using evidence to inform their decisions', Banerjee voiced with confidence.[21] Despite the discernible moral and political reasoning that we will discuss later, the randomistas have always been asserting that they are not bound together by certain political ideas about the effectiveness of specific forms of aid, but rather by their collective belief in the power of a particular methodology to trump all others.

In technical terms, the randomistas represented a refocus from macro to micro. From large-scale aid-funded budget support programmes or sector programmes towards smaller experimental interventions that could prove certain effects without providing broader explanations found in questions of 'why' something happens. They transformed complex and perhaps multi-solution problems of development into technical matters of hard evidence, thereby reducing the uncertainty of social policy and projects, alluring institutions and individuals alike by what can be called *facticity*, the political power of facts and numbers. Replacing one set of expertise with another would prove to be far more than a scientific endeavour, and the true strengths of the randomista movement surely lie in its capacity for networking and institution building, even if its current status as a global Nobel-Prize-winning undertaking was not immediately recognizable in the humbler beginnings at the margins of a discipline.

Empowered by his famous mid-1990s deworming study in Kenya that we met in the introduction to the book, Michael Kremer is widely credited with laying the ground for the randomistas. Nonetheless, it was Esther Duflo who 'set in motion a randomization industry',[22] combining her unique scientific skills with talents of communication and persuasion. It was Duflo's thesis advisor at MIT, labour economist Joshua Angrist, who initially introduced her to work using *natural* experiments. Banerjee, who would later become her life partner, was another of her thesis-advisors. Duflo realized early on that 'economics had potential as a lever of action in the world'[23] while working together with Jeffrey Sachs, whose work she would come to question later in her career. Offered tenure at both Princeton and Yale at the age of thirty, Duflo persuaded MIT to do the same and further commit US$300,000 to create a Poverty Action Lab together with colleagues Banerjee and Sendhil Mullainathan. MIT was and still is the capital of the *lab* in scholarly contexts,[24] and the Poverty Action Lab joined a chorus of labs on anything from robotics to Air-Sea Interaction. The ambition for the new lab was cut in stone for Duflo and her colleagues: 'take the guesswork out of policy-making' and proceed from the two refrains, first, that what works is in fact simple to identify and, second, that what works can be diffused across the world because of causal structures that tend to be uniformly present.[25] 'There are efficiency gains waiting everywhere' in the developing world, Duflo holds in the movement's quest for using experiments to separate good policy influences from bad: 'There is a lot of noise in the world...and what the data is going to be able to do—if there's enough of it—is uncover, in the mess and the noise of the world, some lines of music that actually have harmony. It's there, somewhere.'[26] The ability to produce hard evidence through RCTs accordingly situates the movement in a position able to inform policy makers with knowledge about what works and what does not work, or what the cheapest types of treatment are. It is all 'about allocating resources to the best use. It doesn't seem like a hugely innovative view of the world, but most people who are not economists don't get it', Duflo has explained.[27] By letting economists roam wild in the real world, they are able to find out what works and convert scientific methodology into common cost-effective measures, essentially turning foreign aid into a 'science' of development. Hard evidence, according to this line of thought, is a form of objective information that we have not yet acquired, but whose presence will fill a gap, like the last material piece of a puzzle that reveals the entire picture. The purpose of J-PAL was settled then.

Two years after its inception in 2003, an endowment from Mohammed Abdul Latif Jameel, head of a Saudi conglomerate, truly lifted the J-PAL operations from a being smaller scholarly endeavour to a global institution-building movement, from a 'project that crazy people do in the back yard to something that is institutional and serious'.[28] Over the subsequent years, J-PAL would see immense growth, from four affiliated professors and involvement in thirty-three projects to hundreds of associated researchers and involvement in over a thousand experiments across the world. Duflo won the

John Bates Clark Medal in 2010, largely considered a preamble for the Nobel Prize she was awarded nine years later as the youngest recipient ever. That same year, the *New Yorker* portrayed her as resembling a demi-goddess among mere humans: describing a situation on a business trip to India, the journalist noted that Duflo 'was purposeful: a steady gaze, an orderly mind (she would often ask for 'a second of focus' while collecting her thoughts, to fend off the sins of repetition and digression); and a tolerant, regretful sympathy for those around her whose heads were filled with idle thoughts or low-quality data.'[29]

For Duflo, who calls herself an institution builder, the aim from the outset had been to expand across the world, engaging partners from all sides of the private and public arenas, far beyond the research community. That meant evolving J-PAL into a wider epistemic community based on a shared belief in the verity and applicability of particular forms of knowledge and perceived truths,[30] central to all participants is experimental practice and a lexicographic preference for the RCT. The ambition to turn hard science into policy and implementation was received with open arms among many emerging and established players in global development, and the randomistas have more or less moved from strength to strength since. On the ten-year anniversary of J-PAL, former World Bank economist Lant Pritchett noted how 'The rise in the number of people using rigorous methods—including randomized control trials—to examine development interventions is just astonishing.'[31] Since then, their rise has only increased in pace. Celebrated by media, politicians, and elite institutions, the movement continues to receive massive financial support (the Gates Foundation has pledged tens of millions of dollars alone), not just for experimental projects or evaluation but for essential infrastructure that helps facilitate the growth of experimental methodologies and policies. As specialists in moving from research programme to policy programme to implementation programme, the randomistas work tirelessly to tip the balance of power in both science and development in their favour, breaking with other traditionally dominant voices in the field. As a popular story goes, Jeffrey Sachs, after establishing himself as critical towards the ambitions of J-PAL, came 'back' to Duflo and asked for her Lab's help to evaluate his famed Millennium Villages Project. Duflo's reaction was a methodological bullet to his economist heart—'the design of your project has not accommodated randomized testing and hence there is nothing I can do.'[32]

*

Every morning, a chicken is fed by the farmer. From experience, the chicken knows nothing but this, and the delivery of food each day by the farmer becomes a general rule, a law, for the chicken its entire life. This anticipated causality simply reflects all the evidence the chicken has ever observed. That is until Christmas morning when circumstances suddenly change and it loses its head, ending its days as a supper for the farmer's family. British philosopher Bertrand Russel used the example of the chicken to discuss the limitations to simple extrapolation from successful replication. What is the degree of uniformity of nature and what makes something count as evidence? These are perhaps the two greatest questions posed to the randomistas, whose ambitions, as we already know, are to identify 'what works' and what does not, based on the assumption that RCTs allow us to extrapolate from findings and replicate these elsewhere. Empiricists such as David Hume would, of course, argue that we never observe any laws of nature, but simply make observations from which we infer and make assumptions about law-like propositions. Now, this problem of induction does not apply, so to speak, if we do not adopt a view that works with such law-like propositions but instead acknowledge exceptions to expectations built into all forms of knowledge and evidence. In the praxis of development this means the always present probability of unexpected changes in socioeconomic structures or in individual choice-systems that we could not foresee, entailing that a programme or project will not have the same effects everywhere. Randomistas, on the other hand, maintain an immensely strong faith in reproducibility, replication, and generalization. To repeat what Esther Duflo stated when interviewed immediately after being awarded the Nobel Prize: 'We keep running into the same problem from place to place to place, in India, in Africa, even in France, we have the same problem. And the solutions, in a sense, then can be the same.' Same problems, same solutions, everywhere in the world.

Even if the rise of the randomistas was predicated on a looming criticism of dominant approaches to global development, there is no way it could have happened without a simultaneous set of important changes occurring inside the discipline of economics. Both economics broadly and development economics specifically went through major changes towards the end of the twentieth century and immediately afterwards. A *credibility revolution*, emerging from within labour economics in the early 1990s, brought with it calls to take the 'con out of econometrics'[33] by recentring attention on research designs and causal effects in empirical microeconomics. Economics concurrently went through an 'empirical turn' in the late 1980s and early 1990s that spurred interest in work other than theoretically informed modelling and coincided with the rise of behavioural economics and the credibility revolution's aim to explore notions of causal inference, that is, the documentation of causes and effect and the isolation of specific factors and variables within them. While behavioural economics was susceptible to critique for its preference for lab-like conditions for experiments, the empirical turn pushed RCTs forward as a new way to bring experiments into the real world, just as causal identification became much more manipulable[34] in the hands of a researcher who was in theory able to isolate variables.

It was amidst some of these major changes that the randomistas began circling around how developing countries could prove to be ideal testing grounds for the future of the discipline. The group jumped headfirst on to these *credibility* and empiricist developments with ambitions of minimizing the scientific questions pursued, shifting from the role of economic institutions, political dynamics, and social progress to evaluating whether bed-nets for mosquitoes should be free or have a low price to ensure uptake and use. They did so by challenging existing views that the poor are inherently less rational than everyone else, instead maintaining how the conditions of poverty magnify the effects of cognitive biases and weaknesses.[35] So, while everyone shares these weaknesses and biases, they are just more pronounced in poor people because of the structural circumstances of poverty. This means poverty as a structural condition remains a problem, but it also means individuals are able to escape their so-called efficiency deficiencies themselves. Accordingly, policy makers ought to design interventions that correct decision-making and enhance rationality, shaping presumed motivational structures of the poor. Farmers, as an example, are locked in poverty traps because they spend their earnings immediately instead of saving them for productive investments the next season, that is, it is behavioural biases that limit their lives and their potential. Taking very seriously the view that economics is a scientific endeavour capable of explaining actual human behaviour,[36] randomistas focus on shaping incentive structures so that human behaviour can be channelled in the *optimum* direction that those intervening find socially beneficial. That is, development should essentially be about correcting the behavioural weaknesses of the poor, who are presumed both adaptable and mobile, readily able to be nudged or moved in any direction, with those doing so or arguing to do so gaining legitimation mainly from arguments about the poor's sub-par economic performance and by tracing this performance back to individual concerns. Behaviour is individualized and so too are solutions calling for institutionalizing rational calculation and entailing that small-scale behavioural change works better than large-scale government interventions at transforming the vulnerable poor into resilient economic rational subjects.

These behavioural lines of thought draw on advances made in psychology during the second part of the twentieth century, a discipline that was generally the first of the human sciences to build a tradition of experimental manipulation of human subjects from the 1870s. Behaviourism was largely side-lined during the 1950s and 1960s but gained momentum during the 1970s with advances in cognitive psychology.[37] The 1910s had seen the start of educational experiments among schoolchildren that were easy to administer, controlled by teachers, who were themselves controlled by powerful management. This inaugural period of experimentation in the behavioural sciences witnessed testing on everything from small versus large classes, the gender of teachers, and almost every other conceivable variable. Randomization largely grew out of these efforts and ideas about strengthening impersonality, meaning subjects could not be selected but should be chosen at random, opening the way for generalization as because a result of the supposedly generic findings. The 1970s and 1980s saw the introduction of prospect theory in economics and the idea that people only rely on a limited set of heuristic principles when making decisions in situations characterized by uncertainty.[38] These lines of thought were brought into economics by Richard Thaler who in 1980 published a founding text for behavioural economics on consumer theory. In a context of growing scepticism about the political applicability of neoclassical economics, behavioural economics was able to quickly utilize a window of opportunity to assert itself and its methodological basis.

Over time, the behavioural project has increasingly become a normative project as well of attempting to change the way people behave, beyond merely challenging conventional economic theory. This is something the randomistas have almost perfected while implicitly drawing on concepts such as *nudging*, possibly the ultimate behavioural methodology in the world of politics and administration for shaping people's actions. Forwarding these perspectives not least implies drawing on the dual process model from psychology that is evident in most of the scientific work of the randomistas. The basic tenets of this model are that all individuals either make judgements through a rapid, associative, automatic, and effortless intuitive process or through a slower rule-governed, deliberate, and effortful process. Put bluntly, society is split in two—regular people who rely more on emotions and would be expected to only reach suboptimum outcomes, and then the experts (described by Richard Thaler as *those with PhDs in economics*) who are rational and pursue optimum outcomes.[39] And the poor, because of the structural conditions of poverty, too often fall into the first category. The purpose of development should accordingly be to help those who do not act fully rationally whilst not spoiling things for those who do, that is, providing a 'smart' and individualized solution. The main protagonists of development (expertise) accordingly become those with (scientific) skills to manipulate that behaviour. But before one can induce behavioural changes, a baseline of evidence needs to be established concerning which direction people should ideally be nudged towards. And that is where the RCT rules, brought in from the natural and medical sciences.

'It's not the Middle Ages anymore, it's the 21st century...RCTs have revolutionized medicine by allowing us to distinguish between drugs that work and drugs that don't work. And you can do the same randomized controlled trial for social policy', Duflo has expressed this inspiration from medical science.[40] Many economists love the natural and technical sciences for their *hard* methodologies and approaches to evidence. It is not surprising that the same applies to randomistas, who believe they have found in medicine a 'very robust and very simple tool' as Duflo puts it.[41] And randomistas love the popular story from medicine on why RCTs were introduced there. When first suggested in medicine, many clinicians resisted this new methodological framework that fundamentally challenged their scientific authority by claiming it insufficient to evaluate the efficacy of a new treatment based on their professional opinions. But resistance is futile and in sweeps RCTs, substituting a localized, individual, and *biased* truth with an objective, generalized, and scientific one.[42] Like Banerjee's criticism of the current regime of development donors and policy makers, a group of stubborn practitioners, who refuse to embrace new ways and instead maintain their practices as they have done for their entire careers, stand in the way of progress but are eventually pushed aside by a wave of science itself. This is a very nice framing story accentuating the obvious point that whereas RCTs are democratic knowledge, accessible to and operationalizable by all—at least in theory—subjective expertise resides with the individual, lacks transparency, and cannot be fact-checked. This mathematization of medical knowledge, not least facilitated by the rise of statistics,[43] has always been thought to bring precision and fairness just as it allowed the categorizing of spaces, populations, and diseases, as well as treatments, while maintaining a strong sense of generalizability and average effects through randomization. RCTs in medicine have their own shortcomings, of course, and are also widely criticized just as it has been proven that their adoption was based not only on methodological grounds but—unsurprisingly—also on political grounds.[44] The highly lauded democratic transparency has not exactly burned through in a pharmaceutical business where trial conditions and results are regularly published but only to the bare minimum extent needed to obtain approval by medical authorities for commercialization. Because of clinical and regulatory dependence on RCTs, methodological issues are rarely raised with a view to discrediting or questioning the methodology, but rather with a view to improving it.[45] There is no real alternative, at least for the pharmas for whom RCTs are immensely important and have financial implications. But that is not the fault of the methodology, the argument runs, which seemingly escapes political implications by way of its objective mathematical nature.

The intellectual roots of the movement go back further than the medical science of the mid-twentieth century. Relevant traces can be found in Britain's attempts to introduce payments by results in the mid-1800s and French experimental medicine around the 1850s, even if the obsession with evidence did not make its way into public policy before the 1960s and 1970s (especially in the US under the name of Management by Objectives), where it was seen as a rational and technical break with 'old-fashioned' ideological policies and instruments.[46] From their entrance into the medical sciences, the prominence of RCTs rose and coincided with the diffusion of statistical concepts and methods across genetics, psychology, economics, and physics. Between the 1960s and 1980s, the golden age of the field experiment saw some 245 trials undertaken in the US with famous early studies including the 'Perry preschool program' (1961) and The Rand Health Insurance Experiment across a broad field of trials within employment programmes, electricity pricing, and housing allowances in the US. The same decades, as said, saw early RCTs in developing countries, with experiments employing long time horizons and a focus on large-scale political change within health and education. This first wave consisted mostly of sociologists, psychologists, or health experts from key global US institutions such as the US Agency for International Development (USAID), The Rockefeller Foundation, the Ford foundation, and the Social Science Research Council (SSRC). This first wave did not prove vastly successful, however, and RCTs never broke through the knowledge and evidence regimes in existence at the time. One reason may be that, although the presence of academic economists seems to have been minimal during the 1980s attempt to introduce RCTs as the gold standard in development aid evaluation and decision-making, this group has been identified as representing at least 80 per cent of published authors of RCT studies over the past decades.[47] Not only did the contemporary randomistas focus their RCT efforts on a much smaller scale such as sub-factors of projects, but the movement was also much more heavily ingrained into economics.

*

The core purpose of an RCT is to measure the effect of something. It is not to explore open-ended causal processes of how something happens—it is to prove inference, establishing whether there is an effect or not—in an easily measurable form and with well-established boundaries. Fundamentally, it is about dividing a population into two groups, providing a 'treatment' to one group, and keeping the other for control purposes, with randomization ensuring that the groups are alike. Thus, you either belong to the intervention group or the control group. You experience the proposed change, funding, or treatment, or you do not. How is it decided who gets something and who does not? 'You flip a coin for each person to decide whether she is offered a program or not. If it comes up heads, assign to treatment. If it comes up tails, assign to control. That's it. That's the big secret. The coin does the work for us', as RCT advocates Dean Karlan and Jacob Appel preach randomization.[48] You either get the experimental treatment and get to take part in the poverty reducing experiment, or you do not. A fundamental part of any RCT then, is the r for randomization. Randomization is so important to RCT proponents because it is what in theory ensures the experiment can identify average treatment effects (ATEs), although it does not excuse researchers from considering covariates just as it does not automatically deliver a precise estimate of the average treatment.[49] These elements of the research design are essentially what makes its proponents situate RCTs at the top of what they believe are evidence hierarchies. For many randomistas, furthering their methodologies is as much about proving others wrong, which is why concepts such as *gold standard* are used, making all others secondary. The key reason why all other methodologies are inadequate, the most radical RCT proponents argue, is because of what is called omitted variable bias. In situations where we have not isolated exactly what we are measuring, there will always be a plausible variable that we may have overlooked. Many randomistas argue that *softer* case studies and regressions are unable to provide hard proof and thus have no scientific legitimacy, essentially only providing what they would characterize as anecdotes. On microfinance, for example, Banerjee explains 'anecdotes about highly successful entrepreneurs or deeply indebted borrowers tell us nothing about the effect of microfinance on the average borrower', with single cases only seen to portray extremes or outliers, never representing or able to tell us something about average treatment. RCTs on the other hand come with an assembled inborne certainty: *we know x caused y*, because we ran a randomized trial. RCTs, on this view, do not produce or construct knowledge, they simply lay bare the naturally given effects, and the only plausible questions to be raised are ones about the validity of the methodological design.

The two major issues usually employed to question RCTs are ones of internal and external validity. The first questions whether the findings are reliable in themselves, something economists and econometrists have deliberated on in technical detail far beyond both my comprehension and our purpose here.[50] We can highlight instead the important discrepancy between the stylized version of experiments as they figure in research designs and plans, and the reality of actually conducting trials in the field. Several issues are common in field experiments, including attrition, lack of blinding, unintentional unblinding, post-randomization confounding, and selection biases.[51] And outside the lab, trial samples are much more likely to be the result of local practical circumstance than of scientific unbiased selection. Who was willing to participate? Who can be conveniently reached within the time and financial plans? The same concerns naturally apply to policy and implementation as well, as rolling out policies on the basis of RCTs does not eliminate deviation in implementation.

External validity describes the fundamental question of whether the findings can be transferred elsewhere, and in itself carries some problematic connotations. Not least for its binary assumption that either something (a trial) has obtained external validity, or it has not, implying that either its findings hold everywhere, or they do not. The first point here is that a trial obviously does not have to work everywhere to be considered constructive or productive. So long as it seems to function in a specific context that conclusion may be sufficient. The second point is the discussion of whether something can in fact be so decontextualized that it applies the same everywhere. We can obviously only transfer RCT findings from one context to a radically different one and expect the results to be the same if we believe that all the environmental and human factors in play remain the same. Nonetheless, generalization is a major purpose of RCTs, as we have seen several times already, with randomistas maintaining an intriguing simultaneity of attacking fragmented questions in specific locales while still aiming for a universalization of impact across the world. Randomistas often acknowledge the narrow scope of their experiments, but at the same time believe that the knowledge produced should completely determine the destination of development finance; if an intervention has not been proven effective by way of a *rigorous* RCT, it should not be funded.

Rigorous is important here because it signifies a hierarchy—that some forms of evidence are top notch—legitimate—and that others are not. So what thoughts does the word 'rigorous' trigger and how do people other than the authors of a paper or an evaluation see or use rigorousness? Rigorousness is not necessarily universal, ensuring that a piece of knowledge can be extended to every situation or context across time and space. Still, generalization beyond a single experience is immensely alluring to everyone, not just randomistas. A fundamental part of development policy work has always been to try and find some of those magic bullets that might just work across contexts, and we are all guilty of doing it all the time as we transfer first- or second-hand experiences from one context to another: 'when I worked in Zimbabwe we did x, y, z'. This attitude is naturally based on the hope and assumption that we don't have to start from scratch every time we have to address a problem. Generalization is convincing to a certain extent, it just cannot be taken for granted. Even the greatest internal validity does not ensure generalizability, and there is no cross-contextual generalization without translation. Even if some aspects may be transferred from one context to the next, introducing a programme used successfully elsewhere into a new context potentially remakes it altogether with all its causal connections and variables.

Causal chains are complex and there are dozens of things that can change along them, possibly undermining the potential for full generalization.[52] Those involved, whom we expect to act in precisely the same way as others halfway across the world, may in fact have other preferences, cultural traits, or belief systems that shape their actions and reactions under the programme or treatment. And the institutions on which the programme depends may have different operational procedures or efficiency levels, just as other structural conditions may obviously change and interfere, hence Bertrand Russell's chicken. As such, the aggregate does not always look like the individual. Consider maize farmers in a municipality or region who have been given access to an immensely effective fertilizer, allowing them to increase their yields markedly. The individual case is good for these particular farmers, yet if the project is scaled nationwide or to entire regions, we would expect maize prices to decrease because of inelastic demand. Decreasing prices is bad for the farmers and will not help them to improve their economic situation, thus undermining the intention of the intervention. Extrapolation, of course, is not always necessary or an ambition for those carrying out an RCT. A single-programme evaluation for a donor to explore whether its specific intervention is having an impact is ideal for an RCT and does not immediately require or beg the question of extrapolation. But once those findings have been made, deeming the programme a success or not, they are difficult to control. Even if those asking for the evaluation do not take it forward to new contexts themselves, people in headquarters or working in other country contexts may come to read the evaluation and themselves engage in extrapolation. Thus, we are back at the allure of generalization that everyone working in the field of global development has succumbed to once in a while. We see something working somewhere and think, why not bring it here to see whether we can achieve the same effect, even if we are very much aware of how context-dependence distorts replicability in practice.

It is important then not to take the micro-level focus of most RCTs as a signifier of limited ambitions of influence or impact. The shift to such a focus is often done because of the belief in what we can call intentional fragmentation, the breaking down of every system to its individual parts. In their 2011 book *Poor Economics*, Banerjee and Duflo advise the reader to think of poverty as 'a set of concrete problems that, once properly identified and understood, can be solved one at a time'.[53] Social contexts and real-world situations are seen as systems in which one can understand the different mechanisms and their effects and consequences, allowing us to predict the necessary actions to bring about change in its individual parts. Social issues are thus amendable if we break them down into technical issues, just like an engineering system. In the Gates Foundation's visitor centre in Seattle, the public can participate in games of moving levers into different positions to develop a vaccine, mechanically shifting issues such as 'funding' to different levels to obtain a final effect. These are only games, of course, but also a nod to how such engineering approaches sometimes see social systems as mechanistic ones. The ultimate purpose of these processes of fragmentation, or taking larger systems apart to its smaller parts which are then thought capable to being manipulated for the benefit of those targeted, is to create a sense of control, marginalizing contingency and uncertainty to a degree where these are not considered confounding factors. Attempting to tidy up uncertainty also often includes a move from client-focused to rule-governed implementation, controlling the relevant population for the policy makers by engineering their behaviour because of its suboptimum state.[54] The evidence produced by RCTs thus represents forms of control meant to provide both accountability and improvement. Accountability is concerned with how to prove that government or organizations are working effectively (basically as performance management), not wasting scarce resources; controlling improvement means looking at what works under different circumstances, generating reliable knowledge that provides a basis for effective action. It is tempting to think that this positivist mind-set almost translates into a suppressing of the self, individuality, and desires for the sake of general rules of life and society, with control of nature equalling control of self.

*

Is this not just an ivory-tower discussion of methods and evidence far removed from more pressing issues in the real world? What are the reasons, except for scientific explanations, leading us to these fairly long periods of attention and critique for something that may appear scholastic to the outsider? While the more technical forms of critique noted above are justifiable and necessary in questioning the supposed superiority and *gold standard* of RCTs, they are also insufficient to fully understand the implications of the randomista movement. There is a further level to the technicalities of methods, data collection, and analysis usually targeted in discussions of RCTs, particularly in the context and under the conditions randomistas typically apply them, that is, the Global South and in situations characterized by strong vulnerabilities, whether in poor communities, schools, or refugee camps. These next layers reveal a set of normative ambitions or implications, depending on the degree of deliberateness and force we understand to be propelling them. In the summer of 2020, a group of development economists announced a massive new study on 'Enforcing payment for water and sanitation services in Nairobi's slums', a trial mentioned in Chapter 1. The RCT, funded by J-PAL and the World Bank, was published by the National Bureau of Economic Research (NBER), an American private nonprofit. During the experiment, thousands of landlords, each renting multiple properties to poor Kenyan families living in Nairobi's slums, were tested for how they reacted to soft and hard threats of water closure if they failed to pay their bills. Thirty per cent of the treated landlords ended up disconnecting because of the tested threats, essentially leaving poor families without access to water and the authors with the result that 'enforcement is both possible and able to significantly improve repayment behaviour' and the finding that the intervention succeeded in 'bringing more paying customers into the fold'.[55] In concluding the study, the economists noted how, 'while disconnecting public utility services from those that may need them the most may appear to be antipoor and regressive, the alternative of treating basic services as a "right" may erode [the] incentive for utilities to provide those services in the first place'.[56] Contrary to this cynical formulation, basic services such as water or health care should obviously be treated as 'rights', not as an *alternative* to other approaches but exactly because they are fundamental human rights inscribed in UN conventions signed by almost all countries in the world.

The notion of experimentation not being a dead methodology but being a very active set of social practices carries over into sensitivity to the social, political, and cultural life of methods and methodologies beyond objective factors instrumentalized by researchers. Methods are theories of change and vocabularies of action and discourse that shape how we see the world, and in the context of development, progress, and the roads leading there.[57] The political ramifications become clear when we consider the widely promoted randomista argument that only interventions that have had positive results in experimental trials should be funded by donors.[58] This speaks to a fundamental ambition to change who counts as experts and what counts as expertise from a perspective effectively denying the existence of multiple legitimate knowledge sources in our society, by establishing a clear hierarchy of who is right and who is not, who ought to be considered expert, and who ought not to be. And not only which group of experts 'win', but how their knowledge succeeds in restructuring politics.[59]

Nonetheless, associations expand beyond the influence on policy choices, and so what exactly is mobilized in and through methods?[60] The hegemony of positivist quantitative methods that has developed over the past half century is central here for its preoccupation with rationalizing, categorizing, and ordering factors, variables, and finally interventions.[61] Ordering research becomes ordering interventions becomes ordering society. Randomistas' commitment to reductive metrics[62] and their search for 'averages' and deducing general laws from diverse observations fundamentally roots methods 'into specific modes of knowing embedded in particular cultural configurations'.[63] The strong adherence to experimental practices carries with it a belief system with both implicit and explicit normative aspirations about science, technology, truth, politics, and social change. Conditions and assumptions built into the methodology that are too often erased from the story.

These discussions fundamentally touch upon what has been called economic imperialism.[64] Not that Vasco de Gama arrived at the shores of Southwestern India with ships full of armed and khaki-wearing economists. What it denotes instead is how the discipline of economics over time has been able to expand its core premises and methods into other fields of life and science. Exemplified by economics in the US in the twentieth century and the story of how an academic discipline gained political authority,[65] from World War II seen as an 'economist's war'[66] to economics becoming part of the very language of policy in the country, providing political advice at the highest level of government through the Council on Economic Affairs inside the White House.[67] The power of the randomistas lie not just in specific political outcomes we may be able to identify, such as how many new programmes on deworming have been initiated or the extent of evaluation efforts adopting RCTs as a core standard. It lies equally in how they may incrementally exert influence by extending an economic style of reasoning. Reshaping the focus of development agencies and donors' funding interventions based on a logic of cost-effectiveness is an equally powerful tool in gradually introducing operational and cognitive changes in the field that may, over time, strengthen the case and position of the randomistas. Similarly, the randomista approach can shape institutional positions and future generations of (development) economists by training hundreds of young PhDs. The movement has thus benefited greatly from both historical and contemporary forms of economic imperialism and strategized well on knowledge such as how economists are likely to have the greatest political influence if they are able to turn an issue into a technical matter, allowing them to convert technical authority into moral authority.[68] This includes incremental change in a field such as development by way of subtle (and in some randomista cases not very subtle) changes to systems of measurement, calculation, or evaluation, allowing prevailing economic doctrines to influence policy. Generally speaking, the effects of economics on other sciences, particularly the social sciences but also politics and popular life, is achieved by employing devices for seeing and devices for choosing.[69] Producing numbers and producing models that may, on the basis of these numbers, tell you what interventions appear most cost-effective or otherwise shape policy through sociotechnical tools such as GDP per capita, employment numbers, or inflation rates. But the boundaries between devices that measure and devices that determine ideal policies are not always clear, and devices for seeing are rarely just for that purpose. The very exercise of producing numbers in itself shapes the range of potential policies or interventions to follow from it. Economic ways of approaching problems, including modelling, quantification, individual incentives, or marginal change all benefit from a simultaneous complexity–simplicity when being put to use to influence policy. They are easy to understand at a basic level and often to compare, but difficult to transparently or fully comprehend from a technical standpoint, or to challenge or replicate by non-specialists. That is exactly where they derive their power.

*

'I had two dinners with Bill Gates in two days. It was *efficient*', Duflo told a journalist days after a TED talk. One of those dinners included other notable

Silicon Valley figures including Jeff Bezos, Mark Zuckerberg, Nathan Myhrvold, a former Microsoft executive, and Vinod Khosla, founder of Sun Microsystems. Duflo represents an interesting combination, appearing at the same time inconspicuous and extremely convincing through her deep technical and economic knowledge. The networking and institution-building skills and efforts of the randomistas form a key explanation for their rise, and a reason why, in many ways, we find them at the centre of the movement depicted in this book. Their deep ties to Silicon Valley are equally unsurprising. It is not shocking why an invitation to reduce the messy world we live in to identifiable and manipulable variables and numbers has gained the popularity it has among Silicon Valley moguls and institutions, most of whom largely see the world through a similar lens and desire to fix things within the confines of a predictable system, made possible by technology. Like randomistas, the libertarian actors of Silicon Valley believe in strengthening the autonomous and self-dependent powers of individual actors, freeing them from the bureaucratic and inefficient webs of big government. Collective ownership is a disincentive to investment and risk-taking, many in Silicon Valley believe, and the focus on individualizing both issues and solutions speaks well to that mindset. And like cryptocurrency arguments that trust is a bad human emotion in need of elimination,[70] solved in Silicon Valley by relying on the 'transparent' peer to peer networks that we know from Bitcoin or Ethereum, randomistas wish to generate data on the efficacy of interventions to show *everyone* where the cost-effectiveness of development interventions lies. That means no further need for large-scale programmes and government interventions built on a traditional understanding of expertise, substituting planning with experimentation and expertise with objective measurements of progress. The days of *soft* evaluators should be long gone. Silicon Valley moguls have an aptitude for deflecting attention away from questions of power, inequality, politics, or ideology towards technical solutions and behavioural nudges, allowing implementors to push people in different directions without the need for government intervention or political discussions.

The experimental methodology of the randomistas serves as the glue of institution building among all of the actors explored in this book, a mass continuously expanding in size, presence, and influence, both in elite institutional settings and on the ground in developing countries. This expansion occurs strategically through grants, services to donors, production of RCTs, the publishing of papers and conference presentations, and diffusion to professional milieus through training, handbooks, and direct implementation. And their reach, if we look at the sheer number of organizations, studies, researchers, and partners, is astounding. It may centre around academic institutions such as J-PAL at MIT, IPA at Yale, or CEGA at Berkeley, but beyond these epicentres of influence are institutions such as the International Initiative for Impact Evaluation (3ie), the World Bank's Development Impact Evaluation Unit (DIME), and similar evaluation networks. To these can be added specialized charities such as GiveDirectly, GiveWell, the Centre for Effective Altruism, or the Busara Center for Behavioural Economics, a 130-plus employee 'research and advisory firm dedicated to advancing and applying behavioural science in the Global South' whose President is GiveDirectly founder Jeremy Shapiro. Although the randomistas were initially at odds with the World Bank, who did not see their coming as a revolution, they nonetheless share the Bank's affinity for economists and economics in spite of some initial and occasionally sustained methodological differences, with RCTs still seeing some push-back within the Bank.

Together, these institutions deeply accentuate the age-old mantra that it is not only important how we answer a question, but what questions we ask in the first place. RCTs provide precise answers to very specific questions that explore the effect of specifically isolated variables. But even that fundamental claim is increasingly being questioned. RCTs have their limitations in that they never explain the immensely important *why*, only whether or not something has an effect. Are we therefore asking the right questions? Some of the most vocal RCT critics have pointed to John Tukey's question posed with the rise of mathematical statistics in 1966: 'Far better an approximate answer to the right question, which is often vague, than an exact answer to the wrong question, which can always be made precise'.[71] Take education or health, and the many factors both known and unknown shaping schooling or effective health clinics. RCTs can only try to isolate these we know one by one and attempt to measure their individual impact, hoping to strike cases of either small effects, allowing them to further defunding campaigns, or great effects, pushing for funding for specific programmes targeting this single variable—if the intervention is cost-effective obviously. Criticism has also been rightfully launched at the productive and ethical form of certain conclusions made by the movement, such as precariously hired teachers being more effective than tenured ones. Someone in fear of losing his or her job may be more effective as an Amazon warehouse picker too, but that is neither surprising nor something that necessarily justifies implementation. As we move towards broader questions about political economy, RCTs have little to say about the effectiveness of certain types of intervention. They may prove what type of contracting is most effective in attracting micro finance customers, but they are challenged in telling us whether micro finance schemes are preferable in the first place relative to other intervention types, whether the aim is to generate economic growth or reduce poverty through employment.

These efforts are largely the result of a strategic choice to narrow down the scope of a study to parameters from which it is easier to draw hard evidence. Even if the evidence produced may in the end prove to be less pertinent, the fact that RCTs are able to bring hard evidence to the table strengthens their position and dominance in the evidence hierarchy as well as the institutions behind it. Sure, calls for more data and evidence are great. But they cannot be allowed to mask the fact that not all interventions or solutions are easily quantifiable and that if we only pursue those that fit within the realm of RCTs we risk leaving behind a massive set of pressing questions unchallenged. The danger lies in RCTs becoming ends in themselves, disconnected from larger systems questions. In practice, only a small proportion of development aid programmes are susceptible to randomization, with most interventions focused on institutional or systemic levels unable to be so. You cannot randomize infrastructure locations or conflict situations or even support to taxation systems. And the outlooks for country ownership in deciding development priorities are not particularly impressive if interventions have to be based within the realm of what randomistas deem scientifically feasible and acceptable.

Such limitations may be acceptable for RCTs so long as they are only seen as one type of knowledge production, appreciating the relativity and plurality of methodologies. For the hardcore proponents of RCTs, however, there is no view of science as a process of cumulative understanding. Instead, their own methodology is seen as the only legitimate way to produce knowledge with recurrent calls that only interventions justified by way of randomized experiments should be funded (policy)[72] or that only experimental research should be financed in academia, casting away observational research (science).[73] It is probably difficult for many to buy into such strict evidence and methodology hierarchies that raise certain methods to axiomatic levels. Many researchers still hold that ideal methodologies depend on what you want to explore and explain, that is, what type of knowledge may be suited for the type of question one is asking. But the world of the randomistas is often a binary world of black and white with no nuances of grey: either something works, or it does not. Poor people are either entrepreneurial or slow adopters who suffer from loss aversion and impatience, as the behavioural arguments characteristically go.

Surely, these quantification and objectivist narratives of the randomistas do not release the group from political discussions. Mantras such as 'move from politics to policy' or 'put evidence before politics'[74] are fabricated as though policy is politics' pretty cousin, pure and innocent from the dirty world of politics. Quite the contrary: all policy is politics, and wrestling with ambiguous problems is dirty and difficult. Beliefs in objectivity are as political as anything, with evidence always mediated, never pre-given, and no one 'science' that produces a singular answer to any question. Objectivity, rules, and ordered systems are no guarantee of social progress, and quantification often has difficulty in living up to the democratic expectations that randomistas attribute to it. Simplicity is no guarantee of democratization, and instead of being open and explicit about bias, randomized trials are often clouded in technicalities that make it difficult to see through and understand them. Only so many people have the statistical skills to handle post-RCT processing or to conduct RCTs in the first place, and the randomistas do not introduce a new democracy of policy as much they take one form of elitist expertise and supplant it with another that obviously favours their own institutions.

This question of what kinds of expertise are valued has obvious consequences for the distribution of funds, influence, and power among institutions and individuals, heavily politicizing issues of science, methodology, and evidence. Methodologies are not dead instruments chosen for purely scientific reasons; on the contrary they serve to legitimize certain types of intervention. Here, it sometimes includes market-based solutions, almost always heavily individualized, and with a fixation on cost-effectiveness and incitements for policy makers to save as much money as possible for what are perceived to be similar effects: 'short political attention spans, organisational imperatives to produce "results", and international mandates to achieve targets...generate a net effect, in which the development industry ends of reverse engineering itself, strongly preferring "high initial impact" projects over projects that might actually respond to the problems that poor countries themselves deem a priority, but which are inherently complex, hard to measure and/or necessarily slow to demonstrate positive impact', as Lead Social Scientist at the World Bank's Development Research Group Michael Woolcock has formulated it.[75]

In particular, the relationship between scientists and experimental subjects or trial participants evokes a strong sense of othering of the poor in a mirrored image of the modernized and technologized North. Despite the binary way of thinking evident in the movement, the specific contexts within which randomistas conduct their trials, most often poor communities in the Global South, seem to justify a relativist stance on ethics. Banerjee and Duflo argue that trial participants in these contexts 'are used to the fact that some areas get some programs and others do not',[76] justifying the otherwise fundamentally unfair nature of RCTs because of the ways in which certain people in the treatment group will either not need it or benefit little, whereas some people in the control group will be in a situation of need yet receive no treatment.[77] Former J-PAL director Rachel Glennerster contributes a similar view of the relativity of ethics: 'the perception of the ethics of randomized evaluations is often very different in the US and Europe than it is in developing countries.... The poor are used to scarcity. They understand that there are often not enough resources for everyone to benefit from a new initiative.'[78]

Some, such as World Bank economist Martin Ravallion, have responded to these ethical concerns of RCTs with the argument that there are likely few 'deontological purists' out there who believe that good ends can never justify bad means,[79] drawing on a moral utilitarianism. Yet this obviously depends on whether or not there are any expected welfare benefits from the new knowledge produced. How often is that really the case and for whom? We will soon explore that question with regard to randomized trials in medicine, where those in the Global South who partake in phase 2 or phase 3 clinical trials rarely have access to the medicines for which they put up their bodies for experimentation. Despite the massive amount of evidence and knowledge produced by the randomistas, not much is known about how often trials are followed up by broad-based implementation for entire communities or others who have taken part in the experiments. We likewise seldom know about the involvement of trial participants' inclusion in ethical frameworks as part of research designs. In the story opening up this chapter, we heard of hundreds of households being included in baseline surveys without being told why, because they would later come to form the control group in the experiment, receiving no cash transfers unlike their neighbours. There is clearly abundant room for degrees of transparency when it comes to participants: 'implementers will find that the easiest way to present [randomization] to the community is to say that an expansion of the program is planned for the control areas in the future (especially when it is indeed the case, as in phased-in design)',[80] Duflo and others have suggested.

Herein exists a real risk of inequality that experiments will see subjects as means rather than ends, and even under such perceptions, it is an open question exactly what specific ends subjects are means towards. RCTs are an assemblage and entanglement of research and intervention, acutely concerned with translating scientific authority into policy effects. By way of self-conceived objective and apolitical methodologies of hard science, randomistas see themselves as scientists simply carrying the objective facts and truths to politicians, not only presenting interventions and processes as post-ideological ones, but essentially as post-choice as well: the answer is right there, you don't have to make a decision, science does it for you. This is a defining feature at a time when knowing what to know and what not to know is a key social and political tool for both those in power and those subjected to it. The experimental movement's work may not be ideological in a traditional sense, but it certainly holds strong political ideals far removed from its face as an objective and technical experimental methodology. Having visited the experimental movement's scientific brainchild so to speak, Chapter 4 will take us to what is perhaps the movement's most crucial facilitator and enabler by way of its financial magnitude and generous funding of experimental science and policy: the private foundations, steered not least by one of the world's most famous technological ideologues, Bill Gates, and his massively influential charity.

Notes

1. Dijkstra, 2019. 'Chinese imports "driving fishermen to despair"', 21 March 2019, BBC. Ironically, Chinese small-scale fish-farmers share a similar fate of looming poverty as the Kenyan fishermen, with profits from the aquaculture exports mainly being cashed in at the top of the national value chain.
2. Goldstein, D. 2012. Can 4 economists build the most economically efficient charity ever?, *The Atlantic* 21 December.
3. Goldstein, 2012.
4. Haushofer, J. and Shapiro, J. 2016. The shortterm impact of unconditional cash transfers to the poor: experimental evidence from Kenya, *Quarterly Journal of Economics* 131: 1973–2042.
5. Rayzberg, M. 2019. Fairness in the field: the ethics of resource allocation in randomized controlled field experiments, *Science, Technology and Human Values* 44(3): 371–98.
6. Haushofer and Shapiro, 2016.
7. Haushofer and Shapiro, 2016.
8. de Souza Leao, L. and Eyal, G. 2019. The rise of randomized controlled trials (RCTs) in international development in historical perspective, *Theory and Society* 48: 383–418.
9. Reddy, S. 2019. Economics' biggest success story is a cautionary tale, *Foreign Policy* 22 October.
10. Banerjee, A.V. 2006. Making aid work: how to fight global poverty—effectively, *Boston Review* July–August. http://bostonreview.net/BR31.4/banerjee.html.
11. de Souza Leao and Eyal, 2019.
12. Kremer, M. and Glennerster, R. 2011. Improving health in developing countries: evidence from randomized evaluations. In M.V. Pauly, T.G. McGuire, and P.P. Barros (eds), *Handbook of Health Economics*. Oxford: ScienceDirect, pp. 201–315.
13. See Savedoff, W., Levine, R., and Birdsall, N. 2005. When will we ever learn? recommendations to improve social development assistance through enhanced impact evaluation. Washington, DC: Center for Global Development.

14. OECD. 2008. *Accra Agenda for Action*. OECD.

15. Banerjee, 2006.

16. Duflo, E. and Banerjee, A. 2011. *Poor Economics: A Radical Rethinking of the Way to Fight Global Poverty*. London; New York: Penguin/Public Affairs.

17. Pritchett, L. 2014. An Homage to the Randomistas on the Occasion of the J-PAL 10th Anniversary: Development as a Faith-Based Activity, 10 March. Available here: https://www.cgdev.org/blog/homage-randomistas-occasion-j-pal-10th-anniversary-development-faith-based-activity.

18. Whitty, C. and Dercon, S. 2013. The evidence debate continues: Chris Whitty and Stefan Dercon respond from DFID. Available here: https://oxfamblogs.org/fp2p/the-evidence-debate-continues-chris-whitty-and-stefan-dercon-respond/.

19. Banerjee, A. 2007. *Making Aid Work*. Cambridge, MA and London: MIT Press.

20. Deaton, A. and Cartwright, N. 2018. Understanding and misunderstanding randomized controlled trials, *Social Science and Medicine* 210(August): 2–21.

21. Banerjee, 2007.

22. Parker, I. 2010. The Poverty Lab. *The New Yorker* 10 May.

23. Parker, 2010.

24. Bloomberg. 2010. The pragmatic rebels. Available here: https://www.bloomberg.com/news/articles/2010-07-02/the-pragmatic-rebels.

25. Reddy, S. 2013. Randomise this! On poor economics, *Review of Agrarian Studies* 2(2).

26. Parker, 2010.

27. Parker, 2010.

28. Parker, 2010.

29. Parker, 2010.

30. Haas, P. 1992. Introduction: epistemic communities and international policy coordination, *International Organization* 46(1): 1–36.

31. Pritchett, 2014.

32. Bloomberg, 2010.

33. Angrist, J.D. and Pischke, J.-S. 2010. The credibility revolution in empirical economics: how better research design is taking the con out of econometrics, *Journal of Economic Perspectives* 24: 3–30.

34. I use 'manipulation' throughout not in a derogatory way but with the scientific meaning of inducing some form of change in an environment.

35. Banerjee and Duflo, 2009.

36. Berndt, C. 2015. Behavioural economics, experimentalism and the marketisation of development, *Economy and Society* 44(4): 567–91; Morgan, M. 2002. Model experiments and models in experiments. In L. Magnani and N. Nersessian (eds), *Model-Based Reasoning: Science, Technology, Values*. New York: Kluwer, pp. 41–58.

37. Dehue, T. 2001. Establishing the experimenting society: the historical origination of social experimentation according to the randomized controlled design, *American Journal of Psychology* 114(2): 283–302; for a significant critique, in particular of C.F. Skinner's work, see Chomsky, N. 1959. A review of BF Skinner's *Verbal Behavior*, *Language* 35(1): 26–58.

38. Tversky, A. and Kahneman, D. 1974. Judgement under uncertainty: heuristics and biases, *Science* 185: 1124–31.

39. See also Kahneman, D. 1973. *Attention and Effort*, Englewood Cliffs, NJ: Prentice-Hall; Kahneman, D. 2002. Maps of bounded rationality: a perspective of intuitive judgement and choice, Nobel-Prize Lecture, 8 December; Kahneman, D. 2011. *Thinking, Fast and Slow*, London: Penguin.

40. Duflo, E. *Social experiments to fight poverty.* Ted Talk. 2010. See https://www.ted.com/talks/esther_duflo_social_experiments_to_fight_poverty

41. Duflo, 2010.

42. Goldacre, B. 2013. Building evidence into education. bad science. Available here: http://media.%20education.gov.uk/assets/files/pdf/b/ben%20goldacre%20paper.pdf; Pearce, W. and Raman, S. 2014. The new randomised controlled trials (RCT) movement in public policy: challenges of epistemic governance, *Policy Sciences* 47: 387–402.

43. Moreira, T. 2007. Entangled evidence: knowledge making in systematic reviews in healthcare, *Sociology of Health and Illness* 29: 180–97.

44. Marks, H. 1997. *The Progress of Experiment: Science and Therapeutic Reform in the United States, 1900–1990*. Cambridge: Cambridge University Press.

45. McGoey, L. 2010. Profitable failure: antidepressant drugs and the triumph of flawed experiments, *History of the Human Sciences* 23(1): 58–78.

46. Sandersson, I. 2002. Evaluation, policy learning and evidence-based policy making, *Public Administration* 80(1): 1–22.

47. de Souza Leao and Eyal, 2019.

48. Karlan, D. and Appel, J. 2011. *More Than Good Intentions: How a New Economics Is Helping to Solve Global Poverty*. Boston, MA: Dutton.

49. Deaton and Cartwright, 2018.

50. See Deaton and Cartwright, 2018.

51. See Glass, T.A., Goodman, S.N., Hernán, M.A., and Samet, J.M. 2013. Causal inference in public health, *Annual Review of Public Health* 34: 61–75.

52. See Chalmers, A.F. 2013. *What Is this Thing Called Science?* 4th ed. St Lucia: University of Queensland Press.

53. Duflo and Banerjee, 2011.

54. Pearce and Raman, 2014.

55. Coville, A., Galiani, S., Gertler, P., and Yoshida, S. 2020. Enforcing Payment for Water and Sanitation Services in Nairobi's Slums, Working Paper 27569, National Bureau of Economic Research.

56. Coville et al., 2020.

57. Hacking, I. 1992. The self-vindication of the laboratory sciences. In A. Pickering (ed.), *Science as Practice and Culture*. Chicago: University of Chicago Press, pp. 29–64.

58. Banerjee, 2007.

59. Hirshman, D. and Berman, E. 2014. Do economists make policies? on the political effects of economics, *Socio-Economic Review* 12(4): 779–811.

60. Savage, M. 2013. The 'social life of methods': A critical introduction, *Theory, Culture & Society* 30(4): 3–21.

61. See Savage, 2013; this also reminds us of the 'classical episteme' or Linnaeus and his eighteenth-century classifications. Eugenics was made possible because of advancements in statistics, see MacKenzie, D.A. 1981. *Statistics in Britain: 1865–1930*. Edinburgh: Edinburgh University Press.

62. Savage, 2013.

63. Savage, 2013.

64. Fine, B. and Milonakis, D. 2009. *From Economics Imperialism to Freakonomics: The Shifting Boundaries between Economics and Other Social Sciences.* London: Routledge.

65. Bernstein, M. A. 2001. *A Perilous Progress: Economists and Public Purpose in 20th Century America.* Princeton, NJ: Princeton University Press.

66. Samuelson, P.A. 1972. *Collected Scientific Papers.* Cambridge, MA: MIT Press.

67. Hirshman and Berman, 2014.

68. Hirshman and Berman, 2014; See also Brint, S. 1990. Rethinking the policy influence of experts: from general characterizations to analysis of variation, *Sociology Forum* 5(3): 361–85.

69. Hirshman and Berman, 2014.

70. See Witzig, P. and Salomon, V. 2018. Cutting out the Middleman: A Case Study of Blockchain-induced Reconfigurations in the Swiss Financial Services Industry. Working Paper 1. Université de Neuchâtel.

71. See Tukey, J. and Wilk, M.B. 1966. Data analysis and statistics: an expository overview, *AFIPS Conference Proceedings* 29: 695–709.

72. Banerjee, 2007.

73. Gerber, A.S., Green, D.P., and Kaplan, E.H. 2004. The illusion of learning from observational research. In I. Shapiro, R. Smith, and T. Massoud (eds), *Problems and Methods in the Study of Politics.* New York: Cambridge University Press, pp. 251–72.

74. See Schmitt, D. 2014. Donors should put evidence before politics and diplomacy, 12 June, SciDevNet. Available here: https://www.scidev.net/global/aid/opinion/donors-evidence-politics-diplomacy.html.

75. Woolcock, M. 2009. Toward a plurality of methods in project evaluation: a contextualised approach to understanding impact trajectories and efficacy, *Journal of Development Effectiveness* 1(1): 1–14.

76. Banerjee and Duflo, 2009.

77. Mulligan, C. 2014. The economics of randomized experiments, *New York Times* 5 March.

78. See Glennerster, R. 2014. The complex ethics of randomized evaluations. Available at http://runningres.com/blog/2014/4/9/the-complex-ethics-of-randomized-evaluations.

79. Ravallion, M. 2014. Taking ethical validity seriously, 17 March. The World Bank. Available here: https://blogs.worldbank.org/impactevaluations/taking-ethical-validity-seriously.

80. Duflo, E., Glennerster, R., and Kremer, M. 2008. Using randomization in development economics research: a toolkit. In T. Paul Schultz and John Strauss (eds), *Handbook of Development Economics*, Volume 4. Amsterdam and Oxford: Elsevier, North-Holland, pp. 3895–962.

4

The Gates Effect

Standing in front of a large treatment plant the size of several containers, Bill Gates drinks water made from human faeces. Alongside tubes running in every direction and steam spewing from the top, Gates explains: 'over two and a half billion people have no access to safe sanitation. We asked brilliant engineers to help us solve this problem'. It is 2015 and the engineers at Janicki Bioenergy, a company based north of Seattle and now known under the name of Sedron Technologies, have constructed what they named the Omni Processor. Combining solid fuel combustion, steam power generation, and water treatment, the processing plant is an attempt to revolutionize the waste processing industry in the Global South. The machine removes all pathogens from the waste, the most widespread cause of diseases like diarrhoea, whilst producing outputs of commercial value, including electricity and drinkable water. The sewage is transported up into the plant through a conveyor belt, after which it makes its way through the machine, being treated and boiled. A few minutes later, the end result is ready for consumption and drinkable water may be drained from a tap. The Omni Processor broke headlines when Bill Gates' personal website produced a video under the heading of 'Bill Gates drinks water made from human faeces'. Millions of people were interested in seeing what was behind this peculiar title, although the video itself mainly featured information on the processor and then Gates drinking a glass of water extracted from waste. Even so, the news made its way across the internet, from CNN to fashionable millennial sites, and Gates starred on Jimmy Fallon's popular 'The Tonight Show', where he explained that 'we said it's way too expensive, the way that the rich countries do it [sanitation, ed.], [let's] make something that we can put throughout Africa and get rid of all that sewage'. Fallon went on to taste the water, after a few minutes of joking, and ended up chugging down the glass, prompting cheers from the audience. Only a few months later, in May 2015, the Omni Processor was piloted in Dakar, Senegal, and again featured on gatesnotes.com where a video included local Senegalese sanitation experts explaining that 'with this product, we can make business from sanitation. It's a profitable business'.

The idea of the Omni Processor itself, and the great levels of publicity that surrounded its unveiling in 2015, nicely illustrate the approach of the Bill and Melinda Gates Foundation to development in the Global South. Projects should ideally be generic and decontextualized to the point at which they can be scaled across not only countries but continents, just like the processor is meant for 'all of Africa'. The form of change induced should be driven by the hard sciences, in this case engineering, and should be new, radical, and experimental. It is not enough to replicate systems or solutions as we know them in the West or to just improve certain important practices; changes need to entirely disrupt the system. In fact, these traits do not exclusively belong to the Gates Foundation; instead they embody a new group of private foundations. Out of the immense wealth creation and accumulation that has characterized the past decades, a new group of American philanthropists and private foundations has emerged. With Silicon Valley as their ideological epicentre, these individuals have been characterized as hyper actors with enormous expectations about their ability to change the world, driving what they see as a global revolution through technological experimentation. They are sometimes referred to as philanthrocapitalists or technophilanthropists for their deep belief in the effectiveness of capitalist society and technological innovation.

The new foundations advance a hybrid set of logics that blend scientific progress through experimentation with a belief in businesses and the market as intrinsically efficient, refocusing efforts towards corporate and private influence on, and delivery of, societal progress. Inspired by methodological individualism, many of them consider the social world a system of linear causality where levers and handles can be pulled to change different parts and achieve an anticipated outcome. In this realm of thought, quantification and systematic decision-making, often perceived as apolitical or value-neutral as we saw with the randomistas, form the basis for purposive action today, driven by scientific rationality in designing and executing interventions. Private foundations have historically played a significant role in the diffusion of science, technology, and value systems from industrialized to developing countries. As architects of international networks of scholars and institutions that have produced and disseminated knowledge, they have influenced social and cultural policies on an international scale. But they have also engaged directly in experimentation and the diffusion of science and technology in the Global South. This global political influence has been significant, if fluctuating, since the beginning of the twentieth century. Over the decade of the 2010s, however, their activities in and financial support to global development have increased greatly, strengthening their apparent impact and political influence in all parts of the world. In this new époque since the turn of the millennium, private foundations have been hailed as saviours of global development by some, seemingly representing an alternative to bureaucratically heavy and ineffective state agencies.[1] Others have called for caution and advised especially against the approaches of foundations lead by this new generation of 'philanthrocapitalists' who apply logics and practices from the world of business in their attempts to fundamentally alter the practices and trajectories of development.[2]

Steering this train of thought and action today is the Bill and Melinda Gates Foundation. An immense political and economic force, investing billions of dollars in medical and social research and experimentation, the foundation is currently at full throttle towards shaping the lives of millions of poor people around the world. Bill Gates himself has described the work of the foundation as 'more like Microsoft at age three than at age thirty-three', stressing the experimental nature of much of its work. The foundation is fundamentally built on a logic blending an immense faith in corporate thought and action with that of societal progress through technological innovation. By experimenting with social norms or the development of new toilets to be distributed throughout the Global South, the foundation solidifies a mindset that sees this part of the world as a sort of laboratory in which technical and social experiments and interventions create a force for social progress. In this chapter, we take a dive into the world of private foundations that function as key financial backers and enablers of the experimental movement's interventions as well as diffusors of the experimental scientific ideas that we have met thus far.

*

When the Space Needle, a 180-meter-tall observation tower in downtown Seattle, was built for the city's World Fair in 1962, it attracted great attention as the tallest building west of the Mississippi River. Today, this attention has largely shifted to its most imposing neighbouring building. In June 2012, the Bill and Melinda Gates Foundation moved into its new $500 million, six-story, 7,000 m^2, and 12-acre campus headquarters. The campus houses most of the foundation's 1,700 employees. When the campus was inaugurated one Thursday night in late May 2012, Melinda Gates took the stage and explained to guests at the reception about the deliberate conspicuousness of the headquarters: 'We wanted to make a statement.' Since the Bill and Melinda Gates Foundation opened its doors in 1999, it has distributed more than $60 billion to national and international issues, with grants amounting to more than

$5 billion in 2020[3] and a current massive endowment approaching $50 billion. From an initial focus on education in the US, as well as international spending on vaccine development and delivery, the last decade has seen the foundation venturing into the field of 'global development', where some of its main areas of intervention include agriculture, water and sanitation, and financial services for the poor. The astounding reach and size of the Gates Foundation is underlined by how the foundation accounts for more than half of all global philanthropic giving to development today.[4]

Fuelled by immense ambition and confidence about the potential impact of its fifty-billion-dollar endowment, the world's largest private foundation has embarked on a self-titled expedition to help 'All people live healthy, productive lives'.[5] When employees of the Gates Foundation travel throughout the developed and the developing world, all of them start presentations of their workplace with a particular story. Sometime in the mid-1990s, Bill and Melinda read an article about a simple disease killing hundreds of thousands of children every year from diarrhoea.[6] Eager to find out more, they began to read about the disease, called rotavirus. Unable to grasp that it was in fact a preventable disease, whose main lethality came from the great health disparities between rich and poor, they were eager to do something about it, and sent the article with a note to Gates' father, spelling out, 'Dad, maybe we can do something about this.' Such a story is compelling; it speaks of an undoubted empathy for the world's poorest, and the humility of engaging in not just a complex and tremendous task, but one in a field largely unknown to you. But the story of Gates' call to philanthropy naturally didn't start that day.

After years of public outcry and criticism of Gates for not giving out his exceptionally extensive wealth generated since Microsoft's Initial Public Offering in 1986,[7] the Gates Foundation informally started in the basement of Bill Gates Sr.'s house in the mid-1990s. Here, he would screen incoming requests for charity and pass the most interesting ones on to his son for further inspection and an eventual decision on whether to provide support or not. As the foundation outgrew the basement, it rented scattered and anonymous offices around Seattle, some famously above a pizza parlour. For years, it characterized itself as a small family foundation and was lauded by the *New York Times* for its lean bureaucracy and limited head count,[8] although its endowment grew exponentially to heights above most American private foundations. Today, the Gates Foundation's rise to global prominence is known to most. Or, more precisely, its present-day position as one of the most influential non-state actors in contemporary international political life, both financially and politically, is renowned. More powerful and vastly greater in size than any other foundation in modern history, the Gates Foundation is not simply following a trend of growing influence for foundations, it literally embodies that trend. At present, the foundation is a titanic influence in numerous areas of global development, health, and governance, ever-present in international political discussions in fora such as the UN, OECD, the World Health Organization (WHO), or the World Economic Forum. In the case of the WHO in particular, the Gates Foundation was set to become the largest donor of all, including all member states, when former President Trump announced the withdrawal of the US.

Across all the issues occupying it, the Gates Foundation furthers notions of societal progress through experimentation and technological innovation. And it does so with determination, almost as if it were a global tech-corporation whose very market position and core business depended on it. Whatever the nature or scope of a problem, the solution is often articulated as the necessity to experiment and harness technological innovation in the name of progress.[9] It is fundamentally a paradigmatic example of a philanthrocapitalist organization through its tremendous attention to technological innovation as the central driver of societal progress in the developing world. As an example, the foundation invests more than US$500 million annually in global health research and has invested more than US$530 million in innovative agricultural research and development since 2008. Gates himself generally considers innovation to be 'the most powerful force for change in the world', fundamentally able to shift the 'trajectory of development'.[10] He does not consider it to have played as big a role in development as it could have done, and maintains that although development aid may spur innovation, the real expertise of such 'lies with the private sector'. For Gates, the problem with innovation seems to be that 'a lot of that focuses on the needs of the rich'. This represents a problem when you think that the world will need to 'invent to really make a dramatic difference' on issues such as agriculture in the developing world. Agriculture specifically is conceived by Gates as an 'example of a market that simply does not work for the poor' and one in which change is predominantly to come from innovation in technology because 'digital technology can change that, too'.[11] Finally, Gates thinks that the number of people who can spur innovations is much greater now than in the past and that this will create 'a new era in development'. Speaking to future generations in their 2016 annual letter, Bill and Melinda Gates made it clear whom they see driving poverty alleviating efforts in the future: 'Some of you will become engineers, entrepreneurs, scientists, and software developers. I invite you to take on the challenge of serving the poor'.[12]

These views are mirrored in the foundation. In describing itself, the foundation talks of 'applying new thinking', 'finding solutions', and 'funding innovative ideas', whether in the form of 'innovative financing mechanisms', 'new techniques', or 'innovative technologies'. The founders see the foundation's key role as 'investing in innovations that would not otherwise be funded. This draws not only on our backgrounds in technology but also on the foundation's size and ability to take a long-term view and take large risks on new approaches'.[13] Optimistic about societal progress over the next fifteen years, the two co-chairs of the foundation exclaimed in their 2015 annual letter that the next fifteen years will see major breakthroughs for most people in poor countries and that 'these breakthroughs will be driven by innovation in technology'.[14] Returning to Harvard University, from where he had dropped out to pursue his tech-dreams, Gates told students that 'cutting through complexity to find a solution runs through four predictable stages: determine a goal, find the highest-leverage approach, discover the ideal technology for that approach, and in the meantime, make the smartest application of the technology that you already have'.[15]

Predictable stages or not, the foundation pursues technological or solution innovation that takes the shape of experimentation, holding that its role in global development and health is 'funding a range of ideas with different levels of risk that they could fail'.[16] This is basically the case because 'finding the best ways to help people improve their lives takes many years of research and experimentation'.[17] Innovation, high-risk engagement, and experimentation apply not only to technology, but extend far into the private and social realms of people in the Global South, according to the foundation: 'High-risk innovations require the invention of new tools. Some are at the frontiers of science, such as finding a new drug and running a large trial to see how well it works. Other high-risk efforts involve changing social practices, such as persuading men at risk of getting HIV to get circumcised'.[18] While in a class of its own, the Gates Foundation is situated both in a specific history of philanthropy and global experimentation and in a new group of experimental foundations emerging over the past decades.

*

The historical antecedents of philanthropy and organized giving tread a thousand-year-old path. Every major culture or religion has encouraged not just philanthropic giving, whether to those individuals less fortunate than oneself or to the institutions of society, from churches to hospitals, but also organized forms of giving that have seen vast funds change hands. Whether in China or the US, ancient Rome or Persia, Islam or Judaism, philanthropic endeavours have cut across motives of universal human impulses of altruism, expected responsibility to give back, and the power and influence obtained by gifting away funds and resources. Continuously through history, the accumulation of wealth and private giving in the hands of a few organizations or institutions have caused upheaval and scrutiny. Vast funds have for thousands of years allowed men and women to create institutions in society that can drive the form of change as the founder sees fit, not always for the benefit of the greater good of society.[19] There is a significant difference between the concept of philanthropy and the private foundations dealt with here though, namely that the abstract altruisms affiliated with philanthropy are not exactly guaranteed in the endeavours of private foundations. The word philanthropy itself originates from Greek and can be translated to a 'love of humanity'. It is naïve to expect all private foundations to demonstrate such.

Modern-day private foundations emerged in the late 1900s as some of the world's early billionaires increasingly searched for ways to spend their fortunes. During this golden age of American philanthropy, incredible wealth was generated as rapid industrialization swept across the country. Most famous were the three individuals Andrew Carnegie, John D. Rockefeller, and Henry Ford, the frontrunners of contemporary philanthropic giving.[20] The twentieth century was largely a period of mass-institutionalization and organization of private giving, increasing not just the volume of philanthropy but also systematizing the ways in which it is provided. For many of the older foundations, their gradual evolution over time saw them develop from traditional family-style charities to professionalized institutions, some journeying a great distance from the founders that once provided their initial assets. This part of the history of private foundations is also one of recurrent critique and conflict, especially so in the US, where the influence of these have arguably been felt most strongly. These apprehensions have included democratic concerns over the extent of influence from private foundations, as well as the type of influence exercised, emanating from both sides of the political spectrum. One of the strongest examples was witnessed during the 1960s, when an anti-foundation movement was formed with Texan Congressman Wright Patman at the helm. As a first witness during a 1969 House committee hearing on tax reform, Patman set forth a striking critique that 'Put most bluntly, philanthropy—one of mankind's most noble instincts—has been perverted into a vehicle for institutionalized, deliberate evasion of fiscal and moral responsibility to the nation'.[21]

Wealth creation at the same heights as the late nineteenth century and early twentieth century industrial expansion can be said to have characterized the last thirty years, and it is from this period that we can witness the amassed fortunes of today's billionaires being given away as charity in the Global South. In 1972, Waldemar A. Nielsen in his scrutiny of American Private Foundations wrote that the combined assets of the country's 25,000 foundations, amounting to approximately $20 billion, was a clear sign of megalocephaly. Dwarfing these numbers, there are more than 86,000 foundations today in the US, although the combined assets of these 'only' equal $90 billion, which is less than the numbers for 1972, if allowing for inflation. A private foundation is often understood, based on Frank Emerson Andrews' definition derived from his seminal work on the societal role of these in America in the early 1950s, as a 'non-governmental, non-profit organization having a principal fund of its own, managed by its trustees or directors, and established to maintain or aid social, educational, charitable, religious, or other activities serving the common welfare'.[22] What separates these foundations from the many other types of non-governmental organizations with a mission to do good then, is not least the 'principal fund of its own', allowing it to exercise, in theory, complete self-determination. Through continuous reinvestment of the initial endowment made by the founding individuals, the foundation is excused from external resource allocation. This provides foundations with financial independence, perhaps even making them the most independent institutions in modern society,[23] and strengthening their efforts in terms of experimentation, but it also greatly blurs lines of accountability.

We often hear claims of a direct line between the early philanthropic endeavours in the US and the current generation emanating out of Silicon Valley. For one, overlaps between the 'scientific philanthropy' of Rockefeller and the technological bias of contemporary philanthropists, and especially the Gates Foundation, are pronounced. Although articulated almost a hundred years apart, both the (early) Rockefeller Foundation and the Gates Foundation see science and experimentation as the surest means of advancing society. Both foundations have invested heavily in the development of vaccines against diseases such as hookworm infection, yellow fever, or malaria, and both have (or have had for extended periods), international divisions for health, natural, or medical sciences. Frederick Gates, John D. Rockefeller Sr.'s philanthropic advisor, framed this belief clearly: 'If science and education are the brain and nervous system of civilization, health is its heart. It is the organ that pushes the vital fluid into every part of the social organism, enabling each organ to function and measuring and limiting its effective life.... Disease is the supreme ill of life and it is the main source of almost all other human ills—poverty, crime, ignorance, vice, inefficiency, hereditary taint, and many other evils.'[24] Bill Gates has repeated this view a hundred years after Frederick Gates, telling a Microsoft Faculty Summit in 2013 that 'The average IQ in sub-Saharan Africa is about 82 and that's nothing to do with genetics or race or anything like that—that's disease and that's what disease does to you, and that's why these things are such an extreme poverty trap.'[25]

Aside from their common footprints in science, old and new foundations alike have also acted as strong agents of capitalism. All of them laid the foundations for their fortunes through innovations and different forms of industrial or technological progress, but only cemented their positions because of aggressive business skills, such as buying up all the local newspapers to ensure they would only feature positive product reviews, or controlling the lives of their employees—Ford famously had a large 'social department' investigating employees to ensure no drinking, gambling or 'parental sloppiness'—and the widespread practice of vacuuming up smaller businesses in the same field.[26] This last point deserves a few more words: for several of the magnates, old and new, buying smaller businesses led to strong monopolistic tendencies and accusations of unfair industry domination. Rockefeller, Carnegie, and Gates have all seen charges of illegal monopoly from the US state. Henry Ford, on the other hand, was often able to present himself as an antithesis and anti-monopolist to his contemporaries, although many of his traits, including his strong anti-semitism, leaves him with no better reputation today. Standard Oil, Rockefeller's company, created intense controversy during its entire lifetime for its strong monopolistic behaviour and industry control, including union-busting and responsibility for the Ludlow Massacre—that left some twenty miners and family members dead—underselling competitors, and for innovating a new legal entity that allowed it to gather and control companies in every state of the US under one roof at a time where cross-state operation was illegal.[27] Although many associate Bill Gates with his early days of developing software, Gates was known for the greatest part of his working life in Microsoft for his uncompromising management style and for the company's aggressive product strategies.[28] Aggressive marketing not least led to the 2001 'United States vs. Microsoft Corp.' antitrust case in which the company was accused of abusing monopoly power, and the 2007 'Microsoft Corp vs. Commission' case in which the European Commission accused the company of abusing its dominant position in the market.

As well as these similarities, however, there are also pronounced differences. Industry is perhaps the first and most striking. Whereas early philanthropists made their fortunes in the fires of the industrial revolution—John D. Rockefeller famously revolutionized the petroleum industry, Andrew Carnegie the steel industry, and Henry Ford the automobile industry—the new experimental foundations are built on riches reaped from digital technology and innovation. Obviously with Microsoft at the centre represented by Bill Gates, but also Facebook in the form of Mark Zuckerberg and Jeff Bezos' Amazon, both of whom have launched new foundations and grand ambitions for their aims of changing the world. A second difference relates to spatiality. While the first generation of philanthropists was largely based in the Midwest and further east in Massachusetts, the new generation has emerged on the West Coast of the US, principally in Silicon Valley, in the Bay Area south of San Francisco. Despite both groups shaping the connectivity of people, from cars and railways to computers, email and Facebook, there is also a difference in spatiality that sees the newer generation reaching the far corners of the globe, strengthening the impact of its agenda of experimentation. Lastly, there is an interesting difference in the type of skill or perhaps materiality that underpins the different fortunes. Early philanthropists were deeply affiliated with manual labour, rarely conducting such themselves but widely required by their industries: from the assembly lines of mass production, and the early techniques of drilling, refining, and transporting oil, to the blast furnaces of steel production. In contrast, the new philanthropists have been characterized as nerds or hackers, famously working out of their parents' garages, with their skills being in coding or computer science, something that has come to greatly influence their technological and experimental approach to both philanthropy and social change.

*

Today, new scientific and experimental approaches such as those of the Gates Foundation are emerging, many of them overlapping across notions of strategic philanthropy, creative philanthropy, venture philanthropy, or social (impact) investment. Collectively, these favour the adoption of business techniques to foundation processes, aiming to shift philanthropy from altruistic charity to strategic social impact investment. Rather than just a new scientific philanthropy, the changes in contemporary foundations are perhaps better captured under the heading of philanthrocapitalism. In 2006, Matthew Bishop coined this term to describe what he perceived as a new generation of private foundations and individuals successfully applying a business approach to tackling global problems.[29] This new generation emphasizes efficiency and measurability, and their business-oriented approach can be considered a departure from traditional philanthropic practice.[30] That includes the deployment of diverse sets of financing tools, such as social impact bonds, equity, debt, loans, but also non-financial forms of support through networking and mentoring.[31] Most importantly here of course, this movement is inseparable from technology, carrying with it an innate belief in societal progress through technological experimentation.

The new portrayal as philanthrocapitalism alludes to at least three organizational processes of change that have come to characterize contemporary foundation work and has strategically positioned this group at the forefront of the experimental movement. The first concerns the adoption of proactive and strategic approaches. Traditional forms of grantmaking have long emphasized 'responsive' and bottom-up approaches to philanthropy in which a board or group of selected individuals in the foundation would screen incoming proposals and accept those most convincing and in line with the foundation's mission.[32] Often, at the heart of this approach is a belief in the necessity for grant proposals to emerge more organically from the ground, to ensure ownership of projects, but also a reliance on local civil society to better understand where to intervene and how. Contrary to these forms of thinking, newer approaches to international foundation giving have been described as high-engagement and directive forms of grantmaking, driven by an emphasis on direct involvement, experimentation, and effectiveness, frequently serving the purpose of increasing control over the manner and uses of funding.[33] Being more 'strategic' in this sense implies a top-down approach to grantmaking that almost puts the foundation in the driver's seat when it comes to designing interventions, and thus in the endeavour of social problem-solving. A tangible example of proactivity is the Ford Foundation's announcement that all its grants would now be targeted towards inequality in all its manifestations. Such a proclamation greatly narrows the scope for potential grants and clearly signifies a decision to proactively guide the future work of the foundation in a specific direction. Another tangible example of proactivity is the way in which many of the world's largest foundations today initiate first contact with and approach potential partners with project ideas, rather than awaiting them to submit proposals, often on the grounds of wanting to influence project design from its earliest stage. This not least allows them to actively target and support actors and approaches within the experimental regime.

The second process of change we see in contemporary foundations relates to their in-house capacity and competencies, greatly multiplying their influence in advancing and shaping experimental interventions. Traditionally, those who have been known to take decisions on grantmaking in foundations are often not experts in the field within which the grant is to have an impact.[34] Instead, they have formal power to decide grants by virtue of their organizational position, often on the boards of the foundations. After decisions are made to fund certain proposals, responsibility for grants have traditionally been moved to programme officers whose main competence has been in accounting and making sure that agreements on reporting have been upheld by the grantee; that these could deliver what they had in fact promised. An increased focus on more strategic or proactive modes of grantmaking, on the other hand, requires a higher level of expertise on the part of the foundation, relating this factor to the first. Engaging not just in the identification of relevant partners and issues of intervention, but also in designing, monitoring, and evaluating impact, from beginning to end, requires an immense amount of expertise. Increasingly then, some of the largest foundations have been hiring employees with specific issue-based expertise, not least in the field of development, from agriculture to microfinance to water-management.[35] Issue-specific expertise thus moves from the grantees and partners and to the foundations themselves, greatly strengthening their ability to push for experimental approaches directly through interventions.

The third point of change for today's foundations is an increasing focus on global grantmaking. Perhaps most important because it captures the essence of why foundations are so important in questions of experimentation in the Global South, foundation and philanthropic giving to international causes has significantly increased over the past decade. Foundations have traditionally focused their efforts on the near proximity of their founders or their headquarters, and targeted local libraries, schools, or hospitals. Whilst not fundamentally substituting this pattern of philanthropy, an increasing amount of funding is now targeted towards global interventions, either by directly investing there or by indirectly investing in organizations whose main work is global.[36] Obviously not all foundations are going through the same processes of change and generalizing on account of several hundred thousand foundations around the world is not exactly wise. Yet these fairly transformative processes have not only been experienced by the world's largest foundations, whether that be the Gates or Ford Foundations. In a historically development aid-committed country such as Denmark, for example, many of the smaller foundations are going through similar processes of active strategizing and professionalization, with ambitions increasingly to take the driver's seat in the implementation of their grantmaking,[37] as they target it outwards to all corners of the world. And this move has been widely embraced, with proponents framing private aid as a contrast to the apparently unsuccessful top-down and centrally planned public aid programmes. It is indeed a widespread conception among foundations and their strongest proponents that they are significantly better placed than public aid agencies to experiment, take risks, and seek out 'opportunistic innovations'.[38] And with limited pressure from the accountability-influencing forces of government prompting an insulated culture that accepts and perhaps even encourages inappropriate levels of independence, foundations are exceptionally well-positioned today to act as key financers and enablers of the new experimental regime, armed as they are with plenty of arguments for why the public should not have a say in how they spend their money.

*

Some of the strongest examples of technological experimentation from the Gates Foundation are perhaps its endeavours in the innovation of new toilets and of contraceptives, the latter involving radical changes to social norms. The first of these endeavours was essentially launched as a contest to reinvent the toilet with parameters including suitability for a single-family residence in a developing country and the ability to output waste as drinkable water and turn faeces into energy. The cost of the winning toilet was $1000. In 2014, when Bill Gates recalled ten years of Grand Challenges funding for experimental cutting-edge technology and innovation, his humbling message was that out of the numerous projects sponsored for a total of $1 billion, few had made a significant contribution to improving health in the developing world.[39] But less popularized efforts, such as the innovation of new seeds, are also important technological endeavours of the foundation. Within agriculture, the foundation's most well-known project to innovate technology is likely the Alliance for a Green Revolution in Africa (AGRA), initiated in 2006 with a grant of $150 million in association with the Rockefeller Foundation. AGRA aims to introduce novel technology packages to poor farmers that will allow an increase in agricultural yields, based on a crop-breeding approach that paves the way for genetic engineering technology. The founding of AGRA has not been without controversy however, and critics hold that the inherent genetic engineering could potentially leave smallholder systems more environmentally vulnerable, just as the process of forming AGRA has been criticized for not involving farmers, but mainly seed and fertilizer companies, philanthropic foundations, and multilateral institutions.[40] Responding to criticism, the Gates Foundation has reiterated that it is 'learning all the time' and that a state-of-the-art project on cellular feedback from local farmers would soon allow them to communicate with more than 10,000 stakeholders. Although AGRA is a relative newcomer, it builds upon and forms part of a quasi-public institutional architecture for agricultural research and experimentation that dates back almost a century and includes organizations such as CGIAR, where foundations both serve as members and as core funders, including foundations governed by biotechnology and agribusiness companies. CGIAR has long been a central proponent and funder of genetic crop improvement and has long benefited from having the Gates Foundation as a major financial and political backer. Bill Gates himself has often defended these priorities by referring to the debate for-or-against genetically modified organisms as an ideological battle between those in favour of technology and those opposing it.

Aside from concrete projects, institutional environments are increasingly supported and used by foundations to facilitate global experimental efforts, not least the social innovation labs that we will meet in Chapter 6.[41] The Rockefeller Foundation has been an eager supporter of social innovation labs since 2013; they were used by the foundation to develop new tools and resources for issues such as improvements in livelihoods for small-scale fisheries. According to the foundation, social innovation labs consist of three ingredients—diverse stakeholders, experimentation, and unique tools and processes—and are best used when a problem affects many stakeholders and sectors and can change in unexpected ways.[42] These 'labs' are perceived in opposition to what the foundation deems 'traditional problem solving', in which the problem is clearly defined and confined to a single sector or organization. Likewise, where a traditional planning approach is thought by the foundation to need at least a year to implement its first pilot programme, the social innovation labs can begin prototyping and experimenting with solutions as quickly as within two months. In these 'lab' contexts, subject expertise is often considered unnecessary or even counterproductive, because of disruptive ambitions. In their explanation of the nature of social innovation labs, the Rockefeller Foundation tells a story of how a venture capitalist and an SMS expert came together to design solutions for small-scale fisheries and coastal communities, benefiting from the fact that they had no prior knowledge of the issue, and were thus not constrained by notions such as prior experience or the norms of the field.[43] The absence of prior knowledge certainly gives way for disruptive qualities. As a report funded by the Rockefeller Foundation explains it, 'Social innovation is about profoundly changing or transforming a system rather than adapting or improving it'.[44] Their point of departure is that 'when present solutions do not work, we need to develop new solutions. As it is impossible to predict what works, we need to experiment'.[45] Here, poverty is fundamentally a scientific problem in which solutions can only emerge from experimentation, because of its inherent non-linearity and complexity. These experimental lines of thought are deeply connected to another core Gates Foundation mantra, namely that of constructive failures. In the eyes of the foundation, inspired by Silicon Valley's 'fail fast' culture, failure can be a very positive project outcome as long as it may learn from the failure, deducing from it new approaches or leaving behind those that have proved unsuccessful. The foundation maintains that 'failure is critical to success. When we discover what doesn't work, we gain scientific knowledge that eventually will help us learn what does work. And the feedback from failures helps us continually set new priorities'.[46] As former CEO Jeff Raikes explained upon taking office in 2010, 'Almost by definition, good philanthropy means we're going to have to do some risky things, some speculative things to try and see what works and what doesn't'.[47]

*

Private foundations have historically played a significant role in the diffusion of science, technology, and value systems from industrialized to developing countries, engaging in direct experimentation within the traditional areas of health, agriculture, and education. Agriculture in particular—at the intriguing intersection of germs, fertile land, and geoengineering—has been a prominent historical site of experimentation. Not least because experimentation is at the heart of agricultural practice, historically flowing from biology and chemistry. Unlike the researcher-controlled circumstances of a laboratory, agricultural field experiments are necessarily at the mercy of local conditions, whether the technical equipment, local knowledge, quality and composition of soil, or the weather. Experiments with agricultural inputs, that is finding the influence of specific variables in growing a crop, have consequently remained problematic for their difficulties in translating lab-science to the field. Over time, agricultural experiments have seen a growing distance between farmer experiments, on the ground, and scientific experiments.

The yield gap, the gap between the potential and actual yield of plants, is an example of such translational issues that form a growing concern for agricultural development organizations. Following World War II, food supply was scarce all over the world, in the Global South not least owing to growing populations and recurrent droughts. As an experimental technological response to food shortages, the research and development of new varieties of key crops lead to increased agricultural production from the 1950s and 1960s, a programme that would later be known as the 'Green Revolution', transforming agriculture across the Global South, mainly in India, Pakistan, Bangladesh, Indonesia, and China. The original Green Revolution was not so much a coherent framework for agricultural development as a diverse set of experimental interventions across the developing world that took on many forms. For the Rockefeller Foundation, this work started in Mexico where, in 1941, its Natural Sciences Division began a project to develop new modified varieties of corn and wheat, in particular those with high-yielding capacity, headed by plant pathologist George A. Harrar who would go on to become foundation president twenty years later. During the project period in Mexico, per-acre wheat yields increased by 250 per cent. In the tropics, heavy fertiliza-tion of traditional plant species lead these to shoot up to unnatural heights and collapse, greatly reducing the yield and impeding harvest. In Mexico, the Rockefeller Foundation, in cooperation with the Mexican Government, tested more than 40,000 crossbreeds of plants to find their ideal short-stemmed grain that would allow for heavy fertilization without shooting up, giving way for massive yields. The development of high yielding varieties (HYVs) of rice, wheat, and maize—through plant breeding methods such as cross-pollination— was subsequently pushed from Mexico to Latin America and Asia. Rice alone formed the daily diet for six out of ten people in the world by the late 1960s. Over the next twenty years, the use of HYVs grew substantially, to the point where, by the 1980s half of all wheat and more than half of all rice sown in developing countries used HYV strains, also facilitating a 75 per cent increase in the production of these two crops. The Green Revolution's new varieties brought with them significant improvements to the produced quantities of crops that are immensely important for global food security.

Modern, scientific, commercial, experimental: the Green Revolution had all the elements of success among policy makers and agricultural scientists. But it also entailed a set of undesired ecological consequences. HYVs need large quantities of nitrogenous fertilizer and water, or they will perform worse than original, indigenous varieties. For the Green Revolution, this prompted the use of technological 'packages'. These packages contained different biochemical programmes of disease, insect, and weed control, as well as the necessary chemical fertilizers, that must be complemented by heavy irrigation. The use of biochemicals has since the first introduction of these packages been documented to trigger contamination and degrading of soil, overuse of water as well as water contamination, poisoning from biocides, and decreasing genetic diversity. Soil fertility cannot be restored naturally, and instead fertilizers in ever-increasing amounts are used to ensure fertility. In Indonesia, the use of artificial fertilizers for HYV seeds increased from 25kg per acre in 1975 to 150kg per acre in 1990, with increases in rice yields corresponding more or less linearly to increases in the use of fertilizer. Dependency on pesticides is high because HYVs are based on genetically uniform monocultures and thus rule out the use of crop rotation as a form of protection against infestations. HYVs also require great concentrations of water to be efficient, necessitating the building of wells, canals, and dams for irrigation, both costly and at times necessitating resettlement.

Despite its name, the Green Revolution did not so much reflect nature's green as the clear colour of chemical compounds. Biocides such as pesticides and herbicides are effective killers of pests and weeds, but they are also a health hazard for farmers who are exposed to them through spray, drift, or direct contact because of limited access to safety or protective equipment, just as they leave residues in food crops and drinking water. Several of the pesticides most widely used in the Global South, including DDT and benzene hexachloride (BHC), are either restricted or altogether prohibited in most Western countries. An average of 200,000 people die every year from toxic exposure to pesticides[48] and, according to the UN, the list of illnesses associated with pesticides is long, linking exposure to cancer, Alzheimer's and Parkinson's diseases, hormone disruption, developmental disorders, and sterility.[49] The chronic effects of pesticides may not manifest for months or years after exposure, presenting a significant challenge for accountability, access to an effective remedy, and preventive interventions.

In many developing countries, the lethal effect of pesticides is tragically illustrated by farmers when they use it to commit suicide. Since the mid-1990s alone, hundreds of thousands of Indian farmers have committed suicide, most of them because circumstances such as droughts have ruined their harvests and made it impossible for them to repay the debts from loans they have taken each year to afford new packages of pesticides and seeds. On a visit to Bhubaneswar in the Eastern state of Odisha a few years ago, I learned of several hundreds of suicides in a short period of only a few weeks, because of an extraordinary drought. One of the local farmers was Sushil, whose widow told me that he had come home from the fields one day with severe stomach pains, and later died in the hospital from the several litres of pesticide he had consumed with the intention of taking his own life. Not far from Sushil's piece of land, Somnath, another young farmer in his mid-thirties, had taken his life by hanging himself in a tree on his cashew field. Common to both Sushil and Somnath is that their harvests failed because of the drought, leaving them unable to repay the loans they had taken for pesticide and seeds, and in extension to provide food for their families and school for their children. Facing loss of social status, they took the ultimate and most tragic action.

The socioeconomic impacts of the Green Revolution are even more disputed than the ecological effects of biocides. The necessary technology packages are expensive, and farmers are thus often provided opportunities through monetary systems, some foreign and some indigenous, to take up seasonal loans for new seeds, fertilizer, and water for irrigation. Loans have to be repaid and farmers thus sell their crops, over time diminishing the role of subsistence farming. In general, the technologization and commercialization of agriculture has led many developing countries to shift agricultural policies from food production for local consumption to export-oriented cash crops. This means that instead of food crops, commodity crops such as palm oil and soy are prioritized. Author Vandana Shiva has articulated that the shifts from subsistence to commercial agriculture has 'changed the structure of social and political relationships, from those based on mutual (though asymmetric) obligations—within the village to relations of each cultivator directly with banks, seed and fertilizer agencies, food procurement agencies, and electricity and irrigation organizations. Further, since all the externally supplied inputs were scarce, it set up conflict and competition over scarce resources, between classes, and between regions…this generated on the one hand, an erosion of cultural norms and practices and on the other hand, it sowed the seeds of violence and conflict.'[50]

*

The General Assembly Hall is the largest room in the somewhat confusing building that is the headquarters of the United Nations, by the banks of the East River in New York City. Without a doubt the most imposing, the Hall is a symbol of modern international cooperation and co-existence, but also a site that caters well to the theatrics of hostility, such as Muammar Gaddafi's famous 96-minute rant against the UN Security Council. From the podium, below the golden UN symbol of the world, one has oversight of all the individual desks, each given to a member state. In September 2015, as the Danish prime minister used his gavel to endorse the new Sustainable Development Goals that aim to drive global action against poverty, violence, and inequality towards 2030, Bill and Melinda Gates stood up alongside the 193 UN member states on the floor of the General Assembly Hall and clapped. Observing from the side-lines of the room, I remember being surprised not so much that they were there, big smiles on their faces like everyone else in the crowd, but that their foundation had its own sign and desk on the floor of the Hall, alongside the member states. For a couple (and representing an organization) that used to shrug off the UN as insignificant or even potentially harmful, this was a powerful manifestation of how the foundation's authority today goes far beyond that of a non-state actor and deep into the territory of state action as it advances core mantras of the experimental movement.

Adding to this sensation that the foundation is almost beginning to resemble a state in some of its ways of manoeuvring and influencing world politics, in late January 2017, the Gates Foundation was granted 'official relations' to the WHO despite existing criteria that private actors cannot be permitted such privileges. In elaborating the decision, the WHO Executive Board noted that the breadth of the collaboration between the two organizations would be 'deepened, strengthened and expanded' in the foreseeable future and that the foundation would support WHO's governance reform. Prior to the meeting, a group of civil society organizations had issued an open letter in which they criticized WHO for including the Gates Foundation despite its own rules about conflict-of-interest safeguards and due diligence. Citing the foundation's billion-dollar investments in many of the food, alcohol, and physical inactivity-related consumer products that cause 'the current crisis of preventable heart disease, stroke, cancer, and diabetes' as well as commercial pharmaceuticals, the group accused WHO of undermining its independence from commercial interests.[51] It made no difference in the end and the Gates Foundation now sits in the governing bodies of the WHO, including the Executive Board. The decision was hardly a surprise as the Gates Foundation provided a whopping $600 million out of the organization's $4.5 billion budget the year before, in 2016,[52] and the foundation declared itself honoured that it had 'been invited to establish a formal relationship with the World Health Organization'. The decision was one in a series of culminations of a decade-long process in which the foundation has attempted to establish itself as a major power in the international system. The decision was also a strong indication of the most apparent process of change occurring in the foundation as it has established itself internationally—its growing hybrid ability to shift between different organizational identities, including the adoption of state-like behaviour far beyond its private roots and self-conception as a distinct non-state actor.

Traversing tools of power and influence traditionally associated with different actor types, from states to multinational corporations (MNC) to advocacy

NGOs, the Gates Foundation increasingly practises a hybrid form of 'chameleon politics' to further the ideas and practices of experimentation and technological innovation. Just as the chameleon changes colour to convey a state of mind or body to other animals, the foundation can reinterpret and change its actorness to fit different situations and contexts in which it aims to attain influence. It practises the tools of influence typically associated with non-state actors such as lobbying for its causes in international organizations or uses the celebrity and plutocratic nature of the 'Gates' brand to ensure meetings with and political support from heads of states around the globe. But it also breaks with trad-itional non-profit behaviour by commercially investing its fifty-billion-dollar endowment, employing a weighty corporate power, and by providing inter-national grantmaking of at least $5 billion annually, swaying the priorities of global health and development. In addition, it breaks with traditional foundation behaviour when it aggressively funds core activities and reforms in international organizations such as the WHO or seconds its employees to these to ensure its interests are represented.

The Gates Foundation thus strategically reinforces and strengthens its pos-ition at the top of both international relations broadly and the experimental movement specifically by way of a hybrid shape-shifting authority. But before the foundation assumed such a striking position of influence, it practised a different set of narrow ambitions, far from any grand aspirations of global political power. During the foundation's prefatory period of organizational formation and expansion, from the mid-1990s to well into the 2000s, the foundation in fact largely followed a strategy of isolation that can be hard to comprehend given its contemporary reach. Pursuing action in only a few pro-grammatic areas, and deliberately aiming for isolation in these, the initial idea for the foundation and its leadership was to find underfinanced areas in which it could apply its reasoning of technological progress and entrepre-neurial solutions without too many interfaces with other actors. Reflecting on the belief that the foundation could change the state of its areas of global health by developing *things* that were needed and distributing them on to others for implementation and thus maintain limited contact with other organizations, then CEO Patty Stonesifer later explained how 'Bill, Melinda and I were a bunch of product-development people', and that they had 'assumed others would focus on getting the products we developed to those who needed them'.[53] That quickly turned out not to be the case, and the dis-connect between those developing experimental interventions, vaccines, or emerging technologies and they people who were theoretically assumed to be benefiting from those very same forms of charity only grew, ironically challenging the very fundamentals of anything having to do with cost-effectiveness because of the lack of tangible impact on people's lives.

The Gates Foundation was largely kept in the hands of the family during this time, without much external intervention. Combined with a hesitant approach to publicity, it intentionally favoured isolation all the way up until it became the world's second largest foundation with assets of more than $17 billion at the start of the millennium. It conducted little if any consultation outside of the philanthropic milieu in the US, and Melinda Gates herself acknowledged that when the foundation first opened its doors, a reluctance to work alongside other actors was dominant, maintaining that 'I don't think we had full appreciation for just how important it is to work in close partnership'.[54] 'Full appreciation' is quite an understatement as several people involved during the first years recalled how the attitude towards other organizations was one of fundamental scepticism about both their approaches and motivations, 'The general sense was that we didn't trust them. We may have been a new source of funding in their eyes, but they were mainly an obstacle in ours' as a former Senior Programme Officer has explained it to me,[55] mirroring the other central actors of the experimental movement who see themselves confronting and tearing down old ways and actors. The Millennium Development Goals (MDGs), coming into existence during this time, is a good example of this attitude. Recalling his own and Melinda's view on the MDGs at the beginning of the new millennium, Gates described in 2013 how they initially had strong reservations towards the goals, explaining that the MDGs 'were hardly the first time someone had declared that children shouldn't die' and that 'The UN had passed many resolutions calling for things that never came to pass'.[56] Gates later designated himself and Melinda as having been 'cautious optimists'—in contrast to the way they commonly refer to themselves as 'impatient optimists'. This is likely an understatement as several involved during the early years of turning towards global development recall how foundation leadership perceived of the MDGs as fundamentally restrictive towards the organization's grantmaking. As a former Senior Programme Officer framed it, 'People [in the foundation] thought of the MDGs as a set of principles coming from a group of states that hadn't even been able to live up to their own promises for decades. Why should we respect their opinion?'[57] Over the course of a few years, however, this attitude would change.

Increasingly then, the foundation has come to embrace an expansive repertoire of tools of influence, and today exercises an exceedingly strategic use of its hybrid nature, being very conscious about the effects of such. As a Senior Advisor explained it to me, 'we do consider ourselves a multifaceted organization with many tools at our disposal. It would be silly of us to not use all those tools'.[58] This shape-shifting ability has proven crucial for the foundation to diffuse its values of experimentation and technological innovation to organizations, governments, and communities in the more than 138 countries where it currently works. In the WHO, moving from informal working relations to formal relations grants the organization a further set of options for exercising influence. Amongst many privileges, these include permission to attend meetings of the governing bodies of the WHO, including the World Health Assembly (as a non-voting member), the Executive Board, the six regional committees, and participate in any other meeting organized with the purpose of exchanging views as well as engaging in technical collaboration with WHO on activities, for example concerning product development and capacity building. As mentioned, an alliance of civil society organizations opposed WHO's decision to grant the Gates Foundation because of the corporate investments of the foundation's trust.[59] The investment of its endowment has returned anything between a deficit of $8 billion during the height of the financial crisis in 2008 to a surplus of almost $6 billion in 2013, representing more than 150 per cent of its grant expenses, essentially providing annual net growth of its endowment. Far from exercising a line between pursuing profit and public interest then, the foundation practises a modus operandi that sees the former facilitate the latter. Decisively, the investment of a fifty-billion-dollar endowment is not merely a neutral or passive way of increasing the funds available for charitable activities. Through the commercial investments, the foundation trust is connected to key private sector players in the foundation's areas of engagement, whether pharmaceuticals such as Merck, GlaxoSmithKline, or Pfizer or agricultural giants such as Archer Daniels Midland, Kraft, or Unilever. These connections are crucial for it to maintain a central position as a bridging factor in the experimental movement, between scientists, commercial actors, and policy makers.

In international organizations, the Gates Foundation's efforts to shape political negotiations in the directions of the experimental movement often forms a multi-sided attack that sees it combining the posting of senior technical staff with expertise to shape negotiation texts and engage with national delegations (staff who often have prior experience from representing such country delegations) with a high-level presence of either Bill or Melinda Gates who attract attention and exercise influence at this different level of political and public relations. Negotiation stances are often simultaneously furthered or strengthened through partnerships with think tanks or other knowledge organizations. This construction of knowledge regimes, commonly presented by the foundation as 'best practice' or the result of 'systematic reviews' (by combining several randomized controlled trials), is thus used concurrently by foundation representatives in negotiations and publicly through the co-chairs. These efforts may again be supported by strategic media outlets or by high-profile social media campaigns. But such negotiations only happen so often, and the foundation has increasingly taken steps towards providing financial resources for operational and core backing for many international organizations, often supporting organizational reforms such as the setting up of new offices or departments. This is an ideal way to further a specific priority of the foundation, ensuring that it is prominently featured in the relevant organization by having sufficient resources or by having it include management of a certain level or proximity to the secretary general. In addition to the close talks with management that hundred-million-dollar-donations grant the foundation access to, another way for the Gates Foundation to shape organizational reforms in international organizations is by contributing third party consultants to draft policies, procedures, or to settle decision-making processes. The foundation is itself a pronounced purchaser of external consulting services for internal purposes, and by selecting consultants with prior work experience in the foundation (but who are formally removed from it) it can sustain a degree of influence as to where the organizational reforms or other processes land. This is a widespread practice by the foundation, particularly documented in the field of global health.[60]

The foundation is also increasingly moving into state-territory by scaling up its secondment of foundation employees directly into the heart of the bureaucracies of international organizations. Seconding national employees from member states into the bureaucratic halls of these is a well-versed form of state-action to further national interests. In effect, it implies that individuals already employed by another organization or state bureaucracy are installed into an office or department in the multilateral organization for a fixed period, after which the secondee returns to her or his original organization. While the employee formally works for the organization and, under the rules of declarations of interests for staff (these, however, often only refer specifically to individual interests, not institutional ones), they are still widely used strategically by states to further certain interests through the close connection upheld to their original organization or home country. In late 2015, the first ever review of the WHO's non-state secondments showed that the Gates Foundation was at the time involved in three top-level secondments to management.[61] That is, staff positioned at the highest levels of leadership in the WHO were effectively sent from, and paid for by, the Gates Foundation. The hybridity of the Gates Foundation perhaps represents traits that are becoming increasingly prevalent today; a fluid organizational form given further weight by the increasingly blurred boundaries between private, public, and non-profit organizational forms. Hybridity is an effective strategy for diffusing the values and practices of experimentation to the international political arena, granting access, as it does, to decision-making fora, special rights, and privileges. The ability to project a shifting array of organizational identities across broader categories of public or non-state actors, but also more specific ones like NGOs, MNCs, or private foundations, provides the Gates Foundation with an extensive repertoire of tools and approaches ideal for pushing experimentalist mantras.

One such mantra could very well be the (by now officially former) motto of Facebook and its founder Mark Zuckerberg, for years hanging on the walls of the offices of the tech-giant: 'Move fast and break things'. If not for its overtly aggressive connotations, such a saying might just as well have covered the glass-clad walls of the Gates Foundation's Seattle-headquarters. The foundation sees as its prime guiding line of attack that of disruption, upsetting social systems, and challenging the status quo to evoke radical change and that, within a view that sees such systems as fundamentally closed, allowing them to compose a plan of which levers to pull to produce certain foreseeable consequences. At all times, the Gates Foundation will walk a fine line between being seen as a benefit for, or a negative influence on, society. There is a reason why foundations are more or less exempt for tax, and thus eventually distribute money that at some level belongs to all of us—they are expected to create real value for society. The problem often remains that foundations personify the very thing they should try to oppose, being, as they are, the ultimate testimony to the inequalities of contemporary society. By their very nature then, we can never look at foundations without seeing charity and social justice in tension with each other.

Silicon Valley billionaires have brought with them a renewed vigour of experimentation around the world. Foundations in general, and the Gates Foundation specifically, act both as major financial backers of the experimental movement's key actors, from social norm experiments by NGOs and the randomistas' economics imperialism, and as advocacy and implementing agencies, themselves directly pushing forward an experimental regime on the ground. Randomistas and experimental humanitarian interventions are but two examples of what the new foundations are massively backing today. Next, we move to explore the world of pharmaceutical companies and the growth of global medical trialling, another industry and set of experiments heavily supported by the foundations and contributing towards normalizing experimental practice as an inevitable part of life for the world's poor.

Notes

1. Adelman, C. 2009. Global philanthropy and remittances: reinventing foreign aid, *The Brown Journal of World Affairs* 15(2); Bishop, M. and Green, M. 2010. *Philanthrocapitalism: How Giving Can Save the World*. London: A. & C. Black.
2. Desai, R. and Kharas, H. 2008. The California consensus: can private aid end global poverty?, *Survival* 50(4): 155–68; Edwards, M. 2009. *Just Another Emperor? The Myths and Realities of Philanthrocapitalism*. London: The Young Foundation & Demos; McGoey, L. 2015. *No Such Thing as a Free Gift: The Gates Foundation and the Price of Philanthropy*. London and New York: Verso.
3. Comparably, this figure is far greater than for any other foundation, with e.g. the Ford Foundation (the second largest foundation in the US) awarding grants worth approximately $500 million in 2014 (latest available figures).
4. OECD. 2017. *Global Private Philanthropy for Development*. Paris: Organisation for Economic Co-operation and Development.
5. Bill and Melinda Gates Foundation. 2012. *Annual Report*. Seattle, WA: The Bill and Melinda Gates Foundation.
6. This *article* seems to refer to the 1993 World Development Report, which focused on the interplay between human health, health policy, and economic development from the title of 'Investing in health'.
7. See Fejerskov, A. 2018. *The Gates Foundation's Rise to Power*. Abingdon: Routledge.
8. *New York Times*. 2000. Bill Gates's money. 16 April 2000.
9. See also Gates, B. 2021. *How to Avoid a Climate Disaster*. London: Penguin Books Ltd.
10. Gates, B. 2011. *Innovation with Impact: Financing 21st Century Development*. Report to the G20 Leaders. Personal report to the G20 Cannes Summit, November 2011.
11. Gates, 2011.
12. Bill and Melinda Gates Foundation. 2016. *Annual Letter*. Seattle, WA: The Bill and Melinda Gates Foundation.
13. Bill and Melinda Gates Foundation. 2010. *Annual Letter*. Seattle, WA: The Bill and Melinda Gates Foundation.
14. Bill and Melinda Gates Foundation. 2015. *Annual Letter*. Seattle, WA: The Bill and Melinda Gates Foundation.
15. Remarks of Bill Gates, Harvard Commencement 2007, available here: https://news.harvard.edu/gazette/story/2007/06/remarks-of-bill-gates-harvard-commencement-2007/.
16. Bill and Melinda Gates Foundation. 2010.
17. Bill and Melinda Gates Foundation. 2008. *Annual Letter*. Seattle, WA: The Bill and Melinda Gates Foundation.
18. Bill and Melinda Gates Foundation. 2010.
19. See Arnove, R. 1982. Introducton. In R. Arnove (ed.), *Philanthropy and Cultural Imperialism*. Bloomington: Indiana University Press, pp. 1–23.

20. See Parmar, I. 2012. *Foundations of the American Century*. New York: Columbia University Press; Zunz, O. 2012. *Philanthropy in America*. Princeton, NJ: Princeton University Press; Dowie, M. 2001. *American Foundations: An Investigative History*. Cambridge, MA: The MIT Press.

21. Nielsen, W. 1972. *The big foundations*, New York: Columbia University Press.

22. Andrews, F.E. 1956. *Philanthropic Foundations*. New York: Russel Sage Foundation.

23. Anheier, H.K. and Daly, S. 2007. *Politics of Foundations: A Comparative Analysis*. London: Routledge.

24. Nielsen, 1972.

25. Cnet. 2013. 'Bill Gates on education, patents, Microsoft Bob, and disease, 15 July.

26. See Fleishman, J., Kohler, J.S., and Schindler, S. 2009. *The Foundation: A Great American Secret*. New York: PublicAffairs.

27. Parmar, 2012.

28. See Eichenwald, K. 2012. Microsoft's lost decade. *Vanity Fair* 24 July.

29. Bishop, M. 2006. The birth of philanthrocapitalism, *The Economist* 23 February; see also Birch, K., Peacock, M., Wellen, R., Hossein, C., Scott, S., and Salazar, A. (eds) 2017. *Business and Society: A Critical Introduction*. London: Zed Books.

30. Lundsgaarde, E., Funk, E., Kopyra, A., Richter, J., and Steinfeldt, H. 2012. *Private Foundations and Development Cooperation: Insights from Tanzania*. Bonn: German Development Institute.

31. Moran, M. and Stone, D. 2016. The New Philanthropy: Private Power in International Development Policy? In J. Grugel and D. Hammett (eds), *The Palgrave Handbook of International Development*. Basingstoke: Palgrave.

32. See Fleishman et al., 2009.

33. Jenkins, G. 2011. Who's afraid of philanthrocapitalism?, *Case Western Reserve Law Review* 61(3); Bishop and Green, 2010.

34. Fleishman et al., 2009.

35. See Fejerskov, A. & Rasmussen, C. 2016. 'Going global? Micro-philanthrocapitalism and the engagements of Danish Private Foundations in International Development Cooperation', *Development in Practice*, 26(7): 840–852.

36. Hudson Institute. 2011. *The Index of Global Philanthropy and Remittances 2011*. Washington, DC: Hudson Institute; OECD, 2017.

37. See Fejerskov, A. and Rasmussen, C. 2016. Going global? micro-philanthrocapitalism and Danish private foundations in international development cooperation, *Development in Practice* 26(7): 840–52.

38. Easterly, W. 2006. *The White Man's Burden: Why the West's Efforts to Aid the Rest Have Done so Much Ill and so Little Good*. London: Penguin Books.

39. Fejerskov, 2018.

40. Thompson, C. 2014. Philanthrocapitalism: appropriation of Africa's genetic wealth, *Review of African Political Economy* 41(141): 389–405.

41. For a study on the use of US universities as 'Development Labs' see Collins, C.S. 2017. Development labs: university knowledge production and global poverty, *The Review of Higher Education* 41(1): 113–19.

42. Rockefeller Foundation. 2014. Understanding the Value of Social Innovation Labs: Solutions to Complex Social Problems. Accessed 15 April 2017. Available here http://

visual.ly/understandi ng-value-social-innovation-labs-solutions-complex-social-problems#sthash.uKMftAzM.dpuf.

43. Rockefeller Foundation. 2016. To Save Our Fisheries, We Need a New Approach. Accessed 15 April 2017. Available here https://www.rockefellerfoundation.org/blog/save-our-fisheries-we-need-new/.

44. Westley, F., Laban, S., Rose, C., McGowan, K., Robinson, K., Tjornbo, O., and Tovey, M. 2014. *Social Innovation Lab Guide*. Waterloo: University of Waterloo.

45. Ibid.

46. Bill and Melinda Gates Foundation. 2007. *Annual Letter*. Seattle, WA: The Bill and Melinda Gates Foundation.

47. Associated Press. 2009. New CEO: Gates Foundation Learns from Mistakes. New York: Associated Press. Accessed 15 April 2017. Available here http://www.thestreet.%20com/story/10506452/1/new-ceo-gates-foundation-learns-from-experiments.html.

48. UN. 2017. *Report of the Special Rapporteur on the Right to Food*. New York: United Nations.

49. UN, 2017.

50. Shiva, V. 1999. *Biopiracy: The Plunder of Nature and Knowledge*. Boston, MA: South End Press.

51. The letter, e.g., reads 'According to the United States Government's Securities and Exchange Commission, the Bill and Melinda Gates Foundation Trust endowment—the source of revenue for the Foundation—is heavily invested in many of the food, alcohol, and physical inactivity-related consumer products that cause or treat the current crisis of preventable heart disease, stroke, cancer, and diabetes.... These investments make the Gates Foundation a beneficiary of sales of several categories of products that are the subject of WHO standards and advice to governments related to nutrition and physical activity.' The letter is available here: http://healthscienceandlaw.ca/wp-content/uploads/2017/01/Public-Interest-Position.WHO_.FENSAGates.Jan2017.pdf.

52. In 2019, the foundation provided 12 per cent of the WHO's budget, with a further 8 per cent coming from the Gates-initiated GAVI Alliance.

53. Chronicle of Philanthropy. 2004. A view inside the Gates. 11 November.

54. Bill and Melinda Gates Foundation. 2007. *Annual Report 2007*. Seattle, WA: The Bill and Melinda Gates Foundation.

55. Interview with Gates Foundation Senior Programme Officer, April 2019.

56. Gates, B. 2013. Dream with a Deadline: The Millennium Development Goals. Gatesnotes.com, 18 September.

57. Interview with former Gates Foundation Senior Programme Officer, March 2019.

58. Interview with Gates Foundation Senior Advisor, May 2015.

59. See the letter mentioned in note 51.

60. Storeng, K. 2014. The GAVI alliance and the 'Gates Approach' to health systems strengthening, *Global Public Health* 9(8): 865–79.

61. IP Watch. 2015. Outside Sources: Unease over Seconded Philanthropic Foundation Staff to Top Management at WHO. 15 December 2015. Available here: https://www.ip-watch.org/2015/12/15/unease-over-seconded-philanthropic-foundation-staff-to-top-management-at-who/.

5

Experimental Bodies

As the traffic of Bangkok roars outside, I meet a senior employee of a major contract research organization (CRO), the Swiss army knife of the pharmaceutical industry, for lunch. 'Thailand', he tells me, 'is at that sweet spot, you know, where the medical infrastructure is sufficiently good, while you still have a large population that is both cheap to recruit and willing to partake in trials'.[1] Although the business of pharma has been booming alongside the growing use and availability of drugs for whatever novel purpose imaginable, many pharmaceutical companies have been outsourcing parts of their clinical operations to CROs. It is expensive and only the largest pharmas are able to singlehandedly execute clinical trials from initial exploration to potential final approval by the US Food and Drug Administration (FDA) or other regulatory bodies, the holy grail of all clinical research in the industry. There are simply too many steps, too much specialized knowledge needed, and too much funding required to maintain in-house that sort of capacity. Enter the CROs. As a senior statistician for a global pharma phrased it when I met him a month earlier: 'every service imaginable can be bought for money at the CROs today'. Some CROs focus on laboratory infrastructure to conduct pre-clinical animal testing, others specialize in recruitment, the notorious headache for an industry that is increasingly struggling to enlist subjects for trials, and others are adept at managing data as it flows from studies.

CROs are not only crucial enablers of clinical trials in general, essentially being the *de facto* real-life experimenters of the pharmaceutical business, they have also been fundamental in facilitating the process we refer to as the globalization of clinical trials. In theory, trials in Western countries are preferable for drugs meant to be sold there: potential patients and subjects align, health infrastructures are developed and specialized, and American and European drug authorities greatly prefer results from here. Opposite the risk-taking affinities and cash-burning pace of biotech start-ups (biotech companies raised an estimated \$128 billion from initial public offerings (IPOs), and other sources from 2014 to 2019[2]), many established pharmas mirror the caricatured life of an accountant—risk-averse, level-headed, and with brownish khakis for every occasion. From a strategic perspective that means shaping the business to make it as cost-effective as possible and always starting from where there is money to be made: 'if you're not the World Health Organization, commercial potential will always be the point of departure—marketing strategy and business precedes everything else. It's about singling out that gap which nobody fills up',[3] as the Senior Statistician told me. And drug development is expensive, really expensive. Newer estimates single out the high average price tag of research and development at upwards of US$2.6 billion to take a single drug to market, something only a few clinical programmes achieve.[4] These immense costs grow by almost 10 per cent every year and are elevated by raised regulatory bars on compliance and documentation in the Global North, expensive and difficult subject recruitment (more than 95 per cent of American patients don't want to participate in clinical trials), high standards of care, and growing prices on trial infrastructure. As we will explore later, the calculation of such costs for the experimental endeavour of drug development in itself serves as an instrument of justification for taking trials global, directing attention from the hyperfocus on growth that remains in the biopharma industry, pushing companies at all times to accelerate the licensing of drugs.

Taking these concerns into consideration, the pull factors of the Global South are clear. Fast and treatment-naïve recruitment, a large number of either willing or cheap subjects, weaker regulations and regulatory bodies, and in many trial-destinations struggling public health sectors and high poverty rates entailing a lack of resources and limited access to specialized medicines and treatment (or just the regular health consultations that often come with trial participation). While seemingly low, these barriers of entry are in fact fairly high. There is no such thing as easily entering the Egyptian, South African, or Thai trial markets and subtracting abstract value or concrete results translatable and convincing in FDA applications. Enter the CROs again. In addition to the breadth of their services—that have come to include everything from drug discovery to bioanalytical services and data management—CROs have specialized in different emerging markets and today facilitate trials around the world to relevant buyers. IQVIA, one of the world's largest CROs, claims to have a network of 67,000 experts in more than 100 countries and more than 800 million patient records. The services of the CROs mean even small and mid-size pharmaceuticals can move their trials to regions and countries traditionally out of their reach. For some, that may be Poland in a cautious move to Eastern Europe that provides good trial infrastructure but fewer expenses; for others it may be Spain, whose continued unemployment struggles make subjects readily available; and for others reduced costs make African, South

American, or Asian countries more interesting. Traditionally seen as solo marathons for their commercial secrets and potential, clinical trials today have a more hybrid appearance as CROs weave in and out of pharma operations, often taking on the bulk of their experimental work. And the experiments are not just with new molecules for breakthrough treatments, but there are also trials exploring new combinations, new indications as part of product lifecycles, or new uses of existing drugs to maintain or extend patents lives and keep a steady flow of new products coming to the market. Paracetamol, a pain killer, can be mixed with components such as caffeine to enhance their effect or enable more rapid onset. GlaxoSmithKline's popular Panodil becomes Panodil Zapp or Panodil Extra or Panodil Hot or Panodil Junior to keep the product line dynamic and present in the minds of consumers and to expand its use to other treatment groups such as children.

Squid and fried fish. We're having lunch at a small place in the western part of the Pathum Wan district in central Bangkok, nestled in between the famous Chulalungkorn University, the country's main clinical and pharmaceutical educator, non-profits such as WHO, and the Thai Red Cross, and embassies. The restaurant itself is situated in a hub that also gives a nod to Thailand's potential future as a centre for medical tourism and clinical research, surrounded by several country or regional offices of CROs such as IQVIA, and Bumrungrad International Hospital, a private and major destination for medical tourists. 'We help our clients with whatever they need us to do' my contact tells me, 'regulatory affairs, study design, recruitment, you name it. We provide the services you don't have inhouse or don't want to have. Think about something like patient recruitment. We take the client's ICD-9 codes [international classification of diseases and health problems, ed.] and handle identification and recruitment. We know the local ecosystems, the investigators, the health professionals. Unless you're big, as in really big, there's no way you can run a trial without us or some of the other CROs here'. As pharmas outsource their most experimental work, CROs assume an important position where they develop, refine, institutionalize, and reassert the scientific and societal positions of experimental research and implementation that lies within the boundaries of the clinical trial or the RCT, including expanding its experimental realm into all corners of the world. 'Even if it's only theoretical for some, Thailand does have a universal healthcare scheme that many other countries don't', I say to probe further into the discrepancies among the countries that together make up the setting for 'global trials'. 'Sure', he replies, 'for most African countries it's a totally different thing. Here in Thailand, even if level of care is unequal, most people trust the health system because they have actually benefited from it, in some capacity. At some of the African sites we've worked with, recruitment is not based on trust of doctors and habit of interacting with the system. It's mostly based on not being able to afford regular care. And so, trials become a sort of substitute for treatment.' Normalizing experimentation in everyday bodily life in the Global South then, is what takes centre stage here, as we open up for how some pharmaceutical companies enforce the methodological precedence of RCTs and global trials, directly or indirectly expanding the reach and bolstering the legitimacy of the experimental movement.

*

> KVH provided dedicated research laboratories, a team of technicians, clinical trials all over the Third World, first-class travel, glamorous hotels, respect and money galore. 'For frivolous Kovacs, it was her dream come true. She will drive Rolls-Royces, she will win Nobel Prizes, she will be famous and rich, she will have many, many lovers. And for serious Lara, the clinical trials will be scientific, they will be responsible. They will test the drug in a wide range of ethnic and social communities that are vulnerable to the disease. Many lives will be improved, others will be saved. That will be very satisfactory.' 'And for Lorbeer?' An irritable glance, a grimace of disapproval. 'Markus wishes to be a rich saint. He is for Rolls-Royces, also for saved lives.' 'For God and Profit, then,' Justin suggests lightly.

In John Le Carré's 2001 novel *The Constant Gardener* the main character, Justin Quayle, a garden-loving reserved British diplomat, sets out to unravel the mysterious murder of his activist wife Tessa in northern Kenya. A greater conspiracy unfolds, leading Justin to the reality that Tessa was killed for her work to expose a corporate scandal of medical experimentation by German pharmaceutical company KVH. The book was adapted into a feature film in 2005, scoring four Oscar nominations and a single win to Rachel Weisz for best supporting actress. Le Carré's mixture of multinational corporate greed, pharmaceutical secrecy, and third-world exploitation left a mark in the public imagination and for a brief stint period at least pushed forward a critique that, while somewhat one-sided or conspiratorial, it had some truths to its name.

Despite the millennia-long history of medical experimentation, the first medical RCTs or clinical trials were done within the last hundred years, and it was not until after World War II that commercial trialling really took off. With the 1963 Kefauver Harris Amendments to the US Federal Food, Drug, and Cosmetic Act, advanced requirements were introduced for drug manufacturers in proving the efficacy of new drugs as well as their side effects. The amendments were made in response to the European thalidomide tragedy, which only bypassed the American market by a hair's breadth. More about that later. A 1975 provision permitting the submission of foreign clinical trial (FCT) data to the FDA was the first step, but it was really the exclusion of certain groups for trials that spurred the first wave of globalization. Prior to the 1970s, approximately 90 per cent of drugs licensed in the US were first tested on prison populations.[5] In 1980, this group was banned from most parts of drug testing, and the desperate hunt for other bodies was initiated. Sparked by harmonization of regulatory demands in the European Union at the beginning of the 1980s, talks began with the US and Japan to implement global harmonization standards. In April 1990, the result was The International Council for Harmonisation of Technical Requirements for Pharmaceuticals for Human Use or ICH for short, whose mission and impact was to ease the transferability of data from around the world to be used in regulatory applications in the West by introducing standardization and, well, harmonization in the approach to the quality, safety, and efficacy of trials and their results. CROs too emerged in the early 1990s as the fee-for-service industry we met earlier in the chapter, facilitating the expansion of drug development, production, and distribution from national and regional levels to a global endeavour in the constant pursuit of drug approval.

FDA approval still remains the holy grail of drug development that billions and billions of dollars are invested in every year—not least because the prices of new prescription drugs are unregulated in the US—and something only forty-five drugs obtained in 2019, still prompting headlines of 'friendly FDA here to stay' after a record year of sixty-one approvals in 2018.[6] To be approved by the FDA, global studies, in theory, still need to comport with all relevant regulations as if they were conducted within the US, increasing the demands from global trials. Even so, half of all European drugs currently on the market have been tested outside of Western Europe, the US, or Japan,[7] helped along by standardizations in methodology such as COS-STAR that outlines eighteen items on a checklist considered necessary for trial results to be complete, no matter where they are conducted. An outcome set maintaining minimum standards to be measured and reported on, strengthening the ideas of disease as universal and invariant to time and place, just like the results of any good, controlled trial or RCT.[8] In 2002, 84 per cent of all FDA Regulated Investigators— the specialist term for those responsible for any clinical investigation of a drug, biological product, or medical device—were based in the US. Today, that number is approaching less than half, a watershed moment for the globalization of clinical trials as non-US based investigators will soon form the majority. The global clinical trials registry lists almost 200,000 trials in nearly 190 countries, and the number of countries working as 'study locations' outside the US has more than doubled over the past decade.

The organizational production of global trials in most of these countries is immense, although it often appears more as an improvised rugby match than a beautifully choreographed Russian ballet. Trials run through phases of research and organization, each intensifying in terms of the required resources, whether financial, temporal, or research resources as in trial patients, just as the relative percentage of drugs not making it through a phase increases with every step. From in vitro laboratory research, synthesizing of an eventual substance, and animal testing of efficacy, toxicity, and pharmacokinetics, Phase I studies explore doses and safety of the new drug and how it is absorbed, metabolized, and excreted by a small and select group of human subjects. This initial phase and the laboratory work done up until this point, typically involves greater technological requirements and takes place at *home* for most pharmas, including those who outsource their later-stage trials, although most tend to outsource animal studies. Phase II for clinical RCT studies initiates core experimental scientific methodologies of blinding and randomizing patient groups as well as a scaling of the exercise that potentially includes more than 1,500 subjects whose results help to show the perceived universal nature or average treatment effect of the drug's efficacy. Control groups either receive comparable therapies or a placebo, depending on the nature of the study and the regulatory demands in place. Phase III is the final and crucial stage before regulatory approval, in which the drug must show its efficacy and safety across large quantities of patients, often numbering in the thousands. To save time and speed up the results, Phase III studies are often conducted simultaneously in several different countries—so-called 'multicentre' requirements that are also undertaken because they are thought to reduce bias. Phase II and III are the phases commonly moved to the Global South because of the heavy recruitment needs and costs, making for the easy enrolment of large populations crucial for budgets and timelines. Phase III itself can represent upwards of 70 per cent of the entire R&D budget for a new drug. Finally, a post-marketing Phase IV may be executed for surveillance of the drug's continued safety.

These phased processes are like a patchwork of actors, finance, and experts, both in-house and outsourced. They routinely consist of categories such as sponsors and investigators from the initiating side, and ethics committees and institutional review boards on the reactive or regulatory side, although these do not have to belong to state institutions or be formal regulators. Sponsors assume responsibility for the clinical investigation and are typically pharmaceutical companies or CROs who initiate the trial, but they may also be government agencies such as institutes of health or hospital departments. They are the ones responsible for obtaining ethical permission, for deciding which investigators to use, and for monitoring the trial during its active period to make sure it corresponds to the principles of Good Clinical Practice. Investigators then conduct the actual trial and are formally responsible for obtaining informed consent and for protecting the rights, safety, and welfare of patients enrolled in the trial, and for following the protocol where the study aims are translated into the objectives and actual organization of the trial, including the criteria for selecting subjects, doses, etc. Usually, a protocol synopsis is developed by the sponsor, determining the degree of experimentation in the trial. Finally, before the trial can commence it has to be approved by an institutional review board (US) or ethics committee (EU) that formally monitors and reviews biomedical research involving human subjects, formed to protect patients from harm by ensuring trials live up to the standards of relevant science and ethics. These may be affiliated to hospitals but are also increasingly private in form, potentially blurring institutional affiliations and responsibilities between those meant to oversee the trial and those meant to objectively evaluate its scientific and organizational legitimacy. The form, requirements, and stringency of these review boards naturally depend on where in the world the trial takes place, with vast discrepancies across the trial landscape.

For the sake of explanation, we can split the global trials landscape into at least four major groupings of countries, each with their own composition of actors, types of trials, and predominant phases. The first tier includes the US, Western Europe, Japan, and a few others. These countries are home to most pharmaceutical companies and to the headquarters of most global CROs. This is where the majority of initial laboratory R&D is done, where the commercial potential traditionally resides, and where most pharmas will initially seek approval for their breakthrough drugs, with the FDA (US), EMA (Europe), or the PMDA (Japan). Clinical trials are frequent here, but they are also expensive in their later stages and recruitment is difficult just as it is scientifically troublesome in certain respects, with many trial patients being professionals enrolled in multiple studies—which increases the risks of drug–drug interactions, rendering test results unusable. Researchers at Boston University's School of Medicine and Fairleigh Dickinson University conducted a study showing 75 per cent of study participants admitted withholding or hiding information at least once out of fear that they would not be admitted into a study, stressing the complex relationship between deception, trials, and monetary rewards.

The second tier then includes some of the countries we find just outside of Western Europe. Southern and Eastern Europe, represented by countries such as Spain and Poland, have become popular destinations over the past years for their close vicinity to pharma headquarters, EU membership, and recognition by the European Medicines Agency (EMA). Most have respectable public health care and high standards of living, as well as reasonable patient recruitment because of both financial incentives and the population's habit of interacting with the medical system. Averaging around 400–500 studies per year, Poland began to see a surge of trials as 2019 started, not least facilitated by a simplification of the European Union registration procedure of clinical trials. Still, scepticism of trials remains fairly high in the country, with a 2018 survey showing 40 per cent believing that pharmaceutical companies bribe doctors to conduct trials and 35 per cent being of the opinion that patients in trials are treated as 'guinea pigs'.[9] No matter, it is becoming a favoured destination for many pharmas.

The third tier is represented by the country where we started this chapter—Thailand—but also includes others from Argentina to Russia. Common among these is the combination of well-trained health professionals and a fairly good medical infrastructure that in theory ensures access to a form of basic health care. Most people here are entitled to some form of doctor's visit and essential diagnosis, although some may have to pay a small price for it (hence the 30-baht Thai scheme we will meet). But most of these countries also have multi-tiered coverage systems where the majority of the population have low reimbursement rates on medicine (10 per cent for the majority in Thailand for example), making many treatments and forms of specialized care inaccessible to many sections of the population. And with large populations and relative inequality of access to basic services, recruitment is easy and relatively cheap.

The fourth and final tier includes a whole host of countries that are typically found at the bottom of rankings for health care systems and expenditure. Many of these are sub-Saharan African, including Kenya, Uganda, or Nigeria, but also more well-off African countries such as Egypt are relatively major trial destinations in the Global South. All these countries have struggling health care systems with significant inequality of access, as well as a critical shortage of health care workers and facilities, just as they struggle with social determinants leading to poor health outcomes, including unsafe water and sanitation, gender inequality, and high poverty rates in both urban and rural contexts. Common to all the tiers, however, is that their health systems are characterized by significant inequalities of access and quality of service, carried over into the experimental realm of medical trials.

*

After years of working for global pharmas in Thailand and abroad, clinical research consultant Phamanan[10] returned to government work for the country he believes has given him so much, 'I thought I might give something back to the country before I retire', he tells me laughing. Having dealt with the international and Thai pharmaceutical business and clinical trials for decades, he has seen the rise of CROs and clinical trials in the country, vividly remembering the days of little to no engagement between the global pharmaceutical industry and Thailand. Today his tasks combine inciting international pharmas to take their trials to Thailand and convincing them that they should do everything in their power to uphold standards of good clinical practice, because as he says, 'we have to protect the people, not just take things out of Thailand'. Even for a country lauded for its accessible health care system, inequality is pronounced today and the experimental often appears as the only certain way to access treatment: 'Everyone in Thailand is covered by the Universal Coverage, but that doesn't mean you have access to all medicines. If you don't have the money, [it's] participate in a new trial or die. Life is life' he explains. During the 1990s, the few global trials conducted in Thailand focused on diseases relevant to the country, including HIV, tropical, and infectious diseases. Still, ethical committees based at universities had difficulties in understanding why trials had to be conducted and were reluctant to accept them, much to the frustration of early pharmaceutical companies present such as Bayer, GSK, Pfizer, or Novartis. Other Thai regulatory bodies felt the same and getting devices and drugs into the country was a hassle: 'you can't import drugs that have not been approved yet', was the government response towards the pharmas. Spurred on by industry, the 'five pillars'—industry, investigators, Thai FDA, ethics committees, and institutes at hospitals—came together for an annual congress that runs to this day, under the umbrella of ThaiTECT. Industry led the inaugural congress and outlined the necessity of streamlined understandings of trials, frustrated by how one ethics committee might have rejected a trial approved under another. The solution to that specific problem became FERCT, the Forum for Ethics Committees, and industry pressure to adopt a single international standard across the committees as well as build capacity and institutionalize committee members into the world of trials. A decision of 'don't invent anything, adopt international standards' was made, leading Thai

FDA to adopt ICH Global Clinical Practice standards that the US FDA and most countries abide by, as well as introducing a new category of investigational medical products that granted industry access to a special import licence for experimental drugs, and tax exemption for years. Institutes were incited to improve as well, and Clinical Research Centers (CRCs) were set up to pool resources and allow investigators to charge sponsors while making improvements to universities, aiding the limited resources of investigators. In 2000, the ICH-GCP standards were formally announced in Thailand and today remain the main regulatory reference point as formal national legislation is yet to be adopted.

Since that time in the early 2000s, the number of trials has steadily increased in the country. Even if the past years have reduced the overall number to somewhere around a yearly average of 500, the number of Thai investigators has increased as the government seems to place a growing emphasis on the local development and production of drugs. This includes so-called bio-similar products, cheaper versions of existing drugs, where the competition from Chinese and Korean producers is fierce. A trials registry has been set up and is maintained by the government institution Medical Research Network of the Consortium of Thai Medical Schools or MedResNet for short. It encompasses some 80 per cent of all Thai trials and is implicitly supported by, for example, standards of international medical journals agreeing that they will only publish studies documenting publicly registered trials and the political support that arises from Thailand's position in the regional clinical and medical landscape.

Thailand truly boasts a rapidly expanding and improving medical infrastructure as a key growth driver of its position as a clinical trial destination. Domestically, an ageing population (the third-most rapidly ageing in the world) and a growing middle-class ensures both an increase in purchasing power and a mounting number of patients with heart disease, stroke, cancer, and diabetes. But, equally, medical tourism blossoms, and the more than three million annual medical tourists now contribute some 30–40 per cent of the revenue of private Thai hospitals. Facilities are quickly upgraded, and new players rapidly enter into the market with at least a dozen new private hospitals in the pipeline of what is already the greatest concentration of private hospitals in Asia. More than seventy hospitals and medical centres have accreditation from the Joint Commission International (JCI), the *golden standard* of global health care. Bangkok Dusit Medical Services Plc or BDMS manages close to fifty hospitals and almost monopolizes Bangkok medical services with a company value of tens of billions of dollars. Popular medical services for tourists include cosmetic surgery, dentistry, treatment for cardiovascular diseases, and not least fertility, an industry expected to boom with the newer expansive Chinese child policies in place. Many hospitals have departments speaking different languages and servicing specific nationalities, such as a new hospital recently built purely for Japanese medical tourists, staffed by Japanese medical professionals. Despite the heavy focus on private medical care, the public medical sector is not suffering to the extent one might expect. Doctors working in private hospitals often do so part-time and come from public universities such as Chula, a combination necessary for them to be recognized as the top tier of health professionals. Public employment also seems to reduce the number of trials executed. As many clinics and hospitals do not see the need for trials, doctors are not given much time to act as investigators. In Western countries, doctors may be compensated, and their time spent on research recognized through, for example a 50 per cent split between treatment and research. In Thailand the focus is on routine checks and education, with research being extra. As a consequence, government trials take a long time to finish and most of them rarely do, just as most private clinics only do some trials as there is more money to be won in private clients than trials. For most Thais, however, access to many of these world-class services are far beyond what they will ever achieve, and it is exactly those groups who partake in trials because it may be the only way for them to access novel or advanced drugs.

Thai health care is often lauded for its famous system of universal coverage, especially for most of the population who are put under the '30-baht scheme' ensuring that anyone in theory can access a doctor for less than 2 dollars. The country's coverage system consists of four categories. The 30-baht or Gold Card scheme provides coverage to some 50 million Thais, who can access doctors and very basic treatment, often with no or a low rate of reimbursement on medicines (around 10 per cent as mentioned) that must be paid out-of-pocket. Approximately 10 per cent of the population is covered by the social security scheme for privately employed Thai nationals, another 10 per cent fall under the insurance scheme for military and government officials, and the final 5 per cent of the population have private insurance. Whilst ensuring access, urban–rural divides are significant for the 30-baht scheme, with thousands of patients per health professional in the countryside as opposed to the big cities. And while basic diagnosis may be included, treatments are rarely available under the coverage, instead requiring large co-payments which are affordable to very few.

The reality for most Thais, then, is an inaccessible health care system that may provide a diagnosis after a full day of waiting for a doctor's visit, but where treatment beyond any basic remedy is likely unaffordable. Compared to a system like Korea's 100 per cent reimbursement rate, Thailand only compensates one tenth. Hence the appeal of experimental treatment through global trials. Most trials in Thailand take place in metro areas and in particular in Bangkok, where the population of almost 10 million leaves plenty of opportunity for rapid recruitment. But there are also a large number of trials in central and southern Thailand because of the existence there of major university hospitals. The north-east regions also have a fair share because of their affinity for the dish koi plaa, where small fish caught in rivers are mixed with fresh herbs and eaten raw, creating a population extremely prone to liver cancer because of parasites in the fish, making them an ideal population for all sorts of cancer trials. Some of my interview sources estimated that around 80 per cent of Thai trials fall within oncology today, one of them further elaborating that 'trials in our country now are not just the regular stuff anymore, it's about stem cells, antibodies, CBD and much else'. The last example refers to Thailand's newfound interest in becoming a site for cannabis-related trials and eventual production on its farmlands.

No matter the form of a trial, recruitment is easy in the country through the combined circumstances of lack of access to medicines and treatment, and trust in doctors and the health system. 'Most normal people don't have a choice if they want access to medicines' Phamanan explains, 'and at the same time, they usually get compensated for participating'. Compensation refers to the responsibility that many ethics committees require of sponsors to cover patients' costs. 'One visit normally provides a 'taxi fee' of 1000 bath or around 30 dollars. For those having to travel long, it may not even cover the trip to the clinic (that can include overnight stays), but for those living close by, it can cover three days of work.'[11] From most ethics committees, that responsibility towards patients continues into the domain of providing post-trial treatment, Phamanan explains, where 'ethics committees often ask industry to cover post-trial treatment because there's no way the patients can afford it, but in reality, it is rarely given, even if the drugs are so cheap for the pharmas who produce it for almost nothing. It is about securing the rights of the patients, but unfortunately, it is not the norm', and instead, most trial patients are removed from treatments once the period of their participation is over, with most once again unable to afford the medicine, if it is available at all.

*

The organization of global trials is at all times about negotiating the space between decontextualized standards of experimentation and local circumstance shaping how, when, and where experimental practice takes place. Although often described as a direct transfer of methodological and scientific tools, instructions, and practices, for the sake of seemingly living up to the decontextualized and objective ideals of natural science, trials are not closed packages that simply unfold in the same way no matter where in the world they are conducted. Local cultural, social, or epidemiological differences, as well as organizational ones, significantly shape and translate global ideals in local contexts, even if pharmaceutical companies attempt to design protocols at headquarters level and have these diffuse into local sites of experimentation. One such scientific tool used to strengthen experimental designs is the informed consent we have met many times already. Informed consent is likely to be the most prevalent answer if you ask a medical scientist what makes a trial ethical. The informed consent form, in theory, comes from the sponsor and is approved by an ethics committee, meaning that it cannot always change from its initial shape if the ethics permission is to remain in place. Once signed or agreed to by trial participants, it is kept for showcasing, should the European Commission ever return and ask for it. The form is given to ensure that patients are in control of their participation and that it corresponds with their values and preferences. The global Good Clinical Practices that most investigators are asked to follow specifies that informed consent forms should contain information about the experimental nature of the treatment, the trial's purpose, the probability of random assignment including to placebo, and other information that the investigator finds 'pertinent'. This information may be explained to the potential patient in layman's terms and as 'practically' as possible to make sure that the individual understands the nature of the experiment. But rarely is it sufficient on its own to ensure fair and adequate comprehension of what participation entails.

This idea of informed consent and its current use largely flows from a Western obsession with individual autonomy that we have seen developed not least in American bioethics. The reality of this autonomy of decision-making is obviously much blurrier, no matter whether we are dealing with trials in Western Europe or around the world, or even biometric registration in refugee camps for that matter. The intent may be for a patient to make a voluntary and uncoerced choice of participation, but what does that look like? And how free can a decision be if it is greatly influenced by structural or circumstantial conditions? Wide disparities in education, economic, and social standing, or health care systems may result in a lack of understanding of both the investigative nature of therapeutic products and the use of placebo groups, just as financial compensation for participation may exceed participants' wages and skew the incitement to participate. In many places around the world, patients take advice from family and friends and are influenced by many other factors than their apparent individual motives. But even if the decision is made autonomously, conditions such as poverty and lack of access to health care greatly shape the choice made, not undermining the autonomy of the decision but rather the very ethical nature of the experimental trial. Patients may be given time to explore the document, but if health clinics are far from home, they are more likely to just sign and trust their doctors, eager for a treatment they may not otherwise be able to access. Informed consent is seen by some as necessary in almost all cases, but as sufficient in none,[12] from a perspective that ethics is about ensuring the welfare of the patient throughout the trial and post-trial.

Initially, informed consent was introduced into global regulations governing human trials with the Nuremberg Code that focused on an absence of coercion and favourable risk–benefit ratios following the tragedies of Nazi experimentation in the German and Polish concentration camps. During the Nuremberg trials, Nazi doctors attempted lines of defence that argued for the non-existence of regulations governing medical research on human beings in Germany at that time. While existing rules may have been abandoned during Nazi rule, effectively making this claim true in theory, rules and government expectations about consent had been present in Germany since the turn of the century when the Prussian minister for religious, educational, and medical affairs issued a directive calling on all hospitals to ensure the 'unambiguous consent' of patients before their participation in experimental research.[13] This was followed in 1931 by a set of guidelines for 'new therapy and human experimentation' from the Reich government that included a legal doctrine for informed consent. None of these initiatives came from within the medical profession but were instituted by government following a series of unethical experiments in Germany that drew a large amount of publicity. The events that followed towards the end of that decade both buried and desperately reestablished the need for global regulation on human experimentation.

Following the war, the second of Nuremberg's twelve trials was the Doctor's Trial that saw twenty-three Nazi physicians and administrators accused of human experimentation, medical torture, and mass murder under the guise of euthanasia. On the nature of these experiments, Telford Taylor, principal prosecutor exclaimed:

> the experiments were not only criminal but a scientific failure. It is indeed as
> if a just deity had shrouded the solutions which they attempted to reach with

murderous means. The moral shortcomings of the defendants and the precipitous ease with which they decided to commit murder in quest of 'scientific results', dulled also that scientific hesitancy, that thorough thinking-through, that responsible weighing of every single step which alone can insure scientifically valid results. Even if they had merely been forced to pay as little as two dollars for human experimental subjects, such as American investigators may have to pay for a cat, they might have thought twice before wasting unnecessary numbers, and thought of simpler and better ways to solve their problems. The fact that these investigators had free and unrestricted access to human beings to be experimented upon misled them to the dangerous and fallacious conclusion that the results would thus be better and more quickly obtainable than if they had gone through the labor of preparation, thinking, and meticulous preinvestigation.'

Over the course of 140 days of proceedings, 85 testimonies were given by witnesses and almost 1,500 documents were presented as evidence of the Nazi human experiments. Seven doctors were acquitted, seven received the highest penalty of death, and the remaining nine received prison sentences from ten years to life imprisonment. Out of the trial grew the Nuremberg Code, as a set of internationally defined principles for research ethics. It took a Europe-wide genocide to truly construct an international set of ethics on medical experimentation. While not accepted as law, the code still stands as a cornerstone of modern medical ethics accentuating issues such as: the voluntary, well-informed, understanding consent of the human subject who has full legal capacity, and the need for the experiment to have a positive impact on society with risks being in proportion to the expected humanitarian benefits.

The United States Public Health Service and American authorities in general, however, did not care much for the Code, even if it was inspired by and carried the sturdy stamp of American judges and persecutors in the Nuremberg Trials. And if the Nuremberg Code was not enough, in June 1964 the World Medical Association had endorsed a set of recommendations for conducting human experimentation that has since proved to be perhaps the most influential document on international ethics of clinical research, even if some of its principles are greatly challenged today. In the shadow of World War II and the Nuremberg Trials, physicians from thirtiy-two different national medical organizations met in London in 1946 to discuss the forming of an international association of medical societies, and the World Medical Association (WMA) came into being. With the 'betrayal of medicine by German doctors',[14] WMA greatly concerned itself with questions of ethics, both professional and universal, over its first decade. By 1953, the Royal Netherlands Medical Association asked the WMA's committee on medical ethics to consider the issue of human experimentation, which was also of concern in France, where the French National Academy of Medicine had reviewed features of experiments on human beings.[15] When the committee presented its initial report in October 1954, national differences in the practice of human experimentation became apparent. Austin Smith, an American committee member, objected the suggestion that healthy human subjects be fully informed about experiments they were included in as this would profoundly undermine research in the US. A British and a Danish physician voiced similar concerns. Differences were solved, nonetheless, and the eighth general assembly of WMA endorsed the Resolution on Human Experimentation and the Principles for Those in Research and Experimentation. Discussions continued, often with the Nuremberg Code as the background although no documents made explicit reference to it. When the Draft Code of Ethics on Human Experimentation was presented to WMA delegates in 1962 a major point of dispute was its suggestion to forbid experimentation on institutionalized children and captive subjects; this was especially opposed by the Americans who widely practised such experiments, as we have seen. The chair of the committee on medical ethics on the other hand, British physician Hugh Clegg, held that certain classes of human beings required special protection.[16] Unable to solve the dispute, the 'Ethical Principles guiding Doctors in Clinical Research' became the 'Recommendations guiding doctors in clinical research', with no mention of children or prisoners, and these were ratified by the WMA's Council. The document was given the name 'Declaration of Helsinki'.

Mirroring the Nuremberg Code, the declaration insisted animal and laboratory studies precede human experiments, called for the consent of the subject, and held the right for these to withdraw at any time, just as it was the responsibility of the researcher to discontinue a trial if she could foresee injury to the subject. But it also differed from the Code by distinguishing between therapeutic and non-therapeutic types of experiments and by allowing experimentation on individuals unable to exercise informed consent. An editorial in the *British Medical Journal* in 1963 had warned that a waning of the eventual declaration was underway, spearheaded by the Americans. The unsigned editorial rejected the American argument of profound differences between the experiments of the Nazi Regime and those occurring in American prisons and explained that 'One of the nicest of the American medical scientists I know was heard to say "Criminals in our penitentiaries are fine experimental material—and much cheaper than chimpanzees." I hope the chimpanzees do not come to hear of this.'[17] By 1972, as said, more than 90 per cent of all American investigational drugs were first tested on prison inmates and the experimental research of American doctors was heavily financed by pharmaceutical companies. This meant that not only attempts at public innovation in the form of medical research, such as that by the United States Army, were prevalent, but that companies were allowed to use inmates for their commercial gain. Examples of such include the State Prison of Southern Michigan where Upjohn and Parke-Davis pharmaceutical companies had set up a cooperative drug testing facility for phase 1 studies.

Another side to this story is that the United States Food and Drug Administration's 1966 regulations on granting approval for experimental drugs drew heavily on the Declaration of Helsinki (and also to an extent the Nuremberg Code) and thus cemented its position as the key international document on medical ethics.[18] The new 1966 FDA regulations were not least spurred by the tragic thalidomide case. Thalidomide was a drug sold under a series of trade names, such as Contergan, initially developed and marketed by the German pharmaceutical company Chemie Grünenthal, from 1957 until it was taken off the market in November 1961 following pressure from the press and public. It was prescribed initially as a sedative—importantly, this was a time of general euphoria over pharmaceutical therapies where new popular drugs could quickly gain momentum—and then sold over the counter as a cure against nausea and morning sickness, leading to its widespread use among pregnant women. Not until it had been marketed for some time was it discovered that thalidomide had adverse teratogenic side effects—malformation of the limbs of a foetus while still in the womb (phocomelia is the medical term). The first known victim of thalidomide was the daughter of a Grünenthal employee who was born without ears in 1956. It would still take several years before such cases were connected to the drug. In September 1960, physician Rudolf Wiedemann published a paper documenting twenty-seven cases of infants born with deformities and warned that a contagious epidemic could be the case. At a meeting of the German Pediatric Society in October 1960, physicians Wilhem Kosenow and Rudolf Pfeiffer described two recent cases of malformation. Not until Widukind Lenz decided to investigate the case after having seen similar cases in his practice, were the deformities connected to a drug. Lenz asked mothers about drug use during their pregnancies and soon found his way to Contergan. In November, he phoned Grünenthal's CEO with the evidence, but the drug was not withdrawn until the newsmagazine *Welt am Sonntag* made thalidomide deformities front-page news a few weeks later.

Because of the slow discovery of the relation between thalidomide and phocomelia, 10,000 infants were born with malformed limbs in West Germany and across the world, of whom approximately 50 per cent survived. In most cases, long limbs were not developed and instead took the shape of stumps. Other unknown side effects included peripheral neuritis, damage to the nerves that may impair movement, sensation, or organ function. In the US, thalidomide never made it through the FDA, as inspector Frances Kelsey remained suspicious of incomplete and insufficient data on its safety and effectiveness. Despite pressure from William S. Merrell, the proposed US distributor of the drug (under the name of Kevadon), and from FDA supervisors, Kelsey maintained that the drug was unfit to be set free on the market. This was not least because results from the US clinical trials were not yet available. The clinical trials of thalidomide in the US included the distribution of two and a half million pills to 20,000 patients, at least 207 of whom were pregnant. But trials were not at that point under the oversight of the FDA, and it was not uncommon for doctors involved to lose track of patients. At Grünenthal, thalidomide had been tested on mice and showed extreme low levels of toxicity. No toxic effects were found even at 5,000 milligrams per kilogram of weight in the mice, just as no other tests showed any harmful effects of the drug. Yet, at no point does the drug seem to have been tested on pregnant mice. Not until 2012 did Grünenthal admit their responsibility for the tragic events and provide an apology to the many victims. Until then, they argued that the deformities occurred due to nuclear fallout or botched home abortions. By then thalidomide had actually made an unlikely comeback in the mid-2000s as an effective agent in the treatment of certain inflammatory diseases.

The WMA disputes across the transatlantic have remained, and in 2008 the US FDA stunned parts of the medical world when it publicized a decision to cease compliance with the Declaration of Helsinki for trials outside its borders, dealing a final blow to the declaration they had attempted to weaken for decades. Trials would henceforth only need to live up to the Good Clinical Practices (GCP) that emerged from the International Conference on Harmonisation (ICH), an institution whose voting power rests only with the US, Europe, and Japan as opposed to the WMA's eighty-five medical societies from around the world. The important political differences in what could seem like a technical decision remains that this move essentially bypasses Helsinki regulations concerning limiting placebo studies; requiring public disclosure of trial designs, results, and conflicts of interest; the crucial right for patients to receive post-trial treatment; and for the population on which the drug was tested to benefit from it. Instead of post-trial treatment guarantees, ICH-GCP details that the care to be provided to the control group depends on the population, meaning that what should be matched are just the local conditions. In contexts of limited to no health care, there are thus no obligations for any post-trial care. The importance of post-trial access to treatment, outlined in Helsinki principle 30, is central because the experimental treatment may prove lifesaving and an immediate stop of treatment instead life-threatening. This nonetheless remains the reality in most trials today. Some companies have policies for the availability of the trialled medicine, but it can take years for drugs to make it to the market, and even then, access may be limited because of price levels. Availability has little to do with real-life access, particularly as regards treatment for chronic diseases. The bowel cancer treatment aflibercept, for example, was widely tested in Latin America, but its marketed price is 58 times the monthly minimum wage in Argentina.[19] And availability in countries with low reimbursement rates is continually worsened as the price of medicines continues to increase all over the world. A 2019 study by the Scripps Research Translational Institute found that the costs for popular brand-name drugs doubles every 7–8 years. As an example, the price of Humira, a widely US-prescribed injection to treat rheumatoid arthritis and other conditions, rose from $1,940 in January 2012, to $4,338 by December 2017. In many countries, prices are not regulated nor based on production costs, even if pharmas are good at underlining the massive price tags for medical R&D. In a February 2019 hearing in the US Senate Finance Committee, the CEO and Chairman of Merck, one of the world's largest pharmas admitted that 'the people who can least afford it are paying the most', and that 'we have a system where the poorest and the sickest are subsidizing others'.[20]

The Declaration of Helsinki also includes passages arguing that research on vulnerable groups can only be justified if the trial cannot be conducted among non-vulnerable groups, something that is rarely the case, the justification often being financial from the pharmaceutical side. American regulators then essentially took a leap back in terms of ethical obligations, greatly relaxing the demands on global trials as they decided to bypass the recommendations of the Declaration of Helsinki. At their heart, these discussions concern the schism between ethical universalism and ethical pluralism. Universalism is a strong ideal to ensure that similar regulations govern trials around the world, but if these are increasingly eased to satisfy pharmaceutical industry interests they do little for the safety, fairness, and justice from the perspective of patients. In Thailand, enforcing global standards and regulations speeds up and eases processes of regulatory approval for pharmas, but if the standards followed are those decided by the US FDA, they fail to satisfy Phanaman's claim of a need to protect the interests of the Thai people. Informed consent may be present across all of the fluctuating global regulatory standards, but its presence is only a minimum, not a fulfilment of ethical obligations towards the trial population.

What is more, decisions of informed consent intersect in the organizational conduct of trials with perhaps the most important process in ensuring their successful completion: recruitment. Trial subjects or patients are not just a piece of the puzzle, they are the most central piece, acutely necessary for medical scientists to progress their work and without whom no new drugs could be developed. We have already met the key problems complicating recruitment in the Global North: a massive unwillingness to participate or stay in trials entails that many trials fail to meet their enrolment schedules causing costly time delays; populations characterized by treatment saturation suggest Western bodies are being filled to the brink with medicine; and drug–drug interactions risk ruining trial outcomes because of difficulties isolating variables of effect. To this can be added difficulties of ensuring patients remain compliant with treatment regimens, not least the many professional patients whose financial interest in staying in trials has been found to shape their responses. To give a sense of just how difficult it can be, older numbers document investigators receiving between 7,000 to 13,000 dollars per patient recruited in the US, and that's for Phase III studies where thousands of patients across many, many sites are required.[21]

White males were traditionally the source of medical knowledge from trials, but we have seen efforts towards challenging this ideal and seeking a diversification of subjects for clinical trials in the Global North as well, as research results were wrongly generalized and thought able to treat everyone across age, race, and sex. To avoid deviations in efficacy, something that critically challenges the commercial value of drugs and its potential for FDA or EMA approval, some pharmas are targeting what they call 'hard-to-reach' populations in the US and in Western Europe, but this is proving immensely difficult not least because of historical cases of mistrust in the health care system. What is difficult for some becomes a business opportunity for others to specialize in recruitment and the act of turning living breathing human beings into research material. In the Global North, there has been talk of a science of recruitmentology,[22] simply because of the professionalization of convincing people that they want to be part of clinical trials. CROs are particularly well-positioned to obtain suitable participants and have developed skills in recruitment over the past decade, getting medical researchers the bodies they want. Through local presence and knowledge, including local staff (much like NGOs and their local presence), CROs can gain access to hard-to-reach populations. Adaptive and mobile in changing to new contexts, they may depend on recruitment agencies but also have strong networks to doctors whose networks of patients are themselves wide and provide the CROs with trial material. In the US, the recruitment of minorities and hard-to-reach populations is talked about as a matter of gaining trust and respecting human values.[23] In the Global South, trust varies with the context and plays a far less important role compared to the bare fact of offering experimental treatment representing the only available form of care.

With little to no care available, particularly when it comes to chronic diseases and reimbursement of medicines, the Global South allows for swift recruitment, a diverse patient population, and a much broader array of inclusion and exclusion criteria, meaning it is always possible to adjust the experimental work to benefit the drug being testing. In Thailand, pharmaceuticals talk about keeping patients on treatment regimens for more than ten years at a time, not least spurred on by the strong doctor–patient relations in the country. Elsewhere, this relationship is not needed. In India, so-called OPDs or outdoor patient departments—areas outside of clinical or hospital wards where all patients can come and wait throughout the day hoping to see a doctor—provide lines and lines of patients ready to partake if a trial can grant them access to medicines they would not otherwise be given or be able to afford. These areas are a main reason why there is little need to advertise for trial subjects who are readily available and ready for experimental treatment. The same is true for something like health camps, a widespread sub-Saharan African practice in which clinics and hospitals travel to rural areas, giving patients an opportunity to see doctors for health check-ups, something that may not be feasible in their everyday lives if clinics are far from their homes or are financially inaccessible.[24] Diversifying the patient pool through global trials, of course, does not automatically result in attention being paid to health differences in the design of the experiment, and a pertinent question remains what the primary basis is for deciding which populations to recruit in a study: scientific aims? commercial concerns? Convenience has also shaped recruitment, whether as geographical vicinity, quick, or cheap enrolment. This also concerns the dual role of caregiver and principal investigator common to many doctors who facilitate trials around the world. Conflicts of interest are imminent as the investigator is compensated for recruitment, often obtained by way of the trust between him- or herself and the patients. When a doctor you may have known for years advises you to become part of a trial, the obvious outcome is participation out of trust and respect, putting informed consent and freedom of participation in question. And more importantly here perhaps, it helps to strengthen the feeling that there is no separation of clinical and experimental spaces, consolidating the normalization of experimental practices in everyday life.

*

Global trials emerged in the public imagination at the beginning of the twenty-first century as a posterchild for the troubling effects of medical capitalism and the pharmaceutical industry's insatiable appetite for bodies and profit. And that was replicated in popular media, arts, and culture and in research, from within and outside the medical realm. Over time, the critical exploration of the global biomedical realm has diversified and sophisticated to a point at which not only ethics, but also the medical, social, and organizational production of trials is examined and dissected. Industry still has, by far, the deepest pockets and funds more trials than any other set of institutions today. Even so, public universities and national health institutes continue to play an important role and so too do members of the newer group of non-profits such as the Gates Foundation, Aeras, One World Health, PATH, and more, whose presence and support for global trials can increasingly be felt around the world. Nobody questions the importance of clinical trials essentially used to ensure the safety and efficacy of drugs before these are marketed. And in a reality of experimental treatment or no treatment at all, the schism of access is strong as people are granted medicines that would otherwise not be available for years in their context and perhaps never to them personally. The question remains whether trials help some lucky patients maintain their heads above water in the context of inadequate health care systems or if they help to maintain unequal systems because of (lack of access to) treatment. Even if everyone would prefer to have safe and proven treatment, considering significant inequalities of access to medicines, to care, and to treatment, the difficult issue is whether experimental treatment is better than no treatment whatsoever. Some argue that we are creating a new racialized global under-class, but we are also dealing with poor people who want to obtain access to medicine they otherwise cannot. Who are *we* to deny *them* that? Obviously, it is not as easy as that and one should be careful in equating experimental trial participation with effective treatment. 'If a drug does not cause side effects, it means it doesn't work', an associate director of a Thai medical research institution told me, which of course is not always wholly true. Even if the normalization of experimental drugs has stabilized their use because of lack of access to medicine and treatment, these experimental drugs are still very much that—experimental—and their effects may be both far below what is needed to treat an illness, and far beyond.

If we ask pharmaceutical companies or CROs about the production of global trials, the answer most likely becomes a sanitized or idealized scientifico-organizational one:

> An appropriate question is asked, and a protocol of experiment is developed to satisfy scientific and ethical requirements. Patients are randomly admitted to treatment and control groups. Measurements of effectiveness and toxicity are made, recorded, and analysed sequentially. If the results are satisfactory, a final decision is reached concerning the widespread availability of the new therapeutic agent. The drug may then be released and then monitored for continued effectiveness and for rare manifestations of severe toxicity.

The reality of course is far from such stylized interpretations and sanitizing the clinical trial process by having it abide by scientific and medical rules and norms does not remove its inherent problems of feeding an inequality of access. Trials are not objective and universal. They are heavily shaped by the contexts within which they take place, the investigators and professionals carrying them out essentially functioning not as passive diffusors but as active co-constructors through established scientific practices such as bias-reduction and engineering out of adverse events because of heavy selection bias in recruitment processes. The larger a population of potential patients, the more recruitment can be tailored to fit the needs of the drug being trialled through inclusion and exclusion criteria. This means experiments may be directed to produce the desired effects by containing risks and overdetermining drug value. In the same way as many other forms of knowledge produced by and contributed towards by the experimental movement, clinical trials are not an open field that everyone benefits equally from. There is no global society in which everyone has equal access to medical knowledge or treatment, and publication in Western peer-reviewed journals does not entail an equality of knowledge-sharing or -access, meaning that any attempts from industry to claim general productive effects of trials are inherently miscued. There are no 'fair benefits' when ensuring consent or paying for participation. To obtain fairness, those who bear the risks and burdens of the trials should also be in a position to enjoy its benefits, just as risks ought to be distributed equally.

In theory, Thailand should be ideal because of its universal health care system, but even here there are inequalities and discrepancies between patient groups in terms of resources and access. Trials may address generic questions surrounding chronic diseases that are widespread in the country, but the marketing of any resulting drugs will likely not be done to the population studied. Ethics committees may screen out potentially harmful studies, but they are solely reactive and cannot influence the distribution of trials alongside a broad array of locally relevant diseases. They can only assess individual protocols and experiments. And unlike Thailand, where the phenomenon is yet to occur because of the continuing strong influence of the government, private clinics and health institutions are increasingly creating private ethics committees calling into question transparency and accountability. Many of these do not necessarily report further up in any system, only remaining a theoretical target of monitoring visits that rarely seem to happen (the US FDA for example, visits far less than 1 per cent of all active global trials contained in its registries). Research done in Argentina has shown that over 80 per cent of all trials accepted in the country are authorized by only two ethics committees, both of which are private.[25]

Although Thailand remains both conventional and conservative when it comes to public ethics committees, in all of which pharmas and CROs still pay by cash,[26] the growing privatization of formerly public systems of accountability is only gaining momentum. And like the other actors of this book, the future of global trialling is heavily inspired by movements taking place in Silicon Valley around digital innovation, disruption, and the encroachment of exponential technology deep into people's lives and bodies. 'We need to bring both worlds together [Silicon Valley and pharmas, ed.] so we can learn from one another' is how the broker of PA Consulting frames the future of clinical trials. The ambition is to 'uncomplicate' the experimental practices of the lab by integrating them into existing sites of people's everyday lives—pharmacies, supermarkets, workplaces—allowing for both better and more scaled recruitment, and by having it intersect with technology through the development of personal devices, sensors, or wearables that can facilitate remote or decentralized trials. This development can be driven by new actors in the clinical field: 'large, consumer-oriented companies will be able to bring existing and new offerings to clinical trials', and a company like Amazon 'could leverage their experimental mindset and brand reputation to become the gold standard for delivering investigational drugs'.[27] By moving from paper-based to electronic data collection and towards virtual health tools supported by

mobile technology such as virtual eConsent, 'Clinical research stands to benefit from bolder, large-scale transformation', where 'algorithms can accelerate
initial protocol creation and study design, building data-driven logic into
decisions that today are a mystery to many'. As Josh Rose, VP at IQVIA
explains it, 'Virtual trials are like Uber for investigators.'[28] 'Trials need a
makeover', Julie Dietrich, VP of clinical operation GENFIT Corp. agrees and
in particular one that is informed by Silicon Valley's experimental culture:
'embrace a think big, start small, scale fast mind-set (from start-ups, ed.)'.[29]
Biotech and life sciences companies also increasingly build business strategies
around uniting these two worlds. One example is US-based Schrödinger that
works on computational chemistry, allowing other biotechs to evaluate
compounds *in silico*, able to run through Amazon Web Services and formally
partnering with Google's cloud computing division, leading what it calls a
'digital revolution' that challenges 'traditional methods'.

Clearly, the clinical trial landscape is a moving target. As some emerging
markets see their share of trials grow, pharmas or CROs crowd in and compete
over investigators, who increase their prices. Perhaps regulations become
too bureaucratic because of the growing international attention, leading trials
to gradually move elsewhere. In Europe that means pushing further east beyond
Poland and into Central Asia. This exhaustion phase, as Adriana Petryna has
called it,[30] has yet to make it to most of Asia, Latin America, and Africa. Moving
too, are the three main goals we usually connect to clinical research: an
epistemic goal of bettering whatever the notion of universal medical knowledge
is taken to mean, an ethical goal of increasing the well-being of patients, and a
commercial goal of discovering and forming a commercially viable medical
product that the one instigating the trial may financially benefit from. At all
times changing from one experimental design to the next and from trial to
trial, these are of course idealized but are also an easy tool to remind us of
potential misalignment. Even so, the reduction of trials to matters of abiding
by ethical standards or not does not really address the core of the issue we are
exploring here. Experiments can be done within the confines of what is considered ethical in the pharmaceutical industry and wider medical setting
without necessarily being so in a broader situation of maintaining a system of
unequal access to treatment, legitimizing experimentation as *de facto* stable
practices of care.

Simultaneous medical paternalism—that is, someone else deciding what
treatment is available and for whom—and extraction of biovalue may not even
be unethical according to GCP standards. The response from the medical

professional side, including promises of ending disease, suffering, and vulnerability through scientific progress and technological innovation, is not easily dismissible, even if many of the patients recruited for global trials are at a double disadvantage, both typically belonging to underrepresented groups who may not be able to protect themselves against the irrelevant or harmful effects of trials, just as they do not belong to the target population that may eventually benefit from the new drug. Yet, there is no universalization of social and bodily experiences of patienthood around the world. The medical discourses, power relations, and value production inherent in trials shape behaviour, and experiences of illness differ around the world, as does the pursuit of production of bio-value by corporations. The different forms of experiments addressed in this book have a human, social, or political toll, even if they are done in the name of creating a more equitable global future, offering what appears ato bes a moral vision for progress. The promises of the pharmaceutical industry are to collectively move the world towards the eradication of diseases costing the lives of millions every day. To realize ways of taking away that suffering we need discoveries, and such discovery demands experimentation as the only methodological tool able to identify them. The reality for the industry still remains, however, that some bodies are worth more than others, whether during or after trialling. Pharmaceutical companies are an important example for how the book's actors learn from each other what the science of experimentation looks like, feels like, and how it is implemented, diffused, and defended, the movement altogether contributing to the stabilization of experimental practices, from health care to humanitarian relief to education, as a habitual part of everyday life. Next, we take a step back and travel to the western edges of North America to explore the common denominator that acts as both a techno-material and value-centred glue of the experimental movement: Silicon Valley and its radical dreams of tearing down the old world and its institutions, to witness a new reality rise from its ashes like a digital phoenix.

Notes

1. Interview, Bangkok, February 2020.
2. See https://www.iris.xyz/learn/with-biotech-cash-king.
3. Interview with Senior Statistician, October 2019.
4. DiMasi, J.A., Grabowski, H.G., and Hansen, R.W. 2016. Innovation in the pharmaceutical industry: new estimates of R&D costs, *Journal of Health Economics* 47: 20–33.

5. Petryna, A. 2011. The competitive logic of global clinical trials, *Social Research: An International Quarterly* 78: 3.

6. See https://www.fiercebiotech.com/special-report/2019-s-new-drug-approvals.

7. Berne Declaration. 2013. Clinical Drug Trials in Argentina: Pharmaceutical Companies Exploit Flaws in The Regulatory System. Berne Declaration.

8. Important to note here that not all clinical studies are conducted as RCTs. A large portion are also what is called 'open label' where investigators know what treatments trials subjects are given.

9. See http://scienceinpoland.pap.pl/en/news/news%2C77149%2Cexperts-increase-applications-clinical-trials-drugs-poland-2019.html.

10. Interview, Bangkok, February 2020. Phanaman is not his real name.

11. Interview, Bangkok, February 2020.

12. Emanuel, E.J., Wendler, D., and Grady, C. 2000. What makes clinical research ethical?, *JAMA* 283: 2701–11.

13. Vollmann, J. and Winau, R. 1996. Informed consent in human experimentation before the Nuremberg code, *British Medical Journal* 313: 1445–9.

14. World Medical Association. 1949. War crimes and medicine, *WMA Bulletin* 1: 4.

15. Lederer, S.E. 2004. Research without borders: the origins of the Declaration of Helsinki. In V. Roelcke and G. Maio (eds), *Twentieth Century Ethics of Human Subjects Research: Historical Perspectives on Values, Practices, and Regulations*. Stuttgart, Germany: Franz Steiner Verlag, pp. 199–217.

16. Lederer, 2004.

17. See Pappworth, M. H. 1967. *Human guinea pigs*. Boston, MA: Beacon press.

18. Lederer, 2004.

19. Homedes, N. and Ugalda, A. 2016. Clinical trials in Latin America: implications for the sustainability and safety of pharmaceutical markets and the wellbeing of research subjects, *Salud Colect* 12(3): Jul–Sep.

20. See Caldwell, L.A. 2019. In Senate testimony, pharma executive admits drug prices hit poor the hardest, 26 February. NBC News.

21. Angell, M. 2000. Investigators' responsibilities for human subjects in developing countries, *New England Journal of Medicine* 342: 967–8.

22. Epstein, S. 2007. *Inclusion: The Politics of Difference in Medical Research*. Chicago, IL: University of Chicago Press.

23. Epstein, 2007.

24. Berne Declaration and Sama. 2013. *Exploratory Study on Clinical Trials Conducted by Swiss Pharmaceutical Companies in India: Issues, Concerns and Challenges*. Berne Declaration.

25. Berne Declaration, 2013.

26. Interview with Novo Nordisk senior executive, February 2020.

27. Jakee, K. 2019. Transforming the Clinical Trial to Help Us Live our Best Lives. London: PA Consulting.

28. Miseta, E. 2019. Will virtual trials mean the end of CROs?, 4 November, Clinical Leader.

29. PA Consulting, 2019.

30. Petryna, A. 2009. *When Experiments Travel: Clinical Trials and the Global Search for Human Subjects*. Princeton, NJ: Princeton University Press.

6

The Silicon Valley Way

'There is only one worthy goal for scientific exploration: piercing the tissue that separates life from death.... That is my river. That is my mountain. There I will plant my flag'. So, the scientist Victor Frankenstein frames his grand experimentalist ambitions in Mary Shelley's 1820 novel of the same name. *Frankenstein* is the definitive fictional testament to how over-reaching scientific progress, in which technology appears as the eternal giver of life, can lead to human suffering. But it is also a recognition that such curiosity for reaching and breaking the boundaries of knowledge is an inescapable human condition. Shelley's novel carries the subtitle 'The Modern Prometheus', a nod to the Greek myth of the Titan who is punished by Zeus for stealing the fire of the gods and giving it to humans. Along with his backward brother Epimetheus—whose name means 'afterthought' to Prometheus' own name of 'forethought'—Prometheus is tasked with distributing qualities to man and all living creatures, once the gods have moulded them out of clay and fire. Unwise as he is, Epimetheus distributes all the finite qualities among the animals, leaving man naked and unprotected in a hostile world. To remedy the mistake, Prometheus steals the fire of creative power from Athena and Hephaistos' workshop and passes it on to man, in the shape of a burning stalk of fennel, establishing his renown as an advocate of humanity. Angered by Prometheus' deceit of the gods, Zeus punishes him by having the immortal Titan chained to Mount Caucasus and commanding an eagle to feed on his liver every day, only to have it grow out at night and the torment begin over again in the morning.

The trickery of Prometheus lies both in his ability to challenge Zeus, and equally in his connection to the idea of *mekhane*, using mechanics or machines to trick nature, a tricking of nature that essentially means to progress humankind. The myth of Prometheus then, and its modern form in Frankenstein, accentuates technology not as a neutral set of material objects, but as a power to create; a space of the possible, configuring notions of experimentation, advancement, and future. From Prometheus' fire raged the creation of technology, of industry and progress, and of freedom. But the story of Prometheus is also one of downfall from the eagerness of advancement, a warning of hubris relevant for the techno-scientific experimentality of the actors visited in this book. At the same time, it tells us that technology cannot be thought separate from humankind, and that our confidence in technological progress means we greatly pursue the mastery of or control over nature through technology, to a point where progress creates risk beyond our imagined control.

There are strong connections between the practices and ideas of techno-scientific experimentation in the Global South that we have seen across an array of different actors in the previous chapters, and then a particular part of the US that forms a thought collective more so than a geographic space: Silicon Valley. Increasingly, the dominant and transformative ideas that shape our societies today do not emanate from Washington, Brussels, or Beijing. Instead, they are greatly informed by key actors from Silicon Valley. Whilst politics may have failed to transform humanity, as Franklin Foer has written, the dream is that computers just might.[1] More than a geographical area, Silicon Valley is united by a set of core ideologies and beliefs about society, progress, knowledge, and human life. Despite their obvious differences, the diverse organizations, companies, and institutions explored here are bound together and greatly shaped by these very ideas emerging from the US West Coast across notions of urgency, experimentation and failure, radical change, commercialization, and individualization.

The practices and ideas of Silicon Valley introduce an urgency and a need to move fast; an exasperating tempo of experimentation and intervention in which results have to be achieved today and not tomorrow. It is a mindset in which the patience to let change unfold over time is non-existent, greatly shaping the form and type of efforts undertaken. The synchronous need for experimentation and failure is thought of as an inevitable component of progressing us, the human race, to a higher state of knowing what works and what does not through widespread experimental mantras of 'fail faster, succeed sooner'. In this line of thought, high-risk engagements are crucial and failure a positive outcome as long as the organization may learn from the failure, deducing new experiments or leaving behind those that have proved unsuccessful. It is easy to forget, in the euphoria of testing unproved solutions, that in poor country-contexts, experimentation and failure affect the lives of real people—from one individual to many thousands or more. Experiments are meant to lay the ground for knowledge to facilitate radical change, evoking the former Facebook mantra of 'Move fast and break things'. An immense impatience of transformation—rather than adapting or improving a system—radical change and disruption, whether in technologies or social systems, is about profoundly changing or transforming that system. This is a form of change that may commercialize human life and instrumentalize the body and mind to provide new marketable evidence, data, or other types of information, whether in medical experiments or through biometric registration and monitoring to increase funding and control over certain groups. In this chapter, we examine how we got to this point in time and what fundamental ideas and practices from Silicon Valley we are talking about that have helped to inspire the book's actors and their experimental modus.

*

Governments of the Industrial World, you weary giants of flesh and steel, I come from Cyberspace, the new home of Mind. On behalf of the future, I ask you of the past to leave us alone. You are not welcome among us. You have no sovereignty where we gather.... We will create a civilization of the Mind in Cyberspace. May it be more humane and fairer than the world your governments have made before.[2]

So reads the *Declaration of the Independence of Cyberspace*, as written by the American cyberlibertarian John Perry Barlow in response to the Telecommunications Act of 1996, one of the first US regulatory policies trying to address the forming of the internet. Barlow spoke on behalf of a movement that envisioned the revolution of the internet to produce a more enlightened society, a better and fairer world, in which the peoples of earth shared knowledge, music, thought, and art without the constraints of the physical world or the interference of government. The movement grew from communities of the post-war West Coast of the United States, where counterculture's showdown with traditional industrialized society was at its height from the 1960s and onwards. The new generation felt the social fragmentation in the aftermath of war and had watched as the generation before them lived automated suburban lives of pushing papers and filling filing cabinets. They were hungry for a different emancipation centred around cooperation and collectivism; of being part of holistic systems of the commune and the earth. Psychedelic LSD experiments, strong ideas of self-sufficiency, and imaginaries of technology as tools of liberation brought them to visions of the global village and collectivist conceptions of humankind. Even at the renowned Stanford University, so-called development sessions were kicked into gear by psychedelic drugs, allowing academics and professionals to come together in the hopes of discovering and devising new advanced forms of solidarity and solutions to the world's problems.

These great emancipatory dreams about the future merged into cultural experiments such as the *Whole Earth Catalogue* (WEC), which has been described by Apple's Steve Jobs as the bible of his generation. A popular magazine where articles on self-sufficiency, bio-ecology, and all-around do-it-yourself inventions were mixed with philosophical essays on holistic life and the importance of communion, WEC was perhaps even more about what the tools it presented and discussed enabled, than the tools themselves: 'personal power is developing—power of the individual to conduct his own education, find his own inspiration, shape his own environment, and share his adventure with whoever is interested. Tools that aid this process are sought and promoted by the WHOLE EARTH CATALOGUE'. The government, big business, formal education and the church (as the WEC framed the big adversaries) had failed the young generation, who were now looking to carve out their own future of freedom, driven by a radical individualism in which technology would help set them free and unite them at the same time. The Canadian rock star academic Marshall McLuhan captured the essence of this spirit at the time: 'The computer, in short, promises by technology a Pentecostal condition of universal understanding and unity. The next logical step would seem to be, not to translate, but to bypass languages in favour of a general cosmic consciousness'.[3] This was the mind-set shaping the valley south of San Francisco that has since become known as Silicon Valley.

There was a hunger for freedom and a different life than their parents that the engineers and computer scientists who roamed the local campuses and new technology companies in California shared with the thousands of Vietnam protesters. Contrary to the conservative world of finance on Wall Street in Manhattan, New York, the new Silicon Valley offered an environment of the possible. A milieu that theoretically valued progress, risk, innovations, and outrageous experiments and provided opportunity based on individual skills rather than heritage and family ties. Some came together to build outdoor domes that could facilitate new forms of nomadic living. Others met in societies like The Homebrew Computer Club, where various new technologies were developed. Apple co-founder Steve Wozniak was a key driver of the computer club, where over a thousand members shared and exchanged ideas. When Wozniak developed the first Apple computer with his partner, the later so powerful Steve Jobs, it was here in the club that it was shown for the first time. The *Whole Earth Catalogue* may only have lasted as a publication for four years, but the final words of the last edition, encapsulating the innovative and experimental spirit of its movement, would go on to shape the region to this day: 'Stay hungry, stay foolish'.

The *hungry and foolish region* would not exactly have made a catchy nickname, and instead Silicon Valley was given its characteristic label by a journalist in 1971 after a critical mass of silicon chip producers had settled in Palo Alto, Mountain View, and the surrounding cities. That same year, a company named Intel produced the world's first microprocessor and kick-started a technological revolution, the magnitude of which few foresaw. The first building blocks of what would become the North American innovation hub par excellence were already laid before World War II though. And some will even say they were laid at the beginning of the twentieth century with the invention of the telegraph and the founding of the Federal Telegraph Corporation (FTC) in 1909, which created the world's first global radio communication system. In 1939, Bill Hewlett and David Packard formalized their partnership and flipped a coin to decide the sequencing of their names in the new company. Hewlett won and they went with HP as the company started small in a garage in Palo Alto, where the two young engineers experimented with semiconductors and electronic circuits. Following World War II, more specifically in 1956, American physicist William Shockley moved from New Jersey across the country to his ailing mother and settled in Mountain View, not many miles from the city where HP had started a few decades before. Here he gathered a group of young scientists and PhDs and set in motion work to develop a new generation of semiconductors, leading them to the invention of the transistor in 1956, a central part of what would become the microprocessor and CPU that plays a crucial part in all contemporary computers.

The invention won Shockley the Nobel Prize in Physics, a feat that sent his arrogance through the roof and eventually made a number of his closest employees quit his company over leadership issues. The traitorous eight, as the group of men would be referred to, left Shockley to start their own business under the name of Fairchild Semiconductor. Among this group was Gordon Moore, who would later found Intel and articulate the well-known Moore's law predicting that the number of transistors in an integrated circuit will double every eighteen months. In the years that followed, a large number of technology companies were established in the region—many of which with Shockley's former employees at the forefront, popularizing the name *fairchildren* to describe these new companies—and as we reached the mid-1970s, the area had become well established in the public's imagination as the country's epicentre of innovation and technology. For a number of decades following World War II, the US military and the DoD (Department of Defense) were major investors in Silicon Valley's activities, accelerated by military policies focused on techno-industrial innovation and the growing scientific arms race with the Soviet Union. Large portions of capital would flow to semi-commercial research at local universities, not least Stanford University, whose engineering department had been established during the war by Frederick Terman. The department and the university in its entirety would play a central role in the valley's development as a main provider of ideas and new companies, with Terman known for calling on his students and staff to set up new companies, a line of action that has earned him the title of Silicon Valley godfather in some circles.

Intel's invention of the microprocessor in the early 1970s helped to lure investors and new venture capital firms into Silicon Valley, although Intel itself did not initially realize the potential of their invention and mainly marketed it towards agricultural equipment, elevators, and the like. The customers also changed over time, as computers became smaller, cheaper, and widely used in commercial and personal spaces outside the military. Computer games companies such as Atari were founded and helped to create the first distinct Silicon Valley workplaces, where employees would conduct meetings in hot-tubs, smoke weed at the assembly line, and play computer games when they didn't feel like working. And women were rarely invited inside, laying the foundations for the *Brotopia* and its gender imbalanced chauvinist traditions that still plague Silicon Valley today.[4] The technologies developed shrank in size, had a short lifetime of typically one to two years before a new and up-to-date generation made it to the market, and they demanded greater investments in production if they were to be manufactured at a competitive pace. Apple's IPO at more than $1 billion in 1980 was the final push for venture capital firms, who would now flock to the chip makers and all the other startups. But mounting concerns were also voiced that the growing capital requirements led technology companies towards short-term growth-spurt strategies rather than long-term business models. This concern would turn out to be true, but it would also come to form a fundamental characteristic of the type of business we call startups today. Young companies that do not necessarily base themselves on technological innovation, although they may be located in Silicon Valley, but instead have exponential growth as their ambition. And although many of the new engineers and innovators of the region shared the hunger for freedom with the Vietnam protesters and the wider counterculture that existed in California, the distance between them grew quickly. Whilst freedom meant confronting conventional education and conservative ways of living to the protestors, it meant resistance to unions and government interference, as well as control over income and corporate tax for the technologists. Silicon Valley saw itself as both out of political reach, neither interested in interference by politicians nor in intervening in politics, and as the right revolutionaries through their technological disruption. Gordon Moore himself bleakly established the distance between the groups when he claimed that 'the engineers are the world's true revolutionaries today—not the children with long hair and beards'. Silicon Valley may have been founded on a bed of countercultural yearning for freedom, but it soon turned inconsiderately libertarian.

As we reached the mid-1980s, the rapid pace of growth started to slow down, not least due to declining sales in related industries. The PC market especially was decelerating after years of extreme price competition that saw new personal computers drop in price to only a few hundred dollars, from several thousand just a few years earlier. Some companies in Silicon Valley had to close or release employees whilst waiting for a new recovery. The US had long dominated the semiconductor market, but towards the end of the 1980s, the country's market share fell in favour of a rising Japan that succeeded in simultaneously closing its home market to foreign products and flooding the US market with great volumes of cheap semiconductors at prices well below what Silicon Valley could produce. The concerns reached Washington and the politicians finalized two trade agreements with Japan—so much for the Valley's anti-Washington bias in times where the politicians were not needed—before a new technological development opened a fresh avenue and emerging market: the internet.

*

In 1962, American psychologist and computer scientist J.C.R. Licklider was the first to articulate what he saw as a future Intergalactic Computer Network. In his job as director of the US Department of Defense's Advanced Research Projects Agency or ARPA, Licklider's ideas about the computer as a tool of communication and not just of advanced mathematical calculations led him to the idea of the network. The first real networks, however, were far from intergalactic and mainly had a bureaucratic and practical function. Computers of the time were immensely impractical in size, making it impossible to transport data or information from one place to the next. The solution came to be the construction of a local network between computers, and the US military became the main financer of the ARPANET, the first of its kind, spurred by the Soviet launch of the satellite Sputnik, which suddenly made it theoretically possible to communicate after a nuclear attack. ARPANET was intended for a limited audience, centred as it was around authorities and research institutions that had agreements with the DoD. This meant the search for a network that could embrace a greater public continued. The answer was the new and open network protocol TCP/IP, launched 1 January 1983, seen by many as the internet's real birthday. Still, it was not until the late 1980s that the idea of the World Wide Web and a global information system as we know it today was formed in Switzerland by British scientist Tim Berners-Lee. From there, progress was rapid, and by 1992 more than a million computers were connected to the network, and the first steps towards a web browser could begin.

Alongside the advent of the internet and its diffusion to businesses and people's homes, consumer-friendly electronics saw a surge in sales and development. Technologies became available that everyone could fit in their pocket or at least in their backpack, far from the heavy and cumbersome computers they had known. Apple barely escaped bankruptcy in 1996, and with Steve Jobs returning to the company, it produced the first iMac and roared back into the market. Silicon Valley euphoria regained momentum as we reached the mid-1990s. The internet, in its relatively free and unregulated form, approached a reality, while low interest rates secured large portions of available capital to invest in the new IT companies. Many people got rich in the span of a very short period. At least on paper. The new tech companies cultivated a 'grow big, fast' strategy, which often saw technological innovation fall into the background, replaced by the ability to hype new businesses and capitalize on the investment craze.[5] By 1997, more than a third of US homes were now connected to the Internet, and companies such as Netscape and Yahoo! went public with valuations of billions of dollars. Any company with '.com' in its name (think Pets.com, Webvan.com, or Kozmo.com) was almost guaranteed massive capital injections and soaring valuations, even without necessarily having developed or presented anything that resembled a business model. For young entrepreneurs like Google-founders Sergey Brin and Larry Page, both PhD students at Stanford in the mid-1990s, the tremendous flow of capital seems to have overwhelmed their initial idealistic idea of breaking with the commercialization of search engines. The outlook of massive growth and wealth found in the opportunity to monopolize searches and get the world's businesses to pay for how they would like to be ranked, simply proved too tempting to pass on.

In 1999, several major tech shares rose by more than 1000 per cent, while many traditional shares plummeted as people sold them off to join the dot-com wave. The new tech companies, which for the most part did not make any money, spent all their fresh capital on advertising, expensive launch parties, and large fancy offices. But, by the year 2000, the party ended abruptly after NASDAQ had peaked in March. From then until November 2000, the stock market fell by upwards of 75 per cent. A company like theGlobe.com, a social network of chat rooms and message boards, went public in 1999 and could see its stocks rise by over 600 per cent in a single day, to a price of over $63 per stock. By 2001, the company was taken off the stock exchange, now with a price per share of less than 16 cents. Silicon Valley had been brought to its knees. At least parts of Silicon Valley. Because for many of the companies we know today, the dotcom bubble was just a brief downturn, and perhaps in fact cleared the way to establishing the dominance they currently enjoy. Amazon likely only survived because the company's newly hired conservative Chief Financial Officer argued strenuously for the firm to secure a larger 'cushion' of financial security, if the unstable market was to collapse. Amazon managed to get nearly $700 million from European investors just a month before the bubble burst and NASDAQ collapsed. From here, it would prove virtually impossible for most other companies to attract capital in the immediate aftermath of the crisis, and Amazon's fate might well have followed Pets.com's had they not secured funding just weeks before the bubble burst.

The developments towards the end of the millennium and in the opening of the new can be said to have been the end of the early dreams of community and one world, one people. Silicon Valley's accumulation of businesses, capital, and power has brought with it important changes to dominant ideas and made it a political epicentre, no matter how apolitical it still sees itself. Its contemporary movements, beliefs, and actions are felt at the same time as a sudden earthquake and a slow erosion, when its main actors rethink and challenge everything from how we work, to our social interaction, to the organization of our societies and economies through their disruptive and experimental ways. Silicon Valley remains attached to a freedom-focused political libertarianism that puts the individual at the centre and above all other institutions in society. That implies opposition towards trade unions as well as any kind of regulation or wavering of sovereignty from the individual or the company to government institutions. Community and unity may still be important for a few, but only so long as it does not compromise the individual's ability to maintain full control over one's own life. This is a form of radical idealism that sees the path to peace and growth as a free world where the actions and profits of companies are not bound, just as people should not be. Such idealism also imagines a world where progress is sustained through experimentation, innovation, and technology, based on the narrative that if only people were given access to these services, they would create a positive change in their own lives and for society as a whole.

The legacy of early beliefs in the strength and freedom of the individual rather than of a regulating and controlling state is still evident today, but these thoughts are impossible to disconnect from our knowledge of how this approach is translated into troublesome conditions for low-skilled workers or commercialization of the individual's every digital movement. The radical idealism seems to mainly serve the companies and their shareholders. For those who cannot afford to travel with ride-hailing companies, or who see the cost of their lease skyrocket because the landlord would rather make money on sub-letting to tourists, the state suddenly takes centre stage for the Silicon Valley ideologues. In these situations, they clearly believe in government's responsibility to pick up all the people, that is, those at the bottom, who fail to exploit the advances that their technology companies are otherwise introducing. And while the state is in the process of cleaning up after Silicon Valley, it can appropriately learn from businesses there and adopt more entrepreneur-friendly regulations and tech-inspired execution and policy planning, acting as an agile investor rather than a heavy bureaucracy that constrains people's lives. And, preferably, governments should do this in a way whereby its different branches are in competition with each other, making room for what the new technologists see as 'the outlines of possible new types of dynamic, flexible and adaptive public service'.[6] We only need to look at an area like education, to see a clear set of Silicon Valley ambitions about the need to set the education market free, based on the idea that competition and private investment lead to innovation and better education. But not just any education. Silicon Valley remains a sturdy proponent of vocational education, focused on readying young people (and refugees, as we have seen) with job skills, and preferably those demanded in Silicon Valley. The liberal arts curriculum must be replaced by professional training that enables people to do a job, and education reforms should use digital technology, to allow for long distance and specialized teaching, while state support must be reduced to set the competition free. These arguments interestingly mirror Ronald Reagan's education agenda during his time as governor of California in the late 1960s: 'taxpayers should not subsidize intellectual curiosity', as he famously framed his political project. The purpose of education is rather to prepare young people for the tech business, just as we have seen it in refugee camps, where startups are training people in 'digital skills', mostly reminiscent of factory work.

Whilst not a concept much engaged with in this book, partly because of its elusive and many-sided meanings, Silicon Valley in its purest form appears neoliberal. We do not need clear lines of thought to Reagan to understand that we are dealing with a political ideology borne by free-market fundamentalists, for whom every part of society should ideally be run as a business. Whether it is the education or health care sector, or humanitarian efforts of alleviating poverty, this set of ideas believes that market mechanisms help to introduce greater levels of efficiency, transparency, and ultimately better products and deliverables to citizens. In 1995, just a few years after the invention of the internet, Richard Barbrook and Andy Cameron coined the 'Californian Ideology', as a new political culture driven by extreme individualization and belief in technology's ability to ensure radical advances, built on a foundation of inequality. Ironically, they were both Europeans, and their analysis of the developments that took place in Silicon Valley was not exactly met with affection on the other side of the Atlantic.

The new Silicon Valley is business growth over business ethics, built on a system where companies are more responsible towards their shareholders and investors than towards their employees and the millions of people their companies are impacting. Morality and responsibility are both principles that in theory may constrain experimentation, and which therefore are troublesome concepts for an ideology that furthers the unrestricted actions of commerce. A leaked 2018 internal memo titled 'The ugly', by one of the longest tenured Facebook executives Andrew Bosworth, accentuates that the end justifies the means:

> We connect people. That can be good if they make it positive. Maybe someone finds love....So we connect more people. That can be bad if they make it negative. Maybe it costs a life by exposing someone to bullies. Maybe someone dies in a terrorist attack coordinated on our tools. And still we connect people. The ugly truth is that...anything that allows us to connect more people more often is de facto good. It is perhaps the only area where the metrics do tell the true story as far as we are concerned. That's why all the work we do in growth is justified. All the questionable contact importing practices. All the subtle language that helps people stay searchable by friends. All of the work we do to bring more communication in.... The best products don't win. The ones everyone use win....make no mistake, growth tactics are how we got here.[7]

For workers, the extreme focus on individualization has striking consequences. As founder of the famous startup-school and accelerator Y Combinator Paul Graham has stated, an industry that still has unions has potential energy that can be released by startups. And no one should be able to tell startups how many hours their employees should work: Jack Ma, the founder of Chinese mega online store Alibaba, caused a furore when he publicly formulated his thoughts on the company's 996 system. If you wish to work at Alibaba, you must be ready to work from nine o'clock to nine o'clock, six days a week, that's the gist of the 996 system. Still, as a representative of an industry that pushes its employees over the edge of what is humanly sensible, and where poverty or absence of success is often regarded as a lack of will and drive to sacrifice, Ma's articulation of the need for such a system is not especially surprising and Silicon Valley moguls often repeat the mantra that the ability to start a company is equal for everyone in this world. Silicon Valley represents the art of the possible and an unstoppable pursuit of change, innovation, and growth. Over time, old Valley dreams of freedom, equality, and community have been greatly challenged, if not overridden, by an obsession with growth that seems to have compromised tech companies' ability to understand the impact they have on their employees and on society in a broader sense, whether it is the economy, democracy, or the people living in it. The collectivist utopia and dreams of global progress have been replaced by a competition to accumulate as much capital, power, and market share as possible. The belief that the networked form and connection of the world's peoples would be a democratization of knowledge and life itself has been replaced by the conclusion that digital connectivity today is mainly a means to others' commercial ends.[8] In this contemporary Californian Ideology, we find mirrored the practices and perceptions of experimentation, change, and progress of the actors we have met throughout this book.

*

> We live in an era of great challenges and unprecedented opportunities, institutional failure and inertia, breakthrough innovations and technological change. It's an age of painful endings and hopeful beginnings. It's a time that feels as if something profound is shifting and dying, while something else wants to be born.[9]

So writes a group of authors in 2014 with a definite Promethean vigour reminiscent of Barlow's 1996 Declaration of the Independence of Cyberspace, in the introduction to the book *Labcraft* on the rise and productive power of social innovation labs, the for-profit or non-profit organizations and companies that work as metaphoric laboratories in that they help innovate new technological solutions and products, often targeted towards the Global South. The established institutions have failed us, and the promise lies with innovation and technological change: 'existing institutions are often poorly equipped to respond to the massive challenges and opportunities we face in the 21st century—those that are complex, messy, fast-moving and non-linear'. In his foreword to this social innovation book, founder of Le Laboratoire and Harvard Professor David Edwards directly connects these new labs with Silicon Valley: 'Their approach, indeed their very emergence, parallels the rise (and one hopes, success) of the Internet'. Just as the internet provides a forum for dizzying idea exchange and experimentation, so do these new labs, Edwards writes.

As key brokers between Silicon Valley and development or humanitarian efforts in the Global South, social innovation labs see their response to this uncertain future as the generation of new innovations, pushing forward digital revolutions everywhere. Their work helps to diffuse the ideology of Silicon Valley to donors and organizations working across the spectrum of international development, shaping the very idea of innovation in the Global South with a particular set of ideas about progress. To them, a new world is about to rise in the ashes of the old: 'too many educational, political, cultural and industrial institutions remain fixed to a worldview that is behind us. Thankfully, many leaders are now questioning how their institutions—of all sizes and types—can move to a more contemporary high ground'. Behind the book quoted here is a group of different *labs* from around the world, many of which are prime examples of the crosspollination between Silicon Valley and efforts of development. These labs include inSTEDD who 'design technology to improve health, safety and sustainable development', and inCompass Human-Centered Innovation Lab, a semi-autonomous lab within the international NGO iDE, whose mission is 'to deliver breakthrough solutions for the poor by pioneering and advocating the best practices of human-centered innovation', putting to work a human-centric design (HCD) methodology that 'treat the poor as real customers with a voice'. They bring key practices and ideas of innovation from Silicon Valley into processes of experimenting with and piloting technological solutions, aiming to bring transformation to development challenges. The transformation and lines of inspiration to Silicon Valley also has a very physical-material side to it, for some of these. inCompass describes here how they turned a local house into something more Silicon Valley-savy:

> At inCompass Human-Centered Innovation Lab our initial lab space was an old Cambodian home that was poorly converted into an office with a one-window room and terrible lightning. The daily swarm of mosquitoes that started at 4 p.m. left the team uninspired and wanting to work at nearby coffee shops. We...decided that we needed a physical space close to our partners

and clients.... We knew that we would be putting makeup on a pig, ... we set up homemade movable white-boards around the room and we created an open-concept space with one large homemade white-board table for the team to sit around.[10]

Like the rest of the actors explored in this book, these labs further a heavy focus on experimentation, combined with the materiality of techno-scientific innovation: 'It's vital to experimentation that we introduce some *thing* you can test—something real that can succeed or fail, that can go off the rails, that can have unintended outcomes, that can *break!*', 'what's a laboratory, after all, without experimentation? We don't just use experimentation in order to develop new solutions; it's in our DNA', they argue. And like experimentation, the concept of productive failure, and the mantra of 'fail fast, fail often, and fail early' are deeply embedded in their approach to development work. This is just as it is across Silicon Valley, both in cultural caricatures and in everyday startup life.

ABC is sometimes presented as an abbreviation of 'Always Be Closing', an ironic portrayal of fast-paced salesmen who always seem to be in the midst of closing another deal, talking loudly in their headsets, or rushing through the city with their briefcases, convincingly presented by Alec Baldwin in the movie 'Glengarry Glen Ross' about high pressure in the world of sales, and subsequently making it as an internet meme. In Silicon Valley, ABC is more often used to describe the less fun process of 'assignment for the benefit of creditors', when another insolvent startup assigns its assets, titles, and property to a trustee. Despite the massive success of startups filling up newspaper columns every day, the storage rooms and closets of Silicon Valley history are filled with stories of companies that never made it anywhere. At least 70 per cent of Silicon Valley startups never succeed, some say upwards of 90 per cent, in what has become a trademark failure industry built on the region's heavy preference for experimentation.[11] The famous startup school Y Combinator even refers to itself as 'failure central'. It is this culture of experimentation that development economists and humanitarian actors are increasingly urged to adopt: 'the exploratory and uncertain nature of innovation means that some degree of 'failure' is inherent, as results will often differ from expectations.... [I]n order to increase innovation in the humanitarian sector, organisations and donors will need to become less risk averse and embrace "failing fast" in order to support adaptation and improvement'[12] as authors in a key humanitarian outlet has framed the drive to adopt Silicon Valley ideas and practices.

There are many semantic nuances to this crucial side of the Californian Ideology. Fail fast, fail forward, fail often, the F-word, or 'secret sauce' of Silicon Valley. Pinned to office walls, worn as a proud badge by the serial entrepreneur, repeated everywhere and by everyone, this central guiding ethos speaks directly to the mythology of the American entrepreneurial spirit. Failure is linked to youthful vigour and idealism, something Silicon Valley's white 25-year-old *Brotopia* thrives on, carried by a radical indifference holding there is no such thing as a negative experience.[13] Although often not the case elsewhere, failure is temporary in Silicon Valley in what has been called a collective industrial amnesia, perhaps more reflective of appearances than the psychological toll that a mounting pressure to succeed can have. This culture speaks directly to the breakneck pace of innovation and experimentation in attitudes with mottos of moving fast and breaking things along the way. As an extreme version of trial-and-error practices, the culture of failure conveys conventional lab attitudes of trying out different things to see reactions and consequences, also mirroring the behavioural economic principle of sunk costs. Sunk costs ideas assert that it is better to abandon a project as quickly as possible if it is beginning to derail, taking knowledge and experience from it on to other ventures.[14] In its contemporary form, the mantra stems from innovation and engineering circles, framed by the likes of Jack V. Matson, who in his 1991 book *The Art of Innovation* introduces his concept of intelligent fast failure. Central proponents today include Ryan Babineaux and John Krumboltz, co-creators of the famous Stanford University course 'Fail Fast, Fail Often', who describe the approach like this:

> successful people take action as quickly as possible, even though they may perform badly. Instead of trying to avoid making mistakes and failing, they actively seek opportunities where they can face the limits of their skills and knowledge.... They understand that feeling afraid or underprepared is a sign of being in the space for optimal growth and is all the more reason to press ahead. In contrast, when unsuccessful people feel unprepared or afraid, they interpret it as a sign that it is time to stop, readdress their plans, question their motives, or spend more time preparing and planning.[15]

Central to the philosophy is that you cannot and should not know the effects and consequences of what you are doing before you do it, and that the world, much like the behavioural psychological views of the randomistas, is binary. Either you are experimental, courageous, and (eventually) successful, or you are risk averse, bureaucratic, and unsuccessful.

Failures are idealized and institutionalized in organizational cultures across the actors we have already met. The Gates Foundation had earlier practised the idea of an annual Failfest, in which employees or teams could present their failures at an organizational meeting, in theory celebrating mistakes and lessons learned from them. Similar experiences have made it to social events at bars and other spaces, just as a conference on the matter, Failcon, was instituted in 2009 in San Francisco. The conference ran for four years, before its founder, Cassandra Phillipps, explained in a *New York Times* interview that the 2014 conference had been cancelled because failure talk was now so pervasive among companies.[16] It was 'in the lexicon that you're going to fail'. While cancelled in the US, Phillipps began licensing the conference for a fee to foreign producers, from Brazil to Israel, spreading the message. But productive failures are not for everyone, and there is a multisided privilege to the idea of failure as growth. In the introduction to this section, we heard grand speak of how traditional institutions have failed their promise of bringing improvements to people's lives. But these are not seen as able to revert their failures into success, in the same way that tech-savvy entrepreneurs and startups are, deterministically described as belonging to the past opposite the future promises of new technology. Failure is also a privilege when it comes to personnel. While founders and CEOs may be seen to grow and develop from their experiences with failed companies, failure is certainly not a productive option for the drivers, receptionists, those working in HR or sales, that will carry them onto their next venture with a sensation of progress and growth.

As we heard from the social innovation labs at the beginning of this section, for its proponents, experimentation and innovation in the humanitarian sector present an opportunity to break the 'apparent inertia' of the industry.[17] It 'presents a new pathway to change, free from the political and institutional blockages curtailing other initiatives; creates potential access to new funding and resources, as well as links with dynamic partners in the private sector'.[18] That is why 'at the project level in particular, a myriad of promising innovations is being... tested around the world'.[19] In contrast to the stalled institutions of the humanitarian sector, startups and private sector companies are dynamic and give way for new thinking, funding, and solutions, free from the political constraints of the old world, and mirroring Silicon Valley's articulations of progress. Emergencies are suspensions of normalcy, almost by their very nature calling upon experimentation, the only potential hindrance to progress in fact being the traditional humanitarian actors: 'there is an increasing concern that, despite increased investment in innovation, institutional blockages and perverse incentives in the system present significant challenges to the growth of promising ideas'[20] as some humanitarian actors have articulated it.

*

In 1933, the now world-renowned philosopher Hannah Arendt fled her homeland Germany shortly after a research project on anti-Semitic propaganda led to her arrest, effected by Hermann Göring's recently established Gestapo. Paris, and later New York, became her home until her death in 1975. Not before 1961 did she return to the country where she grew up, this time with a heavy intellectual baggage and a specific task of following the trial of Adolf Eichmann, one of the main architects of the Holocaust. Her objective was to understand what drives human beings to commit such cruel crimes, as had been the case in Nazi Germany. Arendt's conclusion, after meeting and observing Eichmann during his trial, would prove to be both a provocative and persistent thesis in the study of evil and totalitarianism: Eichmann was normal. He was neither perverted nor viciously violent, but rather alarmingly normal, as Arendt accurately described him.[21] The radical evil he was accused of stood in contrast to his almost trivial appearance, although there are discussions of the extent to which this was an act of theatrics for the tribunal. The essence of the evil surrounding Eichmann's persona was not to be found in a form of personal or individual malevolence, Arendt argued, but rather in the way he had assimilated an extreme dehumanizing conformity.

Not that he was innocent, absolutely not. But Eichmann was hypothetically like any other of us. And, as a single case, he spoke to a more general development in our modern society, where automation, anonymity, and bureaucracy leads to a different form of banal evil. When Harry Truman on 6 August 1945 sent out a press release to tell the world of the US nuclear bombing of Hiroshima, his description of the bomb's development and production likewise made the banality of evil clear as crystal: 'Employment during peak construction numbered 125,000 and over 65,000 individuals are even now engaged in operating the plant. Many have worked there for two and a half years. Few know what they have been producing. They see great quantities of material going in and they see nothing coming out of these plants'.[22] Truman's power was not in the small yet exceedingly powerful bomb and its ability to lay cities or countries to waste, but rather in the 'ignorance and incomprehension of its thousands of workers', whose decentralized contributions to a central destructive technology was not necessarily clear to them or interested them enough to explore the actual intentions of their work.[23] A moral blindness facilitated by a combination of bureaucracy, automation, and non-knowledge that figuratively speaks to contemporary discussions about how Silicon Valley and its throng of engineers have led us to a point at which certain technological advances risk having negative effects on democratic and human life, perhaps beyond our comprehension and control.

In a 2016 issue of *Humanitarian Exchange*, a major source of influence and legitimacy among humanitarian actors, a group of humanitarian actors and authors proclaimed that 'this generation of humanitarian actors will be defined by the actions they take in response to the challenges and opportunities of the digital revolution. At this critical moment in the history of humanitarian action, success depends on humanitarians recognising that the use of information communication technologies (ICT) must become a core competency for humanitarian action.'[24] Humanitarian actors will not be defined and judged by the extent, reach, or effectiveness of delivery of their humanitarian support, nor by their work to execute systemwide transformation of the architecture of which they are part. They will be judged by their response to the digital revolution. The old world has proved incapable of delivering on promises made and, in their stead, new powers equipped with a digital arsenal of solutions are needed to deliver progress.

The digital revolution has surely increased the spectrum of action and volumes of data that can be collected and transmitted from disaster-affected areas. Whether in the form of situational awareness through drones, social media monitoring, or mobile phone signal tracking, in addition to traditional forms of humanitarian data collection, such as surveys, camp management, refugee registration, etc. But with these new developments come new vulnerabilities. The dream that constraining social, political, and institutional structures would be replaced by a global community of autonomous individuals, connected by the networks of the new digital age, has proven naïve. Economic growth, technology, and innovation are not sufficient to satisfy the minimum requirements of human lives and may easily exacerbate existing inequalities and construe novel forms. As the classic innovation-scholar Everett Rogers reminds us, 'when a system's structure is already very unequal, it is likely that when an innovation is introduced the consequences will lead to even greater inequality in the form of wider socioeconomic gaps'.[25] Technologies are not dead hardware that only become corrupt through questionable intentions; they may in themselves be deeply political. 'It's just a platform' is a neutrality myth in Silicon Valley accentuating a dangerous belief that technologies are equally available and beneficial to everyone; that the platform and its construction does not in itself hold any inherent inequalities.

Twenty-five years ago, as the Internet was still taking shape and Silicon Valley was in the process of maturing some of the values and characteristics on which it is built today, Barbrook and Cameron dissected the intrinsic exploitation of the Californian Ideology: 'The deprived only participate in the information age by providing cheap non-unionised labour for the unhealthy factories of the Silicon Valley chip manufacturers', and 'this utopian fantasy of the West Coast depends upon its blindness towards—and dependence on—the social and racial polarisation of the society from which it was born'.[26] Today, we can look back and appreciate that this trend was only beginning to take shape during the mid-1990s, and that even if we have substituted chip manufacturers with the new digital kings of social media and AI, distortions seem to be growing. From the thousands of low-paid ride-hailing drivers in the US, to social media moderators in the Philippines and Hong Kong hired to witness the darkest sides of human nature as they sort beheadings from child pornography, to automated bare-life AI workers in Chinese factories or refugees in camps tasked only with tagging pictures of cows and boats, the new digital rulers are creating a global precariat of temporary workers.[27] The technologies that were thought to liberate and give us power over our own lives, evident in the sociotechnical dreams of J.C.R. Licklider who perceived automation as a social good and imagined a 'man-computer symbiosis', have yet to bring emancipation to the Global South, and its experimental aftermath seems to constrain rather than set us free in the West. New technology and science provide spaces of possibility for humanitarian and development actors, but it is at all times a choice as to how one interprets and uses that space, with technology always being an expression of many other interests than the material technology itself. It is not least a fascination of the unprecedented; how that which we do know not, and perhaps do not understand fully, pushes the boundaries of experimental methodologies. Every technological innovation 'has unforeseen effects and consequences while also reconfiguring the parameters of human existence',[28] not least entailing that the relationships of startup founders, or project workers in innovation labs, to technology, fundamentally reconfigures ethical and moral sensibilities.

The practices of experimentation that we have seen throughout this book mirror the approach to innovation that we see from Silicon Valley. Despite Bill Gates' famous words that Silicon Valley was built completely without the intervening hand of the government, history tells a very different story in which state subsidies and massive public investment, not least by the US military, were fundamental to the innovations that made Silicon Valley what it is today. From the computer—IBM essentially built the first digital computer because of a government request during the Korean War—to the internet, central technological innovations were spurred by public funding. The GPS, perhaps the core driver of software platforms for many startups, was not only developed with core funding from the US government, but it is also basically free for all to use today (including for commercial purposes) because states have a clear-cut interest in maintaining it through their own satellites.

Technology and democracy, just like science and democracy, are not opposites, and may in fact greatly invigorate each other. This co-constructive association cannot be taken as given however, and there is a need to ask what the relationships are between democracy, participation, and the practices of technological innovation and experimentation. It is extremely difficult, if not impossible, to balance equality and innovation within capitalism.[29] If we consider democracy in the context of technological interventionism as we have seen throughout this book, at the very least as some form of participation and access, then equality comes to mean something more specific as forms of access to and control over technology. The form of technological innovation and experimentation told of here may, at a rudimentary level, be seen as bypassing democratic institutions because of either the direct intervention of many of these organizations in developing countries or their outright dismissal of these. This makes other forms of governance of technologies the centre of attention, fundamental to which is consent: the power to give or withhold consent helps to define participation. During the processes of technological experimentation we have seen, the inequality of innovation means the intended beneficiaries are often *de facto* unable to exercise influence any other way than *ex post*. They rarely have access to or are heeded during the initial design processes when technologies are developed; such processes mainly involve the funders and the companies tasked with innovating a new product or technology. Since they are not directly involved in the processes of innovation, and nor in decisions about having these technologies intervene in their communities, they may only react to how the technologies shape their lives as the consequences unfold. And participation not only refers to the design or innovation processes themselves but also the outlook of determining whether technology should be considered at all as an answer to the problems encountered in their lives and their communities.

Processes of innovation and differences between technologies relate further to ideas of expertness. A discrepancy can be seen between a group of western scientists building a new toilet for the Gates Foundation, to great complement from its surroundings, and the local Indian populace who refused to use this modern technology This discrepancy may be explained with the assumption that innovations in the form of artefacts are flexibly interpretable (i.e. employing a social constructivist view on technology), and that different social groups will relate differently to the same piece of technology. This essentially means that a technology developed in isolation from those that are supposed to benefit from it cannot be expected to wield predictable outcomes. In this case, we are not only dealing with forms of social construction. There is a difference in material circumstance as much as in social practice when we consider the providing and receiving ends of technology in the Global South. Furthermore, as expertness is a negotiated attribute,[30] everyone may simultaneously be considered an expert and a layperson in different ways. While a negotiated attribute, the asymmetries in knowledge and comprehension of technology between experts and non-experts is a significant issue for the democratic uses of technology in the Global South.[31] Interestingly, as shown earlier, subject expertise is often considered unnecessary or even a hindrance in forms of 'social innovation' and experimentation. Such disruption from the established order of things and thinking can be very effective but casting away prior knowledge or experience is seldom a good way to come up with effective solutions. Too often, Western non-experts are considered a resource for innovation while citizen-involvement in the Global South provides little but an artificial form of legitimacy in an attempt to appear democratic. In the end, this difference in level of expertise acts as both a motor of inequality and a key facilitator of experimentation because of the many unknowns it hides away.

Individuals in the Global South, as everywhere, are not just users of technological tools, engaging with these in terms of distance whereby one can continually attach and detach oneself from a technology. All humans are technological beings, whose very human nature is shaped by it. Humans have not developed into being able to use technological tools but rather developed co-constitutively with and through them.[32] We should not oppose humanity to a technological other, but rather try to understand the effects of technology on the ideas and practices that are pervasive in the fields engaged here. Whether the unaccountable power of top-down innovation or technological determinism, such efforts are about making visible the invisible effects of technology. The ideology of experimentation and technological innovation is centred around disrupting societies and institutions, tearing down the old world, to see a new order and new humanity born. Our inheritance of Promethean foresight metaphorically means we are guided by the Titan's outlook but also by its blindness, the consequences of our actions only revealed by his brother—hindsight.[33] Such forces of pursuing the unknown may be both productive and necessary, but they also tend to include inequality in terms of the willingness to accept being exposed to technological innovations. I can choose to delete my social media accounts, although my data may already have been sold to third-party companies and therefore, in a sense, remain everlasting, but refugees who are required to give up their material and digital identification in order to receive food aid do not have the same option to decline. That is the inequality of exposure. Development is about confronting imbalances, yet technological experimentation and solutionism may risk supporting rather than countering such. There are no inevitable expressions of technoscientific experimentation, no one way to develop and employ technology or experiments. Rather, there will always be multiple futures and logics of action available, not all of which put people at risk by exposing them to new vulnerabilities.

Notes

1. Foer, F. 2017. *World Without Mind*. London: Penguin Press.
2. See https://www.eff.org/cyberspace-independence.
3. Antecol, M. 1997. Understanding McLuhan: television and the creation of the global village, *ETC: A Review of General Semantics* 54(4): 454–73.
4. Chang, E. 2019. *Brotopia: Breaking up the Boy's Club of Silicon Valley*. London: Portfolio/Penguin.
5. Goodnight, G.T. and Green, S. 2010. Rhetoric, risk, and markets: the dot-com bubble, *Quarterly Journal of Speech* 96(2): 115–40.
6. Schroeder, A. and Meier, P. 2016. Automation for the people: opportunities and challenges of humanitarian robotics, *Humanitarian Exchange* 66, April.
7. See BBC, 2018. Facebook 'ugly truth' growth memo haunts firm, 30 March.
8. Zuboff, S. 2019. *The Age of Surveillance Capitalism*. New York: PublicAffairs.
9. Tiesinga, H. and Berkhout, R. (eds). 2014. *Labcraft: How Innovation Labs Cultivate Change through Experimentation and Collaboration*. P. 14. London: Labcraft Publishing.
10. Tiesinga and Berkhout, 2014.
11. Griffith, E. 2014. Why startups fail, according to their founders, *Forbes* 25 September 2015.
12. Obrecht, A. 2016. Separating the 'good' failure from the 'bad': three success criteria for innovation, Humanitarian Exchange 66: April.
13. Chang, 2018.
14. Draper, N. 2017. Fail fast: The value of studying unsuccessful technology companies, *Media Industries* 4(1).
15. Babineaux, R. and Krumboltz, J. 2013. *Fail fast, fail often*. London: Penguin.
16. Martin, C. 2014. Wearing your failures on your sleeve, *New York Times* 8 November 8.
17. Scriven, K. 2016. Humanitarian innovation and the art of the possible, *Humanitarian Exchange* 66: April.
18. Scriven, 2016.
19. Scriven, 2016.
20. Scriven, 2016.
21. Arendt, H. 1963. *Eichmann in Jerusalem: A Report on the Banality of Evil*. New York: Viking Press; see also Stangneth, B. and Martin, R. 2014. *Eichmann before Jerusalem: The Unexamined Life of a Mass Murderer*. New York: Alfred A. Knopf.
22. Müller, C. J. 2016. *Prometheanism*. Lanham, MD: Rowman & Littlefield: 138.
23. Müller, 2016.
24. Raymond, N. and Harrity, C. 2016. Addressing the 'doctrine gap': professionalising the use of Information Communication Technologies in humanitarian action, *Humanitarian Exchange* 66: April.

25. Rogers, E. 1995. *Diffusion of Innovations*. 4th ed. Cambridge: The Free Press, 436.

26. Barbrook, R. and Cameron, A. 1996. The Californian ideology, *Science as Culture* 6(1): 44–72.

27. See Gray, M. and Suri, S. 2019. *Ghost Work*. Boston, MA; New York: Houghton Mifflin Harcourt.

28. Müller, 2016.

29. Papaioannou, T. 2011. Technological innovation, global justice and politics of development, *Progress in Development Studies* 4: 321–38.

30. Bijker, W. E. 1999. Towards politicization of technological culture: constructivist STS studies and democracy. In H. Ansal and D. Çalişir (eds), *Science, Technology and Society: International Symposium*. Istanbul, Turkey: Istanbul Technical University, 37–47.

31. see Hamlett, P.W. 2003. Technology theory and deliberative democracy, *Science, Technology, & Human Values* 28(1): 112–40.

32. As Christopher Müller deduces from André Leroy-Gurhan's paleoanthropological work, see Müller, 2016.

33. Müller, 2016, 117.

7

Experimental Futures

Balram Kumar was a maintenance worker on mobile phone towers in the state of Gujarat, employed almost 2,000 kilometres from his hometown in Bihar's Khagadia district across the country. When Indian Prime minister Narendra Modi appeared on national television on 24 March 2020, to confirm a 21-day lockdown due to rising cases of Covid-19—'there will be a total ban of coming out of your homes' he commanded—Kumar was far from anything he would call home. Incited by his family, Kumar began making the long trip home on foot. After 400 kilometres he, a friend, and several others were helped by police onto the roof of a lorry for the next stretch. But in Rajasthan the driver lost control, ramming the vehicle into a tree, and killing Kumar and his friend, none of whom made it back to their families. With the lockdown, put in effect after only a four-hour notice, India saw a mass exodus out of all major cities where more than 100 million rural migrants live and work. With lockdown enforced, they had nowhere to stay and nothing to earn, sending millions on strenuous journeys on foot towards their home villages. The textile and diamond city of Surat, in the state of Gurajat where Kumar also worked, saw protests, riots, and massive frustration with its more than 7 million daily wageworkers left in a precarious state as many factories closed, most because of government directives but many also because northern multinationals had cancelled their orders. Most of the workers had food rations for one or two days and little outlook of improving their situation, but were not allowed by authorities to go anywhere.[1] Laying bare the harsh realities of modern mobility and its politics, some were forced to go, and some were forced to stay, both groups facing an arduous future as they did so.

At the height of the Covid-19 crisis, one third of the world's population or more than 2.5 billion people around the world found themselves in some kind of lockdown, with Indian government actions among the strictest, attempting to keep its 1.3 billion population under control. To some, the apparent willingness of citizens to follow directions created an image of a strong social contract where *Pater Patriae*-like politicians steered the public onwards through the crisis, defying Thatcherian claims that 'there is no such thing as society'. To others, lockdowns were seen as strongman enforcements causing psychological stress, spikes in violence against women, and a catastrophic loss of income for hundreds of millions. Whilst the direct health effects of the crisis have been catastrophic, the associated preventive measures put in place are just as tragic in their effects: victims of gendered violence being locked up with their perpetrators, closed borders stalling migrants in precarious situations, and Western hoarding of supplies and nationalism disrupting supply chains and vaccine access for many developing countries. The humanitarian needs to counter the detrimental effects of Covid-19 took priority as the early stages of the pandemic raged. It was quickly estimated that as many as 6,000 children could die each day and 270 million people face starvation by the end of 2020, almost doubling the number of people suffering from acute food insecurity, while the UN's Population Fund expected an additional 31 million cases of gender-based violence. In March of 2020, the UN launched a $2 billion coordinated global humanitarian response plan, which quickly grew to a $7 billion appeal and again in July to a $10 billion appeal as the needs surged. It would take only a single per cent of the entire stimulus package that European countries gifted themselves to secure their economies during the pandemic to address the global humanitarian consequences of Covid-19. But Western countries were far too focused on minding their own business.

Among otherwise precautious European countries, Sweden quickly assumed a different liberal position that saw bars, restaurants, workplaces, and most schools open; people not confined with gatherings in the hundreds allowed; and business continuing more or less as usual. National epidemiologists publicly denied pursuing an explicit strategy of creating herd immunity but did acknowledge their strategy to be in close vicinity to such. After a slow start, the death toll started to skyrocket, with the country at one point having the highest number of deaths per capita in Europe, and many times that of neighbouring countries. Despite the political direction being outlined by epidemiologists from the national health institute, more than a thousand other Swedish scientists, including numerous medical and epidemiological professionals, signed a petition urging the government to change course. If ever an illustration was needed of the plural and political nature of the science that some—including several of the actors in this book—find to rest in singular and nature-given conclusions about the world, epidemiologists screaming at each other from separate corners was it. 'I didn't sign my informed consent for this experiment', virologist Cecilia Söderberg-Nauclér of the Karolinska Institute, a medical research centre near Stockholm, told news media.[2] But her reaction does not mean that other courses of action were necessarily any less experimental, despite their attempts to produce an appearance of control and confidence. In Denmark, the careful and conservative neighbour to experimental Sweden, the initial lockdown was announced by Prime Minister Mette Frederiksen on national television with an almost stoic calmness. Flanking her was epidemiologist and head of the national research institute for infectious diseases Kaare Moelbak, who explained that 'the decision made by the government is founded on a mathematical model. There is no guesswork in this'. In other words, the decision taken by the government to enforce a lockdown was in fact not political, it was technical, provided by a model. The model Moelbak referred to was developed by an expert group at his institute and could seemingly be fed with various policy proposals on the reopening of society, and then respond with the infectious effect the measures would have. A kind of tangible anti-politics or post-choice machine made to evaluate policy proposals for their effect in 'reality', thought to take any experimental features out of political responses to Covid-19.

Despite scientific attempts to construct narratives of certainty, the response to the Covid-19 crisis in reality forms the greatest social, political, and economic experiment witnessed in our lifetime. An experiment of reimagining work for those fortunate enough to normally have an office to work from. For many precariously hired, vulnerable, or gig workers, the reality was rather unemployment and loss of livelihood, with none of the benefits or insurance people receive in well-off countries. With the current way social media is monitored and governed, the changes to work also entailed a global experiment of machines policing speech and content online. Platforms and social media were tested as content reviewers and moderators were forced to abandon work and companies increasingly relied on algorithms for sorting and moderating,[3] not exactly an ideal situation given our knowledge of their inherent gender and racial biases. And we know very well that misinformation is much more prevalent in non-English contexts[4] and has far worse consequences in the Global South. It was also an experiment of social order and control with massive trials of surveillance, not least through contact tracing technologies, in the name of progress and survival. A set of 'breaching experiments' were enabled, as Garfinkel coined his attempts to disrupt social orders so as to study social rules and norms, across both democratic and authoritarian states. And the states of emergency allowed scientists to speed up experimental processes to an immense pace, *inter alia* bypassing conventional phases of drug discovery. Ken Duncan, head of the Gates Foundation's Discovery & Translational Sciences team's drug discovery efforts, framed the pursuit of a Covid-19 vaccine this way: 'unlike the normal timeline of drug discovery, which typically takes at least two years from discovery to testing in patients—in this case, we could be into human testing within a few weeks'.

The Covid-19 crisis has seen a noticeable demonstration of politics as scientific instrumentation, at least in its communicated form, and how mathematics and statistics can control countries and billions of people's actions based on an assumed mathematical purity of complex models, seemingly hiding away the experimental qualities of the interventions. Humans are subjective and political, while numbers and machines provide objective truths, according to the logic we have met many times throughout the chapters of this book. The models produced, such as the Danish literal anti-politics machine, are of course that—models—and as such only attempts to turn reality into a controlled system. One isolated reality cannot include the sea of factors and consequences of crisis measures and restrictions that eventually come into play, whether exacerbating existing inequalities, leaving millions to starvation around the world, causing explosions in suicide rates and violence against women in particular, or keeping people from health checks for other serious illnesses such as cancer. The trust in models as we have seen it unfold is a predictable response to uncertainty and ignorance, reaching as we always will be for whatever is able to expand our opportunities to understand what is going on. This applies to both mathematical models and our own conceptions of reality.

This book has demonstrated how emergencies and states of exceptionalism in equal parts justify and incite practices of experimentation. The response to the Covid-19 crisis has formed a striking social experiment across the world, intersecting many different domains of life, from health, relationships, or family to work and livelihoods, just as the exceptionalism it has made way for has entailed an astounding number of experiments being conducted in real time. Whilst the whole-planet nature of Covid-19 stresses the connectedness of globalized human life, the stark reality of the crisis and its response is also a retreat to national isolationism, xenophobia, and exacerbated inequalities. Despite the uncertainty of addressing the pandemic and its unexpected mutations and patterns, there are really no surprises in its strikingly unequal effects: every society produces its own vulnerabilities, as societies always have throughout history. In this case, there are no universal effects of the experimental efforts taken to address Covid-19. Staying safely at home is a privilege, with lockdowns favouring those who can easily afford food for their families, transfer their work home, or use their skills to educate their children. As such, the pandemic has exposed both the fractures within contemporary society and the inherent inequality flowing through experimental practice that I have tried to expose here. The commercial pharmaceutical responses to the pandemic do the same, mirroring the reality of this book: the Maryland-based biotech company Novavax was awarded $15 million in August 2020 to conduct a phase 2b study of their promising Covid-19 vaccine 'NVX-CoV2373'. Although the funding came as a charitable grant from the Gates Foundation, and the US-controlled clinical trial was conducted in southern Africa, the UK government had bought the rights to the first 60 million doses of the vaccine. Beyond the scope of this book, it is difficult to escape the feeling that the failure of politicians, governments, and their citizens—all of us—to address global challenges of climate, inequality, or health is catapulting us into a new age of experimentation, with the outlook that follows being of equal parts uncertainty and inequality.

*

Economists should be more like plumbers, laying the pipes and fixing the leaks. At the 2017 Ely Lecture of the American Economics Association's annual meeting, Esther Duflo presented her initial thoughts on economics as plumbing, an argument that would come to be the foundation of her 2019 book co-authored with Abhijit Banerjee, *Good Economics for Hard Times*. Their argument runs that the broad principles upon which many international institutions and much effort in global development are based—be they democracy, human rights, or good governance—are of little value because they are too general, too vague. Instead, these institutions, and the economists advising them, should adopt the ways of the plumber—focusing on micro-issues and being guided by intuition, experimentation, and guesswork. And for most taps and pipes, she argued, plumbing issues are the same more or less everywhere, creating a universalization of economic knowledge and solutions. Einstein too is famous for voicing that if he had his life to live over again, he'd be a plumber. Not out of dissatisfaction with his life of science, but rather because of the immense implications his work on energy and mass had on the creation of the nuclear bomb, humankind's most destructive technology. The kind of plumbing presently argued for by Duflo, however, is not about minimizing one's impact on the world, as Einstein sometimes would have wished, but rather *vice versa* it is about maximizing that very impact. And about how experimentation plays a key role in such efforts to shape policy and practice around the world.

We have tried to engage here the global terrain of politics constituted through experimentation, exploring the global assemblage of knowledge, people, and instruments that encapsulate a movement bound together by its mindset and practices of experimentation. It is a movement of powerful actors—some in the business of doing good, some just in business—that collectively contribute to the routinization of experimentation, whether in refugee camps, in global health, education or elsewhere. As a scientific project that fundamentally forms a social, political, or moral project as well, staking out as it does tangible imagined futures, the movement sometimes carries a relativism of intervention, arguing or exhibiting that different rules, norms, and values apply across disparate geographies. But also holds little relativism or pluralism when it comes to questions about science and evidence—those very important matters of who can and should inform policy and thus set out future pathways for society. For the hardcore proponents of experiments and especially the randomized controlled trials, there is no outlook of science as a process of cumulative understanding. Either you generate your knowledge from RCTs, or that which you produce has no legitimacy and basis in reality. If anything, this book has laid bare some of the interlinkages between the different actors of the movement to show that these are deeply entangled—funding each other, supporting each other's political claims, and ensuring that what they have in common rises to the top: experimentalism. The legitimacy of each of the actors in the movement also greatly depends upon the others, staging a recognition through collaborations, financial or other forms of resource support. When three individuals from the movement receive the Nobel Prize in Economics, it not only recognizes their individual contributions and positions in the field—it serves as a legitimation of literally all that they touch professionally, including others who employ their methods and promote their worldviews.

Leading the way on the scientific front, the randomistas have proved immensely skilful in converting scientific and technical authority into political and moral authority.[5] They should rightfully be lauded for the mainstream attention they have brought to issues that far too easily fall outside the realm of interest for most Westerners, Western institutions, and media that do not feel a strong actuality around education or water supply or health in the Global South. Still, the methodologically monopolist and disconcerting conception that exactly their—and only their—ways of doing and thinking science fall outside the realm of morals and politics makes them prone to criticism. Ideals of an objective expert-advised democracy are laudable, but the problem remains that what is constituted by 'expert' is too often interpreted to be only themselves. As Keynes wrote in 1931, 'If economists could manage to get themselves thought of as a humble, competent people, on a level with dentists, that would be splendid!'. At the same time, launching a singular critique of the randomistas is almost too obvious and is regularly done. What I have tried to show is how these form part of a larger movement that extends far beyond economics. Although economists may try to limit discussions of RCTs to the economic realm, the implications, power, and costs of these can only be properly understood if viewed through a broader socio-political lens.

Economists in the randomista movement tend to work from a place of privilege, as the design and purpose of their trials often lays bare, sometimes creating the unfortunate image of a strongly elitist form of science. The role and impact of technology can sometimes appear predacious too, particularly in the humanitarian contexts we have visited here. For all its ambitions of bringing us together, emerging technology appears to be tearing us apart through our own false perceptions of control. The experimental introduction of new human–technology configurations—whether we see them unfolding in refugee camps or in health clinics—cause impacts which we only begin to understand as they unfold before our eyes, undermining any sense of control over the experiments. And there is no lack of calls to 'bring more developing states into hands-on experimentation', inciting development actors 'to throw themselves into the discussion and into hands-on experimentation, and fast'.[6] The abstract governing of technological risks to mitigate the potential negative consequences of experimentation—that we often talk about as if it is even a set of actions within our sphere of control and influence—is largely nonexistent, with actors roaming free as they see fit. If anything, such imagined control or governing becomes fragmented to a point where we still have no influence over the larger directions of change. Instrumental views on technology give humans a ready ability to control technology, a falsely comforting sensation that we master and determine technology, not the other way around. Yet we can never understand our relationship to technology if we only consider its technological aspect. A clock is not only the mechanical parts that make its hands move—it is the organization of time in human society, modern bureaucratization and labour, the biology of our bodies, the stress of not being able to sleep, the long wait before a defining event. It is a means to an end. We must be careful not to neglect the normative property of direction, when talking technology and experimentation—and always ask to what ends innovation is pursued, and based on what ontologies.

Becoming increasingly datafied through new technological forms means becoming vulnerable to extraction just as it renders us increasingly governable through the way digital infrastructures instrumentalize data, turning it into deeply politicized knowledge. The constitutive relationship between humans, technology, and politics is crystal clear in the employment we have seen throughout the book of what can be called technologies of hubris. When a UN organization provides registered migrants on Greek islands with prepaid debit cards that only work in a limited radius of the camps where the refugees have been placed, financial technologies suddenly function as ones of control. This control risks disciplining and retaining migrants, beyond whatever humanitarian drives the technologies may immediately have had. Despite serving a stated ambition of granting migrants autonomy, the cards operationalize a purpose of shrinking their mobility and independence, keeping them not only in a country but in an enclosed and constrained space.[7] If this book stresses anything on the nature of the generation and use of data, it is that data does not fall from the sky. Extracting, producing, and otherwise obtaining data is a laborious and political exercise. And it is one characterized fundamentally by inequality in the relation between technology and society, whether in terms of who extracts the data and from whom it is extracted, who is able to produce, understand, or instrumentalize it, or in who the extraction benefits.

The difference between the 'success' of the Manhattan Project and the 'failure' of the Green Revolution, as examples, can be said basically to have been the interaction between technology and society. The atomic bomb *simply* had to be able to detonate and entail massive suffering for it to be a theoretical success.[8] The Green Revolution had not only to develop new high-yielding seed varieties (which it succeeded in), it also had to make sure that its innovations benefited people living in poverty and brought food security to them (which we are not sure it did). There is no separation of technological innovation and experimentation from the people and communities (i.e. society) in which such are implemented and the politics of what kind of change they allow for or direct us towards. And technological risks and uncertainties, in the same way as those of any kind, have a simultaneous localized and delocalized nature. When we attempt to manage or mitigate risks, we often do so through generalized systems of knowledge and operation, or we speak of the uninsurability or unpredictability of modern hazards. Yet once they occur, they do so in extremely localized form, with real consequences for real people. Risks, uncertainty, and ignorance are not abstract notions floating around in outer space as *force majeures* that effect everyone in equal ways. As Covid-19 vividly shows, emergencies have very real repercussions and often also a pronounced difference in how they affect people and groups, commonly along lines of inequality, whether in terms of income, access, or geography.

I have only scratched the surface of the movement's machinery of knowledge production and diffusion. Even so, the deeply political nature not just of experiments themselves, but of the belief systems they carry with them— about science, technology, truth, politics, and social change—come into view. We must look past the scientific face of the experimental movement and see exactly what it does, what values it furthers, and what vulnerabilities and inequalities it may risk creating or retaining through its forms of knowledge-in-action or rather action-through-knowledge. In short, what social and political orders their imaginaries produce, or how they set out *desirable* end states and clearly define the forms of progress needed to take us there, the pursuit of which depends heavily on experimentation. And although they relate to and imagine the future, they are fundamentally about structuring the present— about who should inform policies or about who should benefit from policy shaped by different inequalities, hierarchies, and privileges.

Hierarchical sensitivities are not least intrinsically built into the experimental movement's view to science. The randomistas' almost monopolist imperatives of scientific and policy truth imply little pluralism with little interest in a diversity of knowledges—it is 'our way or the highway'. This methodological totalization means there are few dialogical efforts and little room for a multitude of methodologies. On the contrary, many would likely argue—myself included—that evidence possesses multiple meanings with no one right or pre-given way to obtain or interpret knowledge, providing room for a humility of scientific doubt, recognizing the responsibility of society in doubting, questioning, not being sure.[9] Constructed truths such as those unearthed in this book are inherently ethico-political because of the way they forge relations to themselves and to others. That is why doubt can form a good counterweight by recognizing potential contingencies and uncertainties and the vulnerabilities arising from them, both along the way, that is in the scientific production of outputs and results, and afterwards in the post-trial translation of statistical effects into policy recommendations. Yet, like the algorithm's computational reality of outputs almost always having to be a numeric probability, the randomistas and other actors of the experimental movement are not satisfied with results that introduce doubt. Either there is a documented effect or there is not. Either the statistical result is significant, or it is insignificant. The difference between the experiments we have met here, and the neural networks of AI is that there is always a human in the loop at the start, establishing and forming the trial, whereas subsequently it may be so complex that even the engineers who worked towards its construction do not understand exactly what goes on inside it. The purpose of the forms of experimentation we have explored is to eradicate doubt, condensing a multiplicity of options to a single output that may shape policy and the lives of many.

To the movement, doubt is not least dangerous because it is seen to open a gate to the much-feared notion of subjective bias. Some of the actors explored here believe themselves able to construct walls of separation between science and the *real* world, inherently detaching research from morals, values, or politics, thereby secularizing the experiment. The experimental movement mobilizes neutrality, objectivity, and impartiality, arguing that it simply lays bare the facts of the naturally occurring world, ready for anyone who wishes to follow truths in policymaking. This production of truth is deeply connected to the value-free ideal that sees normative value commitments as a source of bias that pollutes research. The most uncompromising views on this matter maintain that no values whatsoever are allowed to shape research, with more moderate views arguing that we can distinguish between epistemic and non-epistemic values. That is, values *internal* to the scientific community and related to scientific reasoning, such as the scope of research, are accepted whilst values seen as *external* to science, such as politics, moral, or social issues, are not. Yet this demarcation between epistemic and non-epistemic values is unconvincing. Epistemic concerns of accuracy, consistency, scope, or simplicity, even for their appearance as 'neutral', all relate to values that are translatable to social and political concern. The movement may argue that the results it produces and presents are simply objective numbers, measured in transparent ways that can in theory be repeated by others, elsewhere. But values are inscribed in methodological choices long before any documentation of 'neutral' results—and the values that shape what questions we ask in science, how we wish to pursue them and where, do not simply vanish later in the research processes. Moral, political, or other human assumptions are deeply embedded in the sciences in the first place, even when researchers don't pay explicit attention to them. Methodological choices and consequences—fundamentally any choice about what to do research on, how to do it, and why—that may appear to be based on a pure interpretation of science will always be constituted by values. As such, there can be no real distinction between normativity and factuality, just as there is no 'free' research arena detached from sociopolitical worlds. All science is consequential, if in different ways and to different degrees. The value-free ideal must be questioned for its presumptions that science can in any way take place or be practised outside any conception of society and its social, political, cultural, or economic forms. Whether directly or in derivative form, the practice of science will always have implications for someone, somewhere, and carry with it conceptions about how society should be organized and ordered.

This inability to clearly demarcate science from society is what makes the concept of the laboratory so interesting. In theory, laboratories are about the *malleability* of natural objects—that we can manipulate, control, transform or govern that which we experiment with,[10] with no consequences spilling out of the lab. The perceived laboratory that I have focused on here does not provide any easy malleability, where the studied *objects* are detached from their naturally occurring environments or orders. The laboratories we have visited are not isolated truth spots. They are deeply connected beyond the realm of whatever specific locality where they take place. The inside and the outside of both science and experimentation are interwoven then, and experimentation here appears as an assemblage of actors and ideas from across professional realms and geographies. Experiments are not autonomous forms of theory testing but assemblages of cultural patterns, scientific practices, political economies, epistemologies, and many more coming together[11] to create collections of ideas and practices that shape the production of truth, with no separation of the results of experimentation from the making or production of experiments. So much has been clear since the first researchers ventured into laboratories and observed the very mundane practice of experimental science, eventually confronting myths of any nature-given coherence of this. Laboratories are important first and foremost then for what they are seen as producing—a scientific truth whose objective nature is beyond question, emerging largely from what is a centre of calculation.[12] And because of the way laboratory-like efforts spill out and have consequences far beyond their perceived delimited space—with science becoming politics—the *where* of experimentation is of great importance beyond epistemic concerns.

*

'No, there is no such baby'; 'No, we never had it here'; 'No, he couldn't have seen it for fifty cents'; 'We didn't send it anywhere because we never had it'; 'I don't mean to say that your sister-in-law lied, but there must be some mistake'; 'There is no sue getting up an excursion from Milwaukee, for there isn't any Devil Baby at Hull-House'; 'We can't give reduced rates because we are not exhibiting anything'; and so on and on.

As I came near the front door, I would catch snatches of arguments that were often acrimonious: 'Why do you let so many people believe it, if it isn't here?'

'We have taken three lines of cars to come, and we have as much right to see it as anybody else'; 'This is a pretty big place, of course you could hide it easy enough'; 'What you saying that for—are you going to raise the price of admission?'

We had doubtless struck a case of what the psychologists call the 'contagion of emotion,' added to that 'aesthetic sociability' which impels any one of us to drag the entire household to the window when a procession comes into the street or a rainbow appears in the sky.[13]

For six weeks and more of 1916, streams of visitors poured into Jane Addams' Hull House to catch a glimpse of a rumoured Devil Baby. One story talked of an Italian girl who married an atheist, the man soon tearing a holy picture from the bedroom wall, causing the devil to incarnate himself in their coming child. A 'Jewish' rumour mentioned a father of six girls who proclaimed he would rather have a devil in the house than another girl, prompting the devil baby to appear. A national landmark today at the corner of Polk and Halsted in Chicago's Near West Side, feminist social reformer and sociologist Jane Addams' Hull House was a social experiment, a form of radical political practice meant to explore the prospects not least for women's rights and especially for mothers and their infants. To Addams, the interesting effect of the devil baby rumours of 1916 were the ways in which they inspired visiting women in particular to spill their life-stories of suffering, destitute, hurt: of premature birth, 'because he kicked me in the side'; of children maimed and burned because 'I had no one to leave them with when I went to work'. These women had seen the tender flesh of growing little bodies given over to death because 'he wouldn't let me send for the doctor', or because 'there was no money to pay for the medicine'. The devil baby stories from Hull House could secure visitors a hearing of their own tragedies, and allow them to express their longings. The story proved a valuable instrument in their business of living, seemingly acting as a restraining influence for the irrational taboos and savage punishments of marriage conducted against women at the time. The supernatural became a way to create sympathy for the mother of too many daughters and discipline the irritated father, softening the treatment that men accorded to women, as Addams described it.

Inaugurated in 1889 as 'the great experiment' meant to last a hundred years, Hull House mirrored European settlement houses in the way it combined classes, housing educated women and men in a neighbourhood consisting mainly of poor European immigrants. Over time, Hull House would come to encompass a night school for adults, an art gallery, children's clubs, apartments, an employment bureau, and classes on everything from cooking and sewing to English language and American government. By 1907 it consisted of thirteen buildings in Chicago's inner city. Addams saw Hull House as a social experiment beyond the laboratory, testing new paths of improvement of social conditions for poor communities and people in Chicago.[14] Not as inferior but rather superior to the *ideal-type* experiment articulated in the natural sciences. At Hull House, social workers were both observers and experimental intervenors, living and working in the houses. Over time taking on a deeply political form with ambitions to experimentally learn from society within society, Hull House was to Addams 'an attempt to relieve, at the same time, the overaccumulation at one end of society and the destitution at the other'.[15] Through collaborative experimentation, the objective was to fundamentally empower people, confront inequalities, and pursue social justice.

What does a future of experimentation look like, imagined as it is by the movement explored in this book? The most insistent answer is that the experimental movement's scientific arrogance has proven sometimes to form a morality of inequality. That is, if we follow the argument of this book, namely that experimentation and its effect sometimes have an inherently unequal nature, then a first conclusion must be that an experimental future is an increasingly unequal future. As it does with methodologies, experimentation in the forms practised here seems able to create unfortunate hierarchies of human beings. It is difficult to release the practice of experimentation from notions of inequality, race, structural exclusion, and sociopolitical matters of voice and representation. Suffering may be human—*man* even wills it, seeks it out, as Nietzsche bluntly put it—but it is not inflicted in equal doses to everyone. Experimentation is a social relations that in the form explored here remakes socio-spatial realities around the world and may risk institutionalizing hierarchized differences, affording different standards to different people and different geographies, or employing what Richard Rottenburg has called therapeutic domination[16] to the point at which we are left with questions of what voices are silenced in the production and dissemination of experimentation.

Medical science has developed through the past centuries from a patient-centred and -controlled examination modus where the doctor adapted to the social setting of the patient, to one in which patients are inserted into a tangible clinical space where the doctor rules, and the patient does not ask questions. So too appears many of the present experimental practices, where scientists may take their trials into the social settings of the subjects, but where the subjects are at best passive observers of the star economist and his instruments, at worst unaware of being subjects of experimentation altogether. Dyadic relations are substituted by one-way interactions or detached observations, and although the language of the randomistas is not Latin like that of the eighteenth-century clinical doctors, their technical proficiency and the deep complexity of their econometric endeavours is sufficient to decouple subject and experimenter by way of scientific privilege. When some economists have difficulty in seeing through their own methodologies and scientific practices to acknowledge degrees of unequal power or social relations at play, they display a worrying 'theodicy of privilege',[17] a legitimating privilege. To present experimentation as clean, clinical, objective, and apolitical, is also to neglect or suppress the unequal power relations at play. This creates an opacity that serves as an excluding mechanism, defining who can have a say in experiments, strengthening a particular type of scientific authority. The insularity of economics indeed contributes to a 'black box society'.[18]

What ensues in some of the situations we have considered is the experimental becoming the only accessible point of entrance to key basic services such as health care or education. This leads to a stark choice: experimentation or exclusion. Shelley's lab-constructed Frankenstein monster is a 'modern-day prometheus' turned murderous because of the very nature of exclusion and inequality, because society—due to the monster's nature, out of what and where it is born—denies it the basic human needs of social life and friendship. The inequality of experimentation similarly risks alienating or treating its subjects as though they are never full citizens, never something else; they are never excluded from medical trials, but they are never truly included in post-trial treatment. The experimental interventions may not decelerate the lives of the subjects, but they mostly don't accelerate them either. The in-between situatedness of the experimental subjects does not mean they should be treated as an invisible biological substance, as figuratively dead or as mindless victims. Professor of African American Studies, Alexander Weheliye, has strikingly unfolded how widely used concepts of biopolitics, necropolitics, or bare life risk neglecting alternative life in light of subjection, exploitation, and racialization. These forms of domination or subjugation can and must never come to annihilate dreams of freedom, liberation, or resistance that lies in both imagining and pursuing other worlds. This is especially true for lives shaped by great inequalities.

Is there a different path then, we may ask, to a more democratic form of experimentation? In the spirit of Latour's critique of critique, is there a way to turn the perspectives of this book into a productive force for the necessary change, granted a lot of what has passed has been critical. The contemporary experimental movement does not form open-ended or collaborative learning processes characterized by an inclusion and diversity of voices. Rather, it often seems aligned with the interests of the already powerful, bounded in terms of who can and may speak. Still, is there such a different thing as dialogic or participatory experimentation, drawn from a set of relational perspectives and reflexive practices? Outside the natural science realm, experiments, not as producers of axiomatic scientific truths but rather as a political practice through pragmatism, participation, and iterative growth of knowledge[19] have long been explored. Emerging particularly from Chicago and some of the early protagonists of the schools of pragmatic sociology that we have already met—including Jane Addams, John Dewey, and others—experimentation was employed as a political practice deeply rooted in democracy. They saw experimentation as a cooperative inquiry, breaking with the past by intimately binding together science and politics. Historically, attempts to shield science from religious or political interference led to a secularization, autonomizing science from non-experts, during most of the nineteenth century. But after the turn of the twentieth century, some of these urban sociologists from Chicago began grounding their methodological approaches in a political core, extending their research into social policy.[20] Shifting between different degrees of politicization and autonomy, the participatory question as we see it unfolding today began to emerge in the 1960s, led by feminist, anti-nuclear, and ecological movements. These movements intrinsically formed their political ambitions on the basis of scientific efforts. They worked to further strong civic epistemologies[21] or what has been called a 'mode-2 society'[22] where science is increasingly socially embedded and practised as a hybrid form of interaction between scientific and social actors.[23]

In the context of this book, such paths towards democratic experimentation would require deep questions and marked changes to issues such as who is experimenting and who is being experimented upon; how the experiments are conducted and who contributes; and for what and where the experiments produce important sociopolitical insights. Currently, many of the experiments explored have inequality flowing throughout them. *Before*: in matters of planning and design, including decisions on what types of experiments, why experiments, on whom, and in what ways. *During*: with clear demarcation between who does the experiments and who partakes as subject, most often a separation articulated on scientific grounds of wanting 'pure' or 'unspoiled' data. And *after*: where the effects are uneven and uncertain, rarely discussed with subjects or those who might feel the consequences. If ideal efforts of democratic experimentation are found in attempts to 'open up' such processes, the experimental movement does what it can to hermetically close these from outside influence, performing a monologue more than a conversation. Some economists may practise performative participatory processes such as public ceremonies of randomization, but these mainly seem to establish consensual participation, reducing the room for resistance. Aiming for controlled and strategic acceptance, such top-down exercises in legitimation appear more like public education than public empowerment. Participation is often seen as external to the experiments being conducted, with clearly demarcated spaces for the scientists to roam on their own, in isolation from any notion of 'subjects' or a 'public'. Reflexivity likewise is *held* in the experimental movement, seen predominantly to reside with those who possess the technical or methodological knowledge of conducting the experiment, with pregiven norms and assumptions about (the limits of) participation, or ethics, being transferred by the intervening experimenters into the local context.

*

Both of the men had been trained for this moment, their lives had been a preparation for it, they had been selected at birth as those who would witness the answer, but even so they found themselves gasping and squirming like excited children.

'And you're ready to give it to us?' urged Loonquawl. 'I am.' [...] 'Though I don't think,' added Deep Thought, 'that you're going to like it.'

'Doesn't matter!' said Phouchg. 'We must know it! Now!'[...] 'Alright,' said the computer and settled into silence again. The two men fidgeted. The tension was unbearable.

'You're really not going to like it,' observed Deep Thought.

'Tell us!'

'Alright,' said Deep Thought. 'The Answer to the Great Question...'

'Yes...!'

'Of Life, the Universe and Everything...' said Deep Thought. 'Yes...!'

'Is...' said Deep Thought, and paused.

'Yes...!'

'Is...'

'Yes...!!!...?'

'Forty-two,' said Deep Thought, with infinite majesty and calm.

[...]

'It was a tough assignment,' said Deep Thought mildly.

'Forty-two!' yelled Loonquawl. 'Is that all you've got to show for seven and a half million years' work?'

'I checked it very thoroughly,' said the computer, 'and that quite definitely is the answer. I think the problem, to be quite honest with you, is that you've never actually known what the question is.'

In Douglas Adam's 1979 comedic space odyssey *Hitchhiker's Guide to the Galaxy*, Deep Thought is a supernatural computer programmed by a pan-dimensional, hyper-intelligent species of beings (taking the form of white mice on Earth) to answer the Ultimate Question of Life, the Universe, and Everything. The answer to that question, as anyone with even the smallest affinity for science fiction will know, is forty-two. 42. After first facing criticism and then rebuking the hyper-intelligent beings for not understanding the question they asked in the first place, Deep Thought creates another computer so large and of such complexity that life itself becomes part of its computational matrix. This planet-computer and its 10-million-year program is known as Earth. Unfortunately, Earth is destroyed five minutes before the question to the ultimate answer is delivered. On the surface, this is to make room for a space highway, although the real reason behind Earth's destruction seems to have been a group of psychiatrists afraid of going out of business, should the question to the ultimate answer be known.

How the questions we ask matters for the answers we get, as the logical positivist epitome of forty-two will always remind us. This book, of course, has been about more than dubious questions, questionable answers, and singular truths. Instead of assuming experimentation to be self-evidently productive I have tried to unearth its occasional disempowering effects. I have engaged with institutions in society – including ones of science, technology, or charity – that appear to be independent or separate from the state but which likewise structure society in ways that determine who can speak, who can enjoy access, or who has agency to incite change and to exert influence. The potentially disempowering effects inherent in some of the institutions we have looked at are, first and foremost, found in their formulation of libertarian paternalism, forwarding a form of experimental practice that becomes lodged within a symbolically violent calculus.[24] The movement examined forms a modern-day behavioural project running across a multitude of fields, even beyond those

I have engaged with here, that we would intuitively connect to ideas of the 'digital Anthropocene'[25] and the trans-scalar revolution brought about by Silicon Valley across economic, social, and political realms that sees a merging of physical and digital realities. A project that appears to be emerging, radical, and disruptive. Yet, at the same time, the scientific instrumentation of the experimental movement reminds us that not all data are created, gathered, or treated equal and that even the most high-tech of efforts may carry classical tropes of modernization, technical determinism, and mechanical objectivity. The new geographies of development, we are often told, suggest a 'rise of the South' in agency, influence, and independence. These perceptions are explicit in the universal Sustainable Development Goals, themselves often referred to as the most democratic international agreement ever made because of the apparent influence of the Global South. Even so, the stories told here nuance such arguments of what and who shapes the intersectionality of global and local relations. Only so much is *universal* about the world we live in now, something vividly exposed by Covid-19. Yes, all countries and people feel the weight of the pandemic, but in very different ways and to very different degrees of severity.

Experimentation as we have seen it practised then doesn't so much seem to inspire emancipation as uphold unequal relations of power and resources. And it seems difficult today, if not impossible, to separate these instrumentalizations of life and subjectivity from their capitalization. Technological innovation and experimentation itself are fundamentally about forms of value creation inherent in contemporary capitalism. Through technologized humanitarian efforts, refugees become both modern technologized consumers (when provided with credit cards) and contributors to Silicon Valley's 'virtual assembly lines' and value creation when they are educated, connected, and incited to be employed by startups through picture annotation and similar AI-related microwork. It is impossible to escape the feeling that protection increasingly goes hand in hand with integration into the digital economy, both suffering and healing being co-constitutive with yielding and the creation of economic value.

The mirage of determinism that can emerge from such dire conclusions is perhaps the greatest inhibitor of change and action. History is of exceeding importance, absolutely, but the past must not incapacitate the present nor the future. German sociologist Ulrick Beck warned thirty years ago that 'It may be that the next generation, or the one after that, will no longer be upset at pictures of birth defects, like those of tumor-covered fish and birds that now circulate around the world, just as we are no longer upset today by violated values, the new poverty and a constant high level of mass unemployment.'[26] The present can never be separated from the future in that what we do now shapes what will eventually come. We may base our actions on previous experiences, but we equally act based on how we see the future. We live in a time when social order and technoscience are coproducts,[27] necessitating the imagining of alternative futures of experimentation. Many scientific disciplines suffer from a conscious or implicit silencing of knowledge production at the margins of the self. That is, some forms of knowledge is seen to fall outside the imaginary walls of separation erected by certain authorities in these fields, whether individuals or institutions. There is need to work towards a more participatory science and a practice of experimentation that recognizes its inherent inequality of engagement and works productively from that and with that. This form of participatory science leaves room for substantive public contestation and, from a coproduction perspective, sees reflexivity as something that is both relational and distributed, embedding a hybridity of expert and subject identities.[28] Moving beyond the aggregation of preferences of individual subjects or citizens to address justice and equity at a systemic level[29] requires critically reflecting on one's own positionality and impact and taking participation seriously to the extent of appreciating the effects and qualities of the interaction itself to be as important as the eventual end goals.[30] This is a vision of experimentation as a political practice that does not concern itself with control, that *fata morgana* of reductionism.

Instead of focusing on verification and singular truths, attention would be better paid to variance and how differences in results can lead us to inclusive discussions of ideal outcomes. That means embracing doubt as a productive force and trying out different ideas rather than running an RCT from narrow perceptions of being able to reach a singular truth. Options of counterweighting the effects of the current experimental regime then, are not ones of increasingly adopting precautionary principles or merely heightening ethical awareness while maintaining similar methodologies and practices. Rather, it is about radically reconfiguring the methodological regime based on the values of democratization and inclusion. What I am trying to say is that the form of experimentation practised by the movement portrayed here is not the end of history, not the singular form of experimental practice. Despite Silicon Valley's ethos of doom and revolution that sets itself on the verge of something unique and unavoidable to come,[31] we should not abandon competing imaginaries about the future. The future is a haven for ideals, a potential emancipation from past practices and ideas that failed to take humanity forward.[32] Retaining the agency, the influence, to shape the future is a prerequisite for change, of course, but change starts with imagining an alternative outlook, another course of action. And we know that the system, the ideas, and institutions that have helped to create and push forward a time of inequality cannot be the ones to dismantle it. An opportunity exists then— and along with it a responsibility—to formulate a different vision of empowerment through democratic experimentation and scepticism about supposed scientific authority. This not an individualized scientific ambition but a collective imagining built on dignity, inclusion, and justice. And one that is all the more necessary as we step into a future of uncertainty and ignorance, sending us down definite paths of experimentation and inequality.

Notes

1. See https://www.fes-asia.org/news/stories-of-hunger-indias-lockdown-is-hitting-the-poorest/.
2. Ward, A. 2020. Sweden's government has tried a risky coronavirus strategy. It could backfire, vox.com, 16 April.
3. See Facebook. 2020. Community Standards Enforcement Report, August.
4. See Avaaz. 2020. How Facebook can flatten the curve of the coronavirus infodemic, Avaaz.com, 15 April.
5. Hirshman, D. and Berman, E. 2014. Do economists make policies? on the political effects of economics, *Socio-Economic Review* 12(4): 779–811; see also Brint, S. 1990. Rethinking the policy influence of experts: from general characterizations to analysis of variation, *Sociological Forum* 5(3): 361–85.
6. Danish Ministry of Foreign Affairs. 2017. *Hack the Future of Development Aid*. Danish Ministry of Foreign Affairs, Sustainia and Coinify.
7. See Tazzioli, M. 2019. Refugees' subjectivities, debit cards and data circuits. financial-humanitarianism in the Greek migration laboratory, *International Political Sociology* 13(4): 392–408.
8. See Collingridge, D. 1980. *The Social Control of Technology*. London: Pinter.
9. Amoore, L. 2019. Doubt and the algorithm: on the partial accounts of machine learning. *Theory, Culture & Society* 36(6): 147–69.
10. Knorr-Cetina, K. 1995. Laboratory studies: the cultural approach to the study of science, in S. Jasonoff et al. (eds), *Handbook of Science and Technology Studies*. London: Sage; Latour, B. and Woolgar, S. 1986. *Laboratory Life: The Social Construction of Scientific Facts*. Princeton, NJ: Princeton University Press.
11. Rheinberger, H.-J. 1995. *Towards a History of Epistemic Things: Synthesizing Proteins in the Test Tube*, Stanford, CA: Stanford University Press.
12. Latour, B. 1987: *Science in Action: How to Follow Scientists and Engineers through Society*. Cambridge, MA: Harvard University Press.
13. Addams, J. 1916. The devil baby at Hull House, *The Atlantic* October.

14. Gross, M. 2009. Collaborative experiments: Jane Addams, Hull House and experimental social work, *Social Science Information* 48: 81–95.
15. Addams, J. 1961. *Twenty Years at Hull House*. New York: Penguin (orig. pub. 1909).
16. Rottenburg, R. 2009. Social and public experiments and new figurations of science and politics in postcolonial Africa, *Postcolonial Studies* 12(4): 423–40.
17. McGoey, L. and Thiel, D. 2018. Charismatic violence and the sanctification of the super-rich, *Economy and Society* 47(1): 111–34.
18. Pasquale, F. 2015. *The Black Box Society: The Secret Algorithms that Control Money and Information*. Cambridge, MA: Harvard University Press; Algan, Y., Fourcade, M., and Ollion, E., et al. 2015. The superiority of economics, *Journal of Economic Perspectives* 29(1).
19. Ansell, C. 2012. What is a 'Democratic Experiment'? *Contemporary Pragmatism* 9(2): 159–80.
20. Lengwiler, M. 2008. Participatory approaches in science and technology: historical origins and current practices in critical perspective, *Science, Technology and Human Values* 33(2): 186–200.
21. Jasanoff, S. 2003. Technologies of humility: citizen participation in governing science. *Minerva* 41: 223–44.
22. Nowotny, H., Scott, P., and Gibbons, M. 2003. 'Mode 2' revisited: the new production of knowledge, *Minerva* 31: 179–94.
23. Lengwiler, 2008.
24. Amoore, 2019.
25. WBGU. 2019. Towards our Common Digital Future, German Advisory Council on Global Change.
26. Beck, U. 1992. *Risk Society: Towards a New Modernity*. London: Sage.
27. See Jasanoff, 2003.
28. Chilvers, J. and Kearnes, M. (eds) 2015. *Remaking Participation: Science, Environment and Emergent Publics*. London: Routledge.
29. Chilvers and Kearnes, 2015.
30. Gross, M. and Schulte-Römer, N. 2019. Remaking participatory democracy through experimental design, *Science, Technology & Human Values* 44(4): 707–18.
31. Historically, every generation has been on the edge of a technological revolution, putting into question the revolutionary rhetoric we can witness today.
32. Verschraegen G. and Vandermoere, F. 2017. *Introducion: Shaping the future through imaginaries of science, technology and society*, in G. Verschraegen, F. Vandermoere, L. Braeckmans, B. Segaert, *Imagined Futures of in Science, Technology and Society*. Abingdon: Routledge

References

Adams, D. 1979. *The Hitchhiker's Guide to the Galaxy*. Pan Books, p. 29.

Addams, J. 1916. The devil baby at Hull House, *The Atlantic* October.

Addams, J. 1961. *Twenty Years at Hull House*. New York: Penguin (orig. pub. 1909).

Adelman, C. 2009. Global philanthropy and remittances: reinventing foreign aid, *The Brown Journal of World Affairs* 15(2).

Ajana, B. 2013. Asylum, identity management and biometric control, *Journal of Refugee Studies* 26(4).

Alejandro, A. 2018. *Western Dominance in International Relations? The Internationalisation of IR in Brazil and India*. London: Routledge.

Algan, Y., Fourcade, M., and Ollion, E., et al. 2015. The superiority of economics, *Journal of Economic Perspectives* 29(1).

Amoore, L. 2019. Doubt and the algorithm: on the partial accounts of machine learning, *Theory, Culture & Society* 36(6): 147–69.

Amoore, L. 2020. *Cloud Ethics: Algorithms and the Attributes of Ourselves and Others*. Durham, NC: Duke University Press.

Andrews, F.E. 1956. *Philanthropic Foundations*. New York: Russel Sage Foundation.

Angell, M. 2000. Investigators' responsibilities for human subjects in developing countries, *New England Journal of Medicine* 342: 967–8.

Angrist, J.D. and Pischke, J.-S. 2010. The credibility revolution in empirical economics: how better research design is taking the con out of econometrics, *Journal of Economic Perspectives* 24: 3–30.

Anheier, H.K. and Daly, S. 2007. *Politics of Foundations: A Comparative Analysis*. London: Routledge.

Ansell, C. 2012. What is a 'Democratic Experiment'?, *Contemporary Pragmatism* 9(2): 159–80.

Antecol, M. 1997. Understanding McLuhan: television and the creation of the global village, *ETC: A Review of General Semantics* 54(4): 454–73.

Arendt, H. 1963. *Eichmann in Jerusalem: A Report on the Banality of Evil*. New York: Viking Press.

Arnove, R. 1982. Introduction. In R. Arnove (ed.), *Philanthropy and Cultural Imperialism*. Bloomington: Indiana University Press, pp. 1–23.

Associated Press. 2009. New CEO: Gates Foundation Learns from Mistakes. New York: Associated Press. Accessed 15 April 2017. Available at: http://www.thestreet.com/story/10506452/1/new-ceo-gates-foundation-learns-from-experiments.html

Avaaz. 2020. How Facebook can flatten the curve of the coronavirus infodemic, Avaaz. com, 15 April.

Babineaux, R. and Krumboltz, J. 2013. *Fail Fast, Fail Often*. London: Penguin.

Baldassarri, D. and Abascal, M. 2017. Field experiments across the social sciences, *Annual Review of Sociology* 43(1): 41–73.

Banerjee, A.V. 2006. Making aid work: how to fight global poverty—effectively, *Boston Review* July—August. http://bostonreview.net/BR31.4/banerjee.html

Banerjee, A. 2007. *Making Aid Work*. Cambridge, MA and London: MIT Press.

Banerjee, A. and Duflo, E. 2009. The experimental approach to development economics, NBER working paper, No. 14467.

Banerjee, A. and Duflo, E. 2019. *Good Economics for Hard Times*. PublicAffairs.

Barbrook, R. and Cameron, A. 1996. The Californian ideology, *Science as Culture* 6(1): 44–72.

Barrett, C.B. and Carter, M.R. 2014. Retreat from radical skepticism: Rebalancing theory, observational data and randomization in development economics. In Dawn Teele (ed.), *Field Experiments and Their Critics: Essays on the Uses and Abuses of Experiments in the Social Sciences*. New Haven, CT: Yale University Press, pp. 58–77.

BBC. 2018. Facebook 'ugly truth' growth memo haunts firm, 30 March.

Beck, U. 1992. *Risk Society: Towards a New Modernity*. London: Sage.

Beck, U. 1994. *Ecological Enlightenment: Essays on the Politics of the Risk Society*. Amherst, NY: Prometheus Books.

Beck, U. 1997. The world as laboratory. In S. E. Bronner (ed.), *Twentieth-century Political Theory*. London: Routledge, pp. 356–66.

Berndt, C. 2015. Behavioural economics, experimentalism and the marketisation of development, *Economy and Society* 44(4): 567–91.

Berne Declaration. 2013. Clinical Drug Trials in Argentina: Pharmaceutical Companies Exploit Flaws in The Regulatory System. Berne Declaration.

Berne Declaration and Sama. 2013. *Exploratory Study on Clinical Trials Conducted by Swiss Pharmaceutical Companies in India: Issues, Concerns and Challenges*. Berne Declaration.

Bernstein, M.A. 2001. *A Perilous Progress: Economists and Public Purpose in 20th Century America*. Princeton, NJ: Princeton University Press.

Betts, A. and Bloom, L. 2014. Humanitarian innovation: state of the art. OCHA Policy and Studies Series, November 2014, 009.

Bijker, W.E. 1999. Towards politicization of technological culture: constructivist STS studies and democracy. In H. Ansal and D. Çalişir (eds), *Science, Technology and Society: International Symposium*. Istanbul, Turkey: Istanbul Technical University, 37–47.

Bill and Melinda Gates Foundation. 2007. *Annual Letter*. Seattle, WA: The Bill and Melinda Gates Foundation.

Bill and Melinda Gates Foundation. 2007. *Annual Report 2007*. Seattle, WA: The Bill and Melinda Gates Foundation.

Bill and Melinda Gates Foundation. 2008. *Annual Letter*. Seattle, WA: The Bill and Melinda Gates Foundation.

Bill and Melinda Gates Foundation. 2010. *Annual Letter*. Seattle, WA: The Bill and Melinda Gates Foundation.

Bill and Melinda Gates Foundation. 2012. *Annual Report*. Seattle, WA: The Bill and Melinda Gates Foundation.

Bill and Melinda Gates Foundation. 2015. *Annual Letter*. Seattle, WA: The Bill and Melinda Gates Foundation.

Bill and Melinda Gates Foundation. 2016. *Annual Letter*. Seattle, WA: The Bill and Melinda Gates Foundation.

Birch, K., Peacock, M., Wellen, R., Hossein, C., Scott, S., and Salazar, A. (eds) 2017. *Business and Society: A Critical Introduction*. London: Zed Books.

Bishop, M. 2006. The birth of philanthrocapitalism, *The Economist* 23 February.

Bishop, M. and Green, M. 2010. *Philanthrocapitalism: How Giving Can Save the World*. London: A. & C. Black.

Bloom, L. and Betts, A. 2013. The two worlds of humanitarian innovation, Refugee Studies Centre Working Paper Series No. 94.

Bloomberg. 2010. The pragmatic rebels. Available at: https://www.bloomberg.com/news/articles/2010-07-02/the-pragmatic-rebels

Brint, S. 1990. Rethinking the policy influence of experts: from general characterizations to analysis of variation, *Sociology Forum* 5(3): 361–85.

British Medical Journal. 1963. Without prejudice, *British Medical Journal*.

Bulkeley, H., Castán Broto, V., Maassen, A., et al. 2011. Governing low carbon transitions. In H. Bulkeley (ed.), *Cities and Low Carbon Transitions*. London and New York: Routledge Taylor and Francis Group, pp. 29–41.

Butler, J. 1993. *Bodies that Matter: On the Discursive Limits of 'Sex'*. New York: Routledge.

Caldwell, L.A. 2019. In Senate testimony, pharma executive admits drug prices hit poor the hardest, NBC News 26 February.

Chalmers, A.F. 2013. *What Is This Thing Called Science?* 4th ed. St Lucia: University of Queensland Press.

Chang, E. 2019. *Brotopia: Breaking up the Boy's Club of Silicon Valley*. London: Portfolio/Penguin.

Chilvers, J. and Kearnes, M. (eds) 2015. *Remaking Participation: Science, Environment and Emergent Publics*. London: Routledge.

Chomsky, N. 1959. A review of BF Skinner's *Verbal Behavior, Language* 35(1): 26–58.

Cnet. 2013.'Bill Gates on education, patents, Microsoft Bob, and disease, 15 July.

Collingridge, D. 1980. *The Social Control of Technology*. London: Pinter.

Collins, C.S. 2017. Development labs: university knowledge production and global poverty, *The Review of Higher Education* 41(1): 113–19.

Coville, A., Galiani, S., Gertler, P., and Yoshida, S. 2020. Enforcing Payment for Water and Sanitation Services in Nairobi's Slums, NBER Working Paper No. 27569.

Culliford, E. 2021. Rohingya refugees sue Facebook for $150 billion over Myanmar violence, Reuters, 8 December.

Danish Ministry of Foreign Affairs. 2017. *Hack the Future of Development Aid*. Danish Ministry of Foreign Affairs, Sustainia and Coinify.

Deaton, A. and Cartwright, N. 2018. Understanding and misunderstanding randomized controlled trials, *Social Science and Medicine* 210(August): 2–21.

Dehue, T. 2001. Establishing the experimenting society: the historical origination of social experimentation according to the randomized controlled design, *American Journal of Psychology* 114(2): 283–302.

Desai, R. and Kharas, H. 2008. The California consensus: can private aid end global poverty?, *Survival* 50(4): 155–68.

de Souza Leao, L. and Eyal, G. 2019. The rise of randomized controlled trials (RCTs) in international development in historical perspective, *Theory and Society* 48: 383–418.

DiMasi, J.A., Grabowski, H.G., and Hansen, R.W. 2016. Innovation in the pharmaceutical industry: new estimates of R&D costs, *Journal of Health Economics* 47: 20–33.

Dowie, M. 2001. *American Foundations: An Investigative History*. Cambridge, MA: The MIT Press.

Draper, N. 2017. Fail fast: the value of studying unsuccessful technology companies, *Media Industries* 4(1).

Duflo, E. and Banerjee, A. 2011. *Poor Economics: A Radical Rethinking of the Way to Fight Global Poverty*. London; New York: Penguin/Public Affairs.

Duflo, E., Glennerster, R., and Kremer, M. 2008. Using randomization in development economics research: a toolkit. In T. Paul Schultz and John Strauss (eds), *Handbook of Development Economics*, Volume 4. Amsterdam and Oxford: Elsevier, North-Holland, pp. 3895–962.

Dussel, E.D. and Vallega, A.A. 2012. *Ethics of liberation in the age of globalization and exclusion.* Durham: Duke University Press.

Easterly, W. 2006. *The White Man's Burden: Why the West's Efforts to Aid the Rest Have Done so Much Ill and so Little Good.* London: Penguin Books.

Edwards, M. 2009. *Just Another Emperor? The Myths and Realities of Philanthrocapitalism.* London: The Young Foundation & Demos.

Eichenwald, K. 2012. Microsoft's lost decade, *Vanity Fair,* 24 July.

Emanuel, E.J., Wendler, D., and Grady, C. 2000. What makes clinical research ethical? *JAMA* 283: 2701–11.

Epstein, S. 2007. *Inclusion: The Politics of Difference in Medical Research.* Chicago, IL: University of Chicago Press.

Facebook. 2020. Community Standards Enforcement Report, August.

Fejerskov, A. 2018. *The Gates Foundation's Rise to Power.* Abingdon: Routledge.

Fejerskov, A. and Rasmussen, C. 2016. Going global? micro-philanthrocapitalism and Danish private foundations in international development cooperation, *Development in Practice* 26(7): 840–52.

Fine, B. and Milonakis, D. 2009. *From Economics Imperialism to Freakonomics: The Shifting Boundaries between Economics and Other Social Sciences.* London: Routledge.

Fleishman, J., Kohler, J.S., and Schindler, S. 2009. *The Foundation: A Great American Secret.* New York: PublicAffairs.

Foer, F. 2017. *World Without Mind.* London: Penguin Press.

Fonseca, M. 2019. Global IR and western dominance: moving forward or Eurocentric entrapment? *Millennium* 48(1): 45–59.

Foucault, M. 1970. *The Order of Things: An Archaeology of the Human Sciences,* London: Tavistock Publications.

Gates, B. 2007. Remarks of Bill Gates, Harvard Commencement 2007. Available at: https://news.harvard.edu/gazette/story/2007/06/remarks-of-bill-gates-harvard-commencement-2007/

Gates, B. 2011. *Innovation with Impact: Financing 21st Century Development.* Report to the G20 Leaders. Personal report to the G20 Cannes Summit, November.

Gates, B. 2013. Dream with a Deadline: The Millennium Development Goals. Gatesnotes.com, 18 September.

Gates, B. 2021. *How to Avoid a Climate Disaster.* London: Penguin Books Ltd.

Gerber, A.S. and Green, D.P. 2012. *Field Experiments.* New York: Norton.

Gerber, A.S., Green, D.P., and Kaplan, E.H. 2004. The illusion of learning from observational research. In I. Shapiro, R. Smith, and T. Massoud (eds), *Problems and Methods in the Study of Politics.* New York: Cambridge University Press, pp. 251–72.

Gieryn, T.F. 2006. City as truth-spot: laboratories and field-sites in urban studies, *Social Studies of Science* 36(1): 5–38.

Glass, T.A., Goodman, S.N., Hernán, M.A., and Samet, J.M. 2013. Causal inference in public health, *Annual Review of Public Health* 34: 61–75.

Glennerster, R. 2014. The complex ethics of randomized evaluations. Available at: http://runningres.com/blog/2014/4/9/the-complex-ethics-of-randomized-evaluations

Goldacre, B. 2013. *Bad Pharma: How Drug Companies Mislead Doctors and Harm Patients,* New York: Faber & Faber.

Goldacre, B. 2013. Building evidence into education. bad science. Available at: http://media.%20Education.gov.uk/assets/files/pdf/b/ben%20goldacre%20paper.pdf.see

Goldstein, D. 2012. Can 4 economists build the most economically efficient charity ever?, *The Atlantic* 21 December.

Goodnight, G.T. and Green, S. 2010. Rhetoric, risk, and markets: the dot-com bubble, *Quarterly Journal of Speech* 96(2): 115–40.

Gray, M. and Suri, S. 2019. *Ghost Work*. Boston, MA; New York: Houghton Mifflin Harcourt.

Griffith, E. 2014. Why startups fail, according to their founders, *Forbes* 25 September 2015.

Gross, M. 2009. Collaborative experiments: Jane Addams, Hull House and experimental social work, *Social Science Information* 48: 81–95.

Gross, M. 2010. *Ignorance and Surprise: Science, Society, and Ecological Design*. Cambridge, MA: MIT Press.

Gross, M. 2010. The public proceduralization of contingency: Bruno Latour and the formation of collective experiments, *Social Epistemology* 24(1): 63–74.

Gross, M. and McGoey, L. (eds). 2015. *Routledge International Handbook of Ignorance Studies*. London: Routledge.

Gross, M. and Schulte-Römer, N. 2019. Remaking participatory democracy through experimental design, *Science, Technology & Human Values* 44(4): 707–18.

Guggenheim, M. 2012. Laboratizing and delaboratizing the world: changing sociological concepts for places of knowledge production, *History of the Human Sciences* 25(1): 99–118.

Haas, P. 1992. Introduction: epistemic communities and international policy coordination, *International Organization* 46(1): 1–36.

Hacking, I. 1992. The self-vindication of the laboratory sciences. In A. Pickering (ed.), *Science as Practice and Culture*. Chicago: University of Chicago Press, pp. 29–64.

Hacking, I. 2005. Why race still matters, *Daedalus* 134(1) (Winter): 102–16.

Hamlett, P.W. 2003. Technology theory and deliberative democracy, *Science, Technology, & Human Values* 28(1): 112–40.

Hansson, S.O. 2016. Experiments: why and how?, *Science and Engineering Ethics* 22(3): 613–32.

Haushofer, J. and Shapiro, J. 2016. The shortterm impact of unconditional cash transfers to the poor: experimental evidence from Kenya, *Quarterly Journal of Economics* 131: 1973–2042.

Hirshman, D. and Berman, E. 2014. Do economists make policies? On the political effects of economics, *Socio-Economic Review* 12(4): 779–811.

Homedes, N. and Ugalda, A. 2016. Clinical trials in Latin America: implications for the sustainability and safety of pharmaceutical markets and the wellbeing of research subjects, *Salud Colect* 12(3): July—September.

Hudson, N. 1996. From 'Nation' to 'Race': the origin of racial classification in eighteenth-century thought, *Eighteenth-Century Studies* 29(3): 247–64.

Hudson Institute. 2011. *The Index of Global Philanthropy and Remittances 2011*. Washington, DC: Hudson Institute.

Human Rights Watch. 2017. Massacre by the river: Burmese army crimes against humanity in Tula Toli, December 2017.

IFRC. 2013. *World Disasters Report: Focus on Technology and the Future of Humanitarian Action*. International Federation of Red Cross and Red Crescent Societies.

Inman, P. 2018. Should Africa let Silicon Valley in? *The Guardian* 19 May.

Inman, P. 2019. Economics Nobel prize won by academics for tackling poverty, *The Guardian* 14 October.

IP Watch. 2015. Outside Sources: Unease over Seconded Philanthropic Foundation Staff to Top Management at WHO. 15 December 2015. Available at: https://www.ip-management-at-who/

Ivy, A. 1948. The history and ethics of the use of human subjects in medical experiments, *Science* 108: 2 July.

Jacobsen, K.L. 2015. Experimentation in humanitarian locations: UNHCR and biometric registration of Afghan Refugees, *Security Dialogue* 46(2): 144–64.

Jacobsen, K.L. 2017. On humanitarian refugee biometrics and new forms of intervention, *Journal of Interventions and Statebuilding* 11(4): 539–51.

Jakee, K. 2019. Transforming the Clinical Trial to Help Us Live Our Best Lives. London: PA Consulting.

Jasanoff, S. 2003. Technologies of humility: citizen participation in governing science, *Minerva* 41: 223–44.

Jenkins, G. 2011. Who's afraid of philanthrocapitalism?, *Case Western Reserve Law Review* 61(3).

Jumbert, M.G. and Sandvik, K.B. 2017. Introduction: what does it take to be good? In K.B. Sandvik and M.G. Jumber (eds), *The Good Drone*. Abingdon & New York: Routledge.

Kahneman, D. 1973. *Attention and Effort*, Englewood Cliffs, NJ: Prentice-Hall.

Kahneman, D. 2002. Maps of bounded rationality: a perspective of intuitive judgement and choice, Nobel-Prize Lecture, 8 December.

Kahneman, D. 2011. *Thinking, Fast and Slow*, London: Penguin.

Karlan, D. and Appel, J. 2011. *More Than Good Intentions: How a New Economics Is Helping to Solve Global Poverty*, Boston, MA: Dutton.

Knorr-Cetina, K. 1995. Laboratory studies: the cultural approach to the study of science. In S. Jasonoff, et al. (eds), *Handbook of Science and Technology Studies*. London: Sage.

Knorr Cetina, K. 1999. *Epistemic Cultures: How the Sciences Make Knowledge*. Cambridge, MA: Harvard University Press.

Kohler, R.E. 2008. Lab history: reflections, *Isis* 99: 761–8.

Kremer, M. and Glennerster, R. 2011. Improving health in developing countries: evidence from randomized evaluations. In M.V. Pauly, T.G. McGuire, and P.P. Barros (eds), *Handbook of Health Economics*. Oxford: ScienceDirect, pp. 201–315.

Kremer, M. and Miguel, E. 2004. Worms: identifying impacts on education and health in the presence of treatment externalities, *Econometrica* 72(1): 159–217.

Krohn, W. and Weyer, J. 1994. Society as a laboratory: the social risks of experimental research, *Science and Public Policy* 21(3): 173–83.

Larson, C. 2017. Facebook can't cope with the world it's created, *Foreign Policy* 7 November.

Latour, B. 1987. *Science in Action: How to Follow Scientists and Engineers through Society*. Cambridge, MA: Harvard University Press.

Latour, B. 1988. *The Pasteurization of France*. Cambridge, MA: Harvard University Press.

Latour, B. 2004. *Politics of Nature: How to Bring the Sciences into Democracy*. Cambridge, MA: Harvard University Press.

Latour, B. and Woolgar, S. 1986. *Laboratory Life: The Construction of Scientific Facts*. Princeton, NJ: Princeton University Press.

Lederer, S.E. 2004. Research without borders: the origins of the Declaration of Helsinki. In V. Roelcke and G. Maio (eds), *Twentieth Century Ethics of Human Subjects Research: Historical Perspectives on Values, Practices, and Regulations*. Stuttgart, Germany: Franz Steiner Verlag, pp. 199–217.

Lemke, T. 2005. *Biopolitics and Beyond: On the Reception of a Vital Foucauldian Notion*. Frankfurt.

Lemov, R. 2006. *World as Laboratory—Experiments with Mice, Mazes and Men*. New York: Hill and Wang.

Lengwiler, M. 2008. Participatory approaches in science and technology: historical origins and current practices in critical perspective, *Science, Technology and Human Values* 33(2): 186–200.

Lock, M. and Nguyen, V.K. 2010. *The Social Life of Organs. An Anthropology of Biomedicine*. Chichester: Wiley-Blackwell.

Lorimer, J. and Driessen, C. 2014. Wild experiments at the Oostvaardersplassen, *Transactions of the Institute of British Geographers* 39(2): 169–81.

Lundsgaarde, E., Funk, E., Kopyra, A., Richter, J., and Steinfeldt, H. 2012. *Private Foundations and Development Cooperation: Insights from Tanzania*. Bonn: German Development Institute.

McDermott, R. 2011. Internal and external validity. In J.N. Druckman, D.P. Green, J.H. Kuklinski, and A. Lupia (eds), *Cambridge Handbook of Experimental Political Science*. Cambridge, UK: Cambridge University Press, pp. 27–40.

McGoey, L. 2010. Profitable failure: antidepressant drugs and the triumph of flawed experiments, *History of the Human Sciences* 23(1): 58–78.

McGoey, L. 2015. *No Such Thing as a Free Gift: The Gates Foundation and the Price of Philanthropy*. London and New York: Verso.

McGoey, L. and Thiel, D. 2018. Charismatic violence and the sanctification of the super-rich, *Economy and Society* 47(1): 111–34.

MacKenzie, D.A. 1981. *Statistics in Britain: 1865–1930*, Edinburgh: Edinburgh University Press.

Malloy, P. 2014. Research material and necromancy: imagining the political-economy of biomedicine in Colonial Tanganyika, *The International Journal of African Historical Studies* 47(3): 425–43.

Marks, H. 1997. *The Progress of Experiment: Science and Therapeutic Reform in the United States, 1900–1990*. Cambridge: Cambridge University Press.

Martin, C. 2014. Wearing your failures on your sleeve, *New York Times* 8 November.

Martin, M. and Schinzinger, R. 1988. *Engineering Ethics*, 2nd ed. New York: McGraw-Hill.

Matson, J.V. 1991. *The Art of Innovation: Using Intelligent Fast Failure*. State College: Pennsylvania State University Press.

Michael, M. and Rosengarten, M. 2012. Medicine: experimentation, politics, emergent bodies, *Body and Society* 18(3–4): 1–17.

Mirowski, P. 2002. *Machine Dreams: Economics Becomes a Cyborg Science*. Cambridge: Cambridge University Press.

Miseta, E. 2019. Will virtual trials mean the end of CROs?, 4 November, Clinical Leader.

Montoya, M.J. 2011. *Making the Mexican Diabetic: Race, Science, and the Genetics of Inequality*. Berkeley: University of California Press.

Moran, M. and Stone, D. 2016. The new philanthropy: Private power in international development policy? In J. Grugel and D. Hammett (eds), *The Palgrave Handbook of International Development*. Basingstoke: Palgrave.

Moreira, T. 2007. Entangled evidence: knowledge making in systematic reviews in healthcare, *Sociology of Health and Illness* 29: 180–97.

Morgan, M. 2002. Model experiments and models in experiments. In L. Magnani and N. Nersessian (eds), *Model-Based Reasoning: Science, Technology, Values*. New York: Kluwer, pp. 41–58.

Morning, A. 2011. *The Nature of Race: How Scientists Think and Teach about Human Difference*. Berkeley: University of California Press.

Morton, S.G. 1839. *Crania Americana: Or, a Comparative View of the Skulls of Various Aboriginal Nations of North and South America: To Which Is Prefixed an Essay on the Varieties of the Human Species*. Philadelphia: J. Dobson.

Mozur, P. 2018. A genocide incited on Facebook, with posts from Myanmar's military, *New York Times* 15 October.

Müller, C. J. 2016. *Prometheanism*. Lanham, MD: Rowman & Littlefield.

Mulligan, C. 2014. The economics of randomized experiments, *New York Times* 5 March.

New York Times. 2000. Bill Gates's money. 16 April.

Nott, J.C. and Gliddon, G.R. 1854. *Types of Mankind: Or Ethnological Researches, Based upon the Ancient Monuments, Paintings, Sculptures, and Crania of Races, and upon their Natural, Geographical, Philological, and Biblical History*. Philadelphia, PA: Lippincott, Grambo.

Nowotny, H., Scott, P., and Gibbons, M. 2003. 'Mode 2' revisited: the new production of knowledge, *Minerva* 31: 179–94.

Obrecht, A. 2016. Separating the 'good' failure from the 'bad': three success criteria for innovation, Humanitarian Exchange 66: April.

Obrecht, A. and Waner, A.T. 2016. *More than Just Luck: Innovation in Humanitarian Action*. HIF/ALNAP Study. London: ALNAP/ODI.

OCHA. 2014. Unmanned aerial vehicles in humanitarian response. OCHA Policy and Studies Series, June, 010.

OECD. 2008. *Accra Agenda for Action*. Paris: OECD.

OECD. 2017. *Global Private Philanthropy for Development*. Paris: Organisation for Economic Co-operation and Development.

OIOS. 2016. Audit of the Biometric Identity Management System at the Office of the United Nations High Commissioner for Refugees. Report 2016/181.

Papaioannou, T. 2011. Technological innovation, global justice and politics of development, *Progress in Development Studies* 4: 321–38.

Parker, I. 2010. The Poverty Lab, *The New Yorker* 10 May.

Parmar, I. 2012. *Foundations of the American Century*. New York: Columbia University Press.

Pasquale, F. 2015. *The Black Box Society: The Secret Algorithms that Control Money and Information*. Cambridge, MA: Harvard University Press.

Paynter, B. 2017. How blockchain could transform the way international aid is distributed. *Fast Company*, 18 September.

Pearce, W. and Raman, S. 2014. The new randomised controlled trials (RCT) movement in public policy: challenges of epistemic governance, *Policy Sciences* 47: 387–402.

Petryna, A. 2009. *When Experiments Travel: Clinical Trials and the Global Search for Human Subjects*. Princeton, NJ: Princeton University Press.

Petryna, A. 2011. The competitive logic of global clinical trials, *Social Research: An International Quarterly* 78: 3.

Pisa, M. 2017. Blockchain and economic development: Hype vs. reality. CGD Policy Paper 107, July. Center for Global Development.

Porter, T. 1995. *Trust in Numbers*. Princeton, NJ: Princeton University Press.

Pritchett, L. 2014. An Homage to the Randomistas on the Occasion of the J-PAL 10th Anniversary: Development as a Faith-Based Activity, 10 March. Available at: https://www.cgdev.org/blog/homage-randomistas-occasion-j-pal-10th-anniversary-development-faith-based-activity

Ravallion, M. 2014. Taking ethical validity seriously, 17 March. The World Bank. Available at: https://blogs.worldbank.org/impactevaluations/taking-ethical-validity-seriously

Raymond, N. and Harrity, C. 2016. Addressing the 'doctrine gap': professionalising the use of Information Communication Technologies in humanitarian action, *Humanitarian Exchange* 66: April.

Rayzberg, M. 2019. Fairness in the field: the ethics of resource allocation in randomized controlled field experiments, *Science, Technology and Human Values* 44(3): 371–98.

Reddy, S. 2013. Randomise this! On poor economics, *Review of Agrarian Studies* 2(2).

Reddy, S. 2019. Economics' biggest success story is a cautionary tale, *Foreign Policy* 22 October.

Rheinberger, H.J. 1997. *Toward a History of Epistemic Things: Synthesizing Proteins in the Test Tube*. Stanford, CA: Stanford University Press.

Rockefeller Foundation. 2014. Understanding the Value of Social Innovation Labs: Solutions to Complex Social Problems. Accessed 15 April. Available at: http://visual.ly/understandi%20ng-value-social-innovation-labs-solutions-complex-social-problems#sthash.uKMftAzM.dpuf

Rockefeller Foundation. 2016. To Save Our Fisheries, We Need a New Approach. Accessed 15 April. Available at: https://www.rockefellerfoundation.org/blog/save-our-fisheries-we-need-new/

Rogers, E. 1995. *Diffusion of Innovations*. 4th ed. Cambridge: The Free Press.

Rottenburg, R. 2009. Social and public experiments and new figurations of science and politics in postcolonial Africa, *Postcolonial Studies* 12(4): 423–40.

Rud, S. 2017. *Colonialism in Greenland: Tradition, Governance and Legacy*. Basingstoke: Palgrave Macmillan.

Said, E.W. 1978. *Orientalism*. New York: Vintage Books.

Said, E.W. 1994. *Culture and Imperialism*. New York: Knopf.

Saini, A. 2019. *Superior—The Return of Race Science*. Boson, MA: Beacon Press.

Samuelson, P.A. 1972. *Collected Scientific Papers*. Cambridge, MA: MIT Press.

Sandersson, I. 2002. Evaluation, policy learning and evidence-based policy making, *Public Administration* 80(1): 1–22.

Sandvik, K.B. 2016. The humanitarian cyberspace: shrinking space or an expanding frontier?, *Third World Quarterly* 37(1): 17–32.

Sandvik, K.B., Jumbert, M.G., Karlsrud, J., and Kaufmann, M. 2014. Humanitarian technology: a critical research agenda, *International Review of the Red Cross* 96(893): 219–42.

Sandvik, K.B., Jacobsen, K.L., and McDonald, S.M. 2017. Do no harm: a taxonomy of the challenges of humanitarian experimentation, *International Review of the Red Cross* 99(1): 319–44.

Savage, M. 2013. The 'social life of methods': a critical introduction, *Theory, Culture & Society* 30(4): 3–21.

Savedoff, W., Levine, R., and Birdsall, N. 2005. When will we ever learn? recommendations to improve social development assistance through enhanced impact evaluation. Washington, DC: Center for Global Development.

Schmitt, D. 2014. Donors should put evidence before politics and diplomacy, 12 June, SciDevNet. Available at: https://www.scidev.net/global/aid/opinion/donors-evidence-politics-diplomacy.html

Schroeder, A. and Meier, P. 2016. Automation for the people: opportunities and challenges of humanitarian robotics, *Humanitarian Exchange* 66, April.

Scriven, K. 2016. Humanitarian innovation and the art of the possible, *Humanitarian Exchange* 66: April.

Shah, S. 2006. *The Body Hunters: Testing New Drugs on the World's Poorest Patients*. New York: New Press.

Shapin, S. and Schaffer, S. 1985. *Leviathan and the Air-pump: Hobbes, Boyle and the Experimental Life*. Princeton, NJ: Princeton University Press.

Shelley, M. *Frankenstein*. London: Penguin Classics, pp. 36–7.

Shiva, V. 1999. *Biopiracy: The Plunder of Nature and Knowledge*. Boston, MA: South End Press.

Small, A. W. 1921. The future of sociology, *Publications of the American Sociological Society* 15: 174–93.

Stangneth, B. and Martin, R. 2014. *Eichmann before Jerusalem: The Unexamined Life of a Mass Murderer*. New York: Alfred A. Knopf.

Storeng, K. 2014. The GAVI alliance and the 'Gates Approach' to health systems strengthening, *Global Public Health* 9(8): 865–79.

Tazzioli, M. 2019. Refugees' subjectivities, debit cards and data circuits. financial-humanitarianism in the Greek migration laboratory, *International Political Sociology* 13(4): 392–408.

Teele, D. (ed.) 2014. *Field Experiments and Their Critics: Essays on the Uses and Abuses of Experiments in the Social Sciences*. New Haven, CT: Yale University Press.

Thompson, C. 2014. Philanthrocapitalism: appropriation of Africa's genetic wealth, *Review of African Political Economy* 41(141): 389–405.

Tiesinga, H. and Berkhout, R. (eds). 2014. *Labcraft: How Innovation Labs Cultivate Change through Experimentation and Collaboration*. London: Labcraft Publishing.

Tukey, J. and Wilk, M.B. 1966. Data analysis and statistics: an expository overview, *AFIPS Conference Proceedings* 29: 695–709.

Tversky, A. and Kahneman, D. 1974. Judgement under uncertainty: heuristics and biases. *Science* 185: 1124–31.

UN. 2017. *Report of the Special Rapporteur on the Right to Food*. New York: United Nations.

UNICEF. Humanitarian drone corridor launched in Malawi, see https://www.unicef.org/stories/humanitarian-drone-corridor-launched-malawi

van de Poel, I. 2011. Nuclear energy as a social experiment, *Ethics, Policy & Environment* 14(3): 285–90.

Vollmann, J. and Winau, R. 1996. Informed consent in human experimentation before the Nuremberg code, *British Medical Journal* 313: 1445–7.

Ward, A. 2020. Sweden's government has tried a risky coronavirus strategy. It could backfire, vox.com, 16 April.

WBGU. 2019. Towards our Common Digital Future, German Advisory Council on Global Change.

Westley, F., Laban, S., Rose, C., McGowan, K., Robinson, K., Tjornbo, O., and Tovey, M. 2014. *Social Innovation Lab Guide*. Waterloo: University of Waterloo.

WFP. 2018. Tech for Food wins big at the 'Innovate for Refugees' awards ceremony in Amman. 31 January.

Whetham, D. 2015. Drones to protect, *The International Journal of Human Rights* 19(2): 199–210.

Whitty, C. and Dercon, S. 2013. The evidence debate continues: Chris Whitty and Stefan Dercon respond from DFID. Available at: https://oxfamblogs.org/fp2p/the-evidence-debate-continues-chris-whitty-and-stefan-dercon-respond/

Witzig, P. and Salomon, V. 2018. Cutting out the Middleman: A Case Study of Blockchain-induced Reconfigurations in the Swiss Financial Services Industry. Working Paper 1. Université de Neuchâtel.

Woolcock, M., 2009. Toward a plurality of methods in project evaluation: a contextualised approach to understanding impact trajectories and efficacy, *Journal of Development Effectiveness* 1(1): 1–14.

World Medical Association. 1949. War crimes and medicine, *WMA Bulletin* 1: 4.

Zuboff, S. 2019. *The Age of Surveillance Capitalism*. New York: PublicAffairs.

Zunz, O. 2012. *Philanthropy in America*. Princeton, NJ: Princeton University Press.

Index

For the benefit of digital users, indexed terms that span two pages (e.g., 52–53) may, on occasion, appear on only one of those pages.